AF395617

# Working in Art

# Working in Art

## How to Build a Career in the Art World

## Alexandra Steinacker-Clark

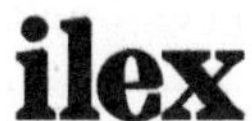

First published in Great Britain in 2026 by Ilex, an imprint of
Octopus Publishing Group Ltd
Carmelite House
50 Victoria Embankment
London EC4Y 0DZ
www.octopusbooks.co.uk

An Hachette UK Company
www.hachette.co.uk

The authorized representative in the EEA is Hachette Ireland,
8 Castlecourt Centre, Dublin 15, D15 XTP3, Ireland (email: info@hbgi.ie)

Text Copyright © Alexandra Steinacker-Clark 2026

Distributed in the US by Hachette Book Group
1290 Avenue of the Americas, 4th and 5th Floors
New York, NY 10104

Distributed in Canada by Canadian Manda Group
664 Annette St., Toronto, Ontario, Canada M6S 2C8

All rights reserved. No part of this work may be reproduced or utilized
in any form or by any means, electronic or mechanical, including
photocopying, recording or by any information storage and retrieval
system, without the prior written permission of the publisher.

Alexandra Steinacker-Clark asserts the moral right to be identified as the author of this work.

ISBN: 978-1-84091-954-7
eISBN: 978-1-85675-956-1

A CIP catalogue record for this book is available from the British Library.

Typeset in 11.5/14.5pt Garamond Premier Pro by Six Red Marbles UK, Thetford, Norfolk

Printed and bound in Great Britain.

1 3 5 7 9 10 8 6 4 2

Commissioning Editor: Ellie Corbett
Senior Developmental Editor: Rachel Silverlight
Copy Editor: Sarah Hulbert
Art Director: Ben Gardiner
Production Manager: Caroline Alberti

This FSC® label means that materials used for
the product have been responsibly sourced.

"You will never get a job in the arts . . ." is a lie.

For my mother, who taught me that no dream
of mine is too far-fetched to make a reality,
and for my father, who showed me how to be creative.

# CONTENTS


Introduction   1

1. Building a Strong Foundation   9
2. Working in Museums   24
3. Working in Curating   45
4. Working in Responsible Culture   63
5. Working in Framing and Art Handling   77
6. Working in Commercial Galleries   96
7. Working in Artist and Studio Management   118
8. Working as an Art Writer   140
9. Working for an Art Fair   160
10. Working in an Auction House   174
11. Working in Art Law   194
12. Working as an Art Advisor   206
13. Working in Content Creation in the Arts   221
14. Conclusion (and Some More Careers)   244

Resource Library   250
Acknowledgments   255
Index   257

Disclaimer:

Although written mainly for emerging arts professionals, the information within this book is relevant for artists, established arts professionals, and readers not at all involved in the arts (yet) who wish to learn more about what professionals do in this sector. The scope of the book covers the art worlds in the USA, the UK, and mainland Europe (Austria, France, and Italy, mainly, while being connected internationally to other regions). It can be relevant for an international audience; however, this book does not cover the art worlds in the Global South or East, such as South America, Asia, or Africa, which also have booming art scenes. This geographical scope reflects the author's professional experience and access to industry contacts in these markets, ensuring the authenticity and depth of the perspectives shared. The author hopes this foundation will inspire readers to explore and contribute to the rich dialogue about arts professions in their own regional contexts and that they will feel supported embarking on a career in the sector no matter where they are.

# INTRODUCTION

*"You can only have a career in the arts if you're rich."*
*"You will never make any money if you study Art History."*
*"Either you work in a gallery or a*
*museum — those are the only options."*
*"You're getting a degree in Art History?*
*What was your first degree? You'll need it."*

In October 2017, I had just taken the plunge to move to London from a small city in Austria to study Art History at University College London. The city was expensive and loud — I had no idea what I was doing, but I knew I was excited. On a mild October evening at the beginning of my first academic year, I headed over to one of the university bars on campus to meet some friends. It was a dingy but charismatic basement bar on Gower Street and I was sitting on one of the squishy sofas that was permanently sunken-in from all of the other students who had sat there before me, when I was approached by a guy. He started to chat to me, telling me he was doing a master's degree in business — or maybe it was law? Engineering? I can't fully remember. He asked me what I was studying and a huge grin spread across my face as I proudly stated I was pursuing a bachelor's degree in History of Art and it was my first year. He raised his eyebrows and scoffed, then proceeded to say: "You're getting a degree in Art History? What was your first degree? I really hope you have one, because if you don't, that's one way to make sure you never get a job."

This wasn't to be the last time I had to hear skeptical statements and disrespect in relation to my education. The problem is, these statements are not only discouraging, they are also incredibly misled. Very little validation is placed on the cultural sector from a professional standpoint to its detriment because, in reality, you *can* have a successful career in the arts. Plenty of people have done so. They have made incredibly meaningful contributions to society through their work, and you can do it, too—if you know where to look to learn and seek development.

Growing up, I wasn't exposed to going to galleries or museums and engaging with art. The first time I set foot inside a gallery exhibiting post-war art was in 2017 when my university professor took us to an exhibition with works by Jean Dubuffet in Mayfair. I still remember the quote by the artist on the wall in grey vinyl lettering: "Art by its very essence is of the new. And the view on art must also be of the new. There is only one healthy diet for artistic creation: permanent revolution." This quote has stuck with me throughout the years. Back when I first read it, I absorbed it, accepting the statement as truth. Now, I don't fully agree—does art have to be new? Why does the view on art have to be new, is it not important to take the past into consideration when viewing new art? What does "of the new" even connote?

Art functions as a prompt for thought and introspection, for dialogue and conversation, and for societal and historical education. And yet pursuing a career in art is actively discouraged, not only by boys in bars, but also by the government. In the UK, we have seen a 28.5 percent decline over the past decade in students pursuing History of Art degrees. Arts subjects have seen a 47 percent drop at GCSE and 29 percent drop at A level since 2010, and fewer than 8 state schools in the country currently offer History of Art at A level[*] (for those of you who are international readers, A levels are akin to AP courses and exams in the USA, the Baccalauréat in France, or the Abitur or Matura in the

---

[*] Riah Pryor, "Is Art History Under Threat? UK universities see 28.5 percent drop in the subject in past decade" *The Art Newspaper,* 1 January 2020.

DACH realm). Even in Austria, where I lived from the age of 14, I had only encountered art history in my final year of high school because of a teacher at my school. Some schools didn't teach it at all.

That was where my passion for art history was ignited, as my teacher was an artist named Gerold Tusch. Gerold not only encouraged my passion for art once he saw it, he also wrote my recommendation for my application to University College London. When I graduated high school, he wished me good luck and gave me Susan Sontag's *On Photography*. Without Gerold, I can say without a doubt I would not have studied art history. I would have been unaware of the university course, let alone that it would be possible to have a career in art in the way that I do. I feel like, nearly a decade later, there is still astonishingly little to encourage professional development in the creative industries, and more so the sub-industry of the arts.

When I moved to London, I didn't know what the Tate was, or everything else the city had to offer with its booming local art scene. In my first year as an undergrad, I was hired to work at the front desk of Sotheby's Auction House, which was my magical "foot in the door." I had been an attractive candidate because I had worked in high-end retail as a teen, which goes to show you never know what transferable skills you may be bringing to a potential job. I was hired the day I went to interview, on a casual contract (meaning zero-hours, quite useful for a student as it allows for flexibility, but of course less stability). When I started working there, I was juggling a job as a barista at the time, too. A few months down the line, it felt really good to hand in my notice at the café because I was being given enough regular shifts at the auction house to pay my rent—but it had taken a bit of time and some grafting to get to that point. I stayed working at Sotheby's part time for four years throughout both my bachelor's and master's degrees, being promoted to the Bids Department and travelling to France and Switzerland for some of the sales.

During the summers, I did a few internships to gain more experience.

My first internship was at a small modern art gallery* where my travel and lunch expenses were paid for, but I didn't receive an actual wage. I did this for six weeks, and worked at Sotheby's on the weekends to make sure I could cover my bills. This was also during exams in my first year at UCL, so I took a day off from the internship to sit the last few exams I had, and then worked a month straight. At the end of that stint, I took a weekend off to travel to Austria, and started an internship at Galerie Thaddaeus Ropac in Salzburg the following Monday (for which I was paid a living wage). I was unbelievably tired, but I was proud of the fact that I had already completed two internships and had Sotheby's on my resumé as I embarked on the second year of my bachelor's degree.

Somehow, after all the study and all the internships, I still was under the impression that the only two career options in the sector were working in a commercial gallery or auction house, or as a curator at a museum. It was then, as I was in the process of finishing my master's degree, that the Covid-19 pandemic hit. I felt like I was lacking clarity as to the possibilities that were available to me to pursue a long-term career, and suddenly I had a bit more time on my hands. While working and studying from home, I made the decision to find out more about different jobs in the arts and how the people in those positions got there.

And so began the *All About Art* podcast. I realized that I couldn't be the only person who wanted these answers. Instead of having Zoom calls and making notes that only I could access, I decided to record my questions and put them out into the world for any others who might be as confused as I was. It turned out I was right: I *wasn't* the only person who wanted these answers. *All About Art* quickly gained a following I hadn't expected. A pinch-me moment happened in early 2024 when I purchased an art book on eBay from a London-based seller. When the book arrived, it was packaged in brown wrapping paper and, to my

---

* Modern art is generally considered to be art made in the late 19th and early 20th centuries.

surprise, had "*PS I love your podcast*" written on the back. It was a small gesture that had a huge impact on me. I felt like I was making a positive difference in an industry, that it was reaching the exact people I was making it for.

In the beginning, the podcast was more about me speaking to my peers that I admire, which was wonderful in its collaborative nature. As time went on, *All About Art* began to grow into a project that gave me the opportunity to speak to professionals I would have never dreamed of meeting. Their stories have been career-defining not only for me, but also for listeners. The feedback I receive on a regular basis has encouraged me to keep *All About Art* running when, statistically, 90 percent of podcasts discontinue after their third episode. I continue to produce it, knowing that it motivates listeners to pursue a career or continue working in a sector that can, at times, be unforgiving.

In 2023, I was reading the news one morning and came across an article about the "ones to watch" in the art world. There were a few people in the article one could classify as "nepo babies" — coming from wealthy art-collecting families or well-known art-business tycoons. One of them was asked to give a piece of advice to people wanting to start a gallery, and in their response they suggested to "go for broke." The advice, I assume, was intended to mean that you should give it all you have when you are trying to break into a sector you are passionate about. But statements like these are not helpful for arts workers from less privileged backgrounds who cannot afford to "go for broke," as going for broke for some people means not being able to afford housing or food, a precariousness that the interviewee in the article had most likely never experienced. It was a tone-deaf statement that led to some backlash online, but it also fueled an important conversation about class in the cultural sector. Through the podcast and now this book, my mission is hopefully to provide support to prospective cultural workers in an industry where the practical advice can feel opaque and the barriers to entry can feel quite high.

When we engage with art, emotions of concern, sympathy, compassion, even outrage can be ignited.* People's experiences of the stories conveyed in art serve as an emotional lens through which they're encouraged to perceive the world as someone else perceives it. Through engaging with the creative outputs of people throughout history, but also with people around the world in cultures different from our own, we grow our understanding for experiences and lives that are not just ours. In the world we live in, within capitalist socioeconomic structures, there needs to be more support shown not just to people wanting to contribute to the sector through purchasing art or buying a ticket to an exhibition (although those things are great), but to people who are dedicated to their role within the art ecosystem. The lack of prioritizing art has a cyclical effect on diminishing the sector. Not enough people engage? This leads to less government-allocated funding to schools and universities. Not enough funding? That leads to a lessened ability for people to develop sustainable careers or discover art history early enough to pursue it as a career. This results in a lack of professionals in the sector, and there will be fewer exhibitions, fewer opportunities to both see and show art, and fewer artists who can practice full time and afford to pay their rent. This book is my way of positively contributing to the initial stages of that cycle in prioritizing the sector as a rewarding professional avenue and giving people useful tools to practically navigate it.

The art world is not always welcoming to newcomers. It can feel intimidating standing in a gallery and reading a text on the wall that barely makes sense — it can cause a sense of feeling out of place (I am speaking from experience). My mission is to give anyone who wants it the support to work in a sector that, in my opinion, makes us feel more human.

---

* On International Women's Day 2023, I was privileged to stand in the red circle for a TEDx Talk to answer the question "Can Consuming Art Increase Empathy?" I answer that question and more in the talk.

As you will discover in the following chapters, there is often no linear way to go about getting a job and progressing in the arts. It is still an industry based on little black books where sometimes, yes, someone with a stellar education and years of experience will not get the sales-director job because another person who barely got their bachelor's degree in a non-art subject comes from a wealthy background and has potential clients in tow. I aim to circumvent this by giving people more knowledge about careers so that you, the reader, have more of an overview, negotiating power, and ability to pivot if needed in order to survive and thrive in the arts.

I want to acknowledge that this book does not cover all of the careers the arts and cultural sector offers. It was not in my purview to create an extensive survey of art jobs, and thus although this book covers international regions, it was not possible, for example, to include Asia's, Africa's, or South America's thriving art scenes in my research. Within this book you will read interviews from professionals in the US, UK, and various countries in mainland Europe. I have done my best to show as much versatility as possible in the framework of this publication and have endeavored to include different viewpoints and experiences.

The quotes listed at the beginning of this chapter don't come from out of the blue. The sector can be underpaid and competitive, allowing space only for those with safety nets to take unpaid internships or low-paying jobs to gain experience. Instead of feeling discouraged, I see all the more reason to encourage the integration of new talent and foster budding arts professionals who have the potential to make positive change. My goal with this book, as well as the *All About Art* podcast, has been to encourage those within the sector to work towards our mission to bring art to everyone while broadening the professional art industry to become more inclusive, accessible, and prosperous. I hope that you, the reader, will feel supported with the information within this book to embark on your career in the arts sector—let's continue to build this industry together.

# CHAPTER 1

# BUILDING A STRONG FOUNDATION

There are plenty of ways an aspiring arts professional can set a good base for their professional endeavors. In this chapter, I will outline various components any aspiring arts professional needs to consider, covering education, introductory work experience (internships, volunteering, freelancing), extracurricular education and training, networking, as well as a conversation surrounding money and job progression. In the subsequent chapters, you will discover interviews with arts professionals who have gone through different versions and combinations of these components; and in some way or another, for both artists and art professionals, the beginning of your career can very much define the trajectory for the rest of it.

## EDUCATION

If you are asking yourself whether you should get a formal education in a humanities subject, it's a tricky question that I can't necessarily answer for you. In my experience, having bachelor's and master's degrees has been a huge advantage when applying for full-time jobs, along with strengthening my validity as an expert in my field. It has taught me so much about art history, art theory, art business, and writing, all valuable knowledge that I use in my career today. I understand, however, that the ability to pursue a degree is a privilege, both when it comes to finances as well as time. There are a few options, such as part-time courses that allow students to work alongside them, and if you happen to live in Europe, there are many undergraduate and postgraduate courses that are affordable in comparison to those in the United States, for example.

I approached the team at art recruitment agency Sophie Macpherson Ltd (which from now on will be referred to as SML) about the importance of their candidates having a university degree. Their spokesperson stated:

While a formal education in art history can be beneficial, it is not always a strict requirement for securing a role in the commercial art market. Many successful candidates come from diverse academic backgrounds, including literature, history, law, and economics, and later transition into art-related roles. For some positions, employers may require either a degree in art history (or a related field such as fine art) or relevant industry experience — such as working in a gallery, auction house, or other art-related environment. In certain circumstances, having an academic foundation in art history can provide a competitive advantage, particularly for those looking to specialize in specific areas. Ultimately, while formal education is valued, practical experience and expertise in the field can be equally important in securing a role.

Specific areas that could require an art history degree include working in the curatorial department at a museum, or in the research department in an art gallery. However, I know of a few industry professionals who studied non-art subjects. After university, they took part in an internship scheme and ended up working their way into established positions at their respective organizations. This is more likely to happen in a commercial organization than a non-profit such as a museum, and may be linked to other factors, such as a candidate's pre-existing network that presents opportunities to sell artworks, instead of capitalizing on a candidate's art historical knowledge.

Looking at the data, higher education does not always lead to higher earnings. The SML Art Market Talent Report 2025 (produced by Sophie Macpherson and ArtTactic, a London-based art market analysis firm) looked at the UK and Europe and concluded that candidates with master's or PhD degrees often earn the same or even less than colleagues with only a bachelor's degree. This can be for a number of reasons. For example, when someone has a PhD they often pursue a career in academia or an institution like a museum, which generally pays less than the commercial art sector. Even if that is the case, depending on the area of the arts you wish to pursue a career in, practical experience and early career entry may benefit you more from a financial point of view than getting additional formal education would, which I will discuss later on in this chapter.

## GAINING INTRODUCTORY WORK EXPERIENCE

### 1. Writing

Internships and volunteering are useful routes to get your foot in the door in the industry. However, I first want to talk about the career benefits of writing. You can do so many things as a writer, including writing books, but also publishing articles, columns, or blogs which can earn you visibility. You can work in copywriting, or contribute to catalog entries (for auction houses, for example), and more. The skill of writing is one I properly learned while at university, but I have also needed to refine it through practice. It's a skill I have needed time and time again for my work—and not just for this book.

It's important to understand the different types of writing, and to be aware of what is often referred to as "International Art Speak", something author Bianca Bosker (who you will hear from in chapter 8 on working in art writing) references in her book *Get the Picture*. The art world has a tendency to write about things in a convoluted way. Even I have trouble reading some of the wall texts in galleries, and I basically have a degree in International Art Speak! However, in order to develop your own voice, reading other arts writers' work is an integral part of understanding what sort of writing you want to do. You don't *have* to be a writer in the arts, don't get me wrong, but I do believe it is an invaluable skill for any role. You can not only supplement your income through freelance writing opportunities, but you can position yourself as someone with an opinion and an ability to ignite a discussion. This ability, to discuss art on the page as well as to do so in conversation, is a key activity required of you as an arts professional and will most likely be instrumental in your future career no matter which area of the arts you choose to work in.

## 2. Volunteering

Another way to gain experience in the arts is by volunteering at an arts organization. You will typically come across these opportunities offered at non-profit institutions, smaller organizations, or independently organized projects.

In the summer of 2019, I completed a four-week volunteership at the Kunsthistorisches Museum in Vienna. I was working in the Director's office as well as in the Imperial Treasury department, where I gained experience in researching image rights for a publication the museum was producing. I was volunteering, so I was not paid a wage. The rent in Vienna was affordable for the month (as one of the most livable cities in the world, voted year on year), and I had saved up to cover any other costs while there.

The volunteering position was not published on the museum's website anywhere, so you may be asking yourself how I could have known that it existed. I had applied for a multitude of internships that summer but I didn't get any. I was late in finding a position, panicking that I wouldn't gain any work experience over the summer break, so I called around. Amongst those calls, I spoke to my classmate who I knew had volunteered at the museum before. I had the intention of simply asking them how they got the position. (Was it advertised? Who do I get in touch with to ask?) But they kindly offered to send in a recommendation.

I told them they should do so only if they were comfortable with it, but that I would be incredibly grateful. I didn't get the volunteership through the traditional means of applying via the museum's website, or filling out a long-winded form. It took a combination of previous rejection, vulnerability, communication, and help from others to get there, but it paid off as it allowed me to meet amazing people while bolstering my resumé. It led to a podcast interview with the then-director, Dr. Sabine Haag, and is also where I met Paula Marschalek, founder of Marschalek Art Management, who you will hear from in chapter 7 on artist management.

When speaking to SML, I wanted to ask if, from a recruiter's perspective, they feel that potential employers value it when their candidates have volunteered:

Employers generally value volunteering, especially when it helps candidates develop relevant skills, build networks, or gain industry-specific experience. However, no one should feel obligated to work for free in order to get their foot in the door. While [Sophie Macpherson doesn't] typically recruit volunteers, we acknowledge that volunteering can be beneficial if it opens doors to new professional connections or provides hands-on experience that aligns with your career goals. If you're looking for opportunities, consider industry-related non-profit organizations, professional associations, or community initiatives that align with your field.

## 3. Internships

The most widespread form of work experience is internships. In my opinion, this is one of the best things you can do early on in your career. I asked the team at SML if they agreed with me, and the answer was a resounding yes:

Internships certainly play a key role in the art world, providing hands-on experience, industry exposure, and valuable connections. Candidates who stand out often leverage internships to demonstrate their passion and commitment, making them more competitive in a field where practical experience is highly regarded. Additionally, if structured well, excellent performance in an internship can often lead to a full-time opportunity at that business.

They added:

We solely advocate for paid internships and believe that no one should have to do an unpaid internship to establish an art world career. It's much more important to conduct thorough research and demonstrate your dedication, passion, and drive to succeed in this industry.

Reiterating the statement from SML, an internship can also lead to a job—maybe not in that organization specifically, depending on the circumstances, but the connections you make can facilitate future opportunities. They are also great for learning the basics. Although your role as an intern will probably involve a lot of data entry and running errands (at least in the gallery world, which we will hear more about in chapter 6, on working in commercial galleries), you will also learn how to use the operating systems in different art businesses and how teams are structured, alongside the theoretical knowledge you will build when working with the art in whichever organization you intern in.

I have worked in contemporary art galleries, as well as galleries that deal in impressionist and modern art, but also, as I mentioned earlier, at the Kunsthistorisches Museum, where I learned a lot about historic tapestries and even got to visit their warehouse to see how artifacts are stored. The internships I did were invaluable in developing my industry knowledge as well as finding out which area of the arts I am most passionate about. I also began to build a network that I have nurtured over the following years. It's important to remember that you may not see the results of those connections right away. It takes time to build relationships, build trust, build a reputation for yourself professionally. View it as planting seeds, and with the right environment and regular watering, many of those seeds will blossom into a garden. This is true for internships, but it is also true in relation to any professional opportunity that may come your way.

## IF YOU ARE PIVOTING
## FROM ANOTHER SECTOR

There are plenty of professionals who have worked in an art-adjacent or completely different industry for a few years, and are interested in or have pivoted into the arts. There are ways, such as freelance work while building a network and becoming familiar with the industry, to build a successful career that don't involve going from running your own team to being tasked with photocopying and doing coffee runs. Internships are not the only way to kickstart a career in the sector, and SML further substantiated this:

> Aspiring professionals can also strengthen their *curricula vitae* through independent initiatives, such as freelance writing, curating online exhibitions, managing art-focused social media pages, or engaging in academic research. Demonstrating dedication, knowledge, and creativity through these alternative paths can be just as effective in securing opportunities.

Internships are not the be-all-and-end-all of embarking on a career in the arts, especially when someone has a decade's worth of transferable skills they could bring to an arts organization. From a recruiter's perspective:

Transitioning into the art world from another industry is becoming a much more common occurrence, and many art businesses value the diverse perspectives and transferable skills that professionals from other sectors bring. When professionals are moving industries, our clients often want to know what the motivator is, therefore it is key to demonstrate a genuine passion for the arts and a long-term commitment to the industry. Attending art world events, enrolling in art-related courses, and staying informed about market trends can help establish credibility and show serious interest. Candidates should focus on highlighting their transferrable skills and demonstrating how their previous experience aligns and might add value to the business. It is essential to then tailor your CV and cover letter to emphasize these skills and show how they can bring fresh insights to the art world.

Thus, for students and emerging professionals, as well as mid-career or senior professionals who have transferable skills from another industry, it is beneficial to attend events, join communities, and stay up to date on what is happening in the arts in your area. Important to note, though, is that if you are thinking about coming into the sector from another industry, it is vital to set realistic expectations relating to salary. Jobs in the arts often pay less than other sectors, and SML states:

To avoid starting from scratch, targeting roles which build on your existing skill set, be it in administration, marketing, operations, or business development will offer a more strategic entry route than targeting highly specialized roles, which may require niche expertise. By strategically leveraging existing skills, building a network, and immersing themselves in the industry, professionals can successfully transition into the art world without having to completely restart their careers.

## EXTRACURRICULAR
## EDUCATION AND TRAINING

As we just heard in the previous section, attending art events, enrolling in art-related courses, and staying informed about what is happening in the industry will legitimize your interest to potential employers while providing you with connections and know-how in comparison to those who are not going the extra mile.

A plethora of opportunities for this exist, from memberships to events programmes to accredited short courses. Some of them are free and some require a membership fee, varying from £10 per month to £1,500 over a six-week period, for example. On the one hand, there are opportunities to learn about the sector by immersing yourself in it and networking. You can do this through finding clubs and groups that are self-organized and most often free, or memberships that provide insightful events programmes, networking opportunities, and resources throughout the year. I created a program called NXT GEN, in collaboration with the Association of Women in the Arts, which is an example of the latter. There is a membership fee (because we want to pay our speakers and cover our costs) and we host monthly online and live events, provide online resources, and organize opportunities for networking.

On the other hand, there are opportunities to deepen your industry knowledge through more extensive courses that take place over a certain amount of time. I completed a short course in curating at Sotheby's Institute of Art in London, where I had evening classes over a period of six weeks. I also completed an evening language course for two terms while at university. I paid for both of those courses. However, due to my circumstances at the time, I was able to sign up for discounted rates, which was necessary because I would not have been able to afford them otherwise. Another course at Sotheby's Institute of Art, not one that I have taken myself but one I have taught on, is the intensive course with classes every day for a week, giving you an introduction to art history, art business, gallery management, and more.

Seeking further development can look different for everybody, depending on financial circumstances, time availability, and ways of learning. But no matter what you do, it will benefit your career because of the effort you are putting into your growth.

When I asked the team at SML about this, they gave some advice on choosing the right course for you.

When considering short or online courses, research their value by checking LinkedIn to see if professionals in roles you aspire to have taken similar courses. Additionally, ask course administrators about the specific skills and knowledge they offer, and look for feedback or testimonials to ensure they align with your career goals. Selecting the right activities can not only expand your expertise but also make you a more attractive candidate to future employers.

## SOCIAL MEDIA

Social media is a funny thing. On the one hand, it has created a lot of professional opportunities for me. I use it to network and have built an incredible community of professionals, artists, and art lovers alike via online platforms like Instagram and LinkedIn. On the other hand, it has been the source of a lot of comparison, stress, and imposter syndrome. I recommend using social media as a professional tool, but I also recommend ensuring you think deeply about your relationship to it and establish boundaries early on so that it benefits you more than it sucks your time and energy.

SML shared their view on how a social-media presence can affect someone's job prospects:

A strong social-media presence can be a powerful asset in a job search, helping candidates discover opportunities, connect with industry professionals, and showcase their expertise and passion. Additionally, digital fluency is increasingly important. Platforms like Instagram and TikTok are key for marketing, networking, and audience engagement, making social-media skills highly attractive to employers. However, candidates should be mindful of their online presence — while a well-curated profile can enhance career prospects, unprofessional content may have the opposite effect. Using social media strategically can significantly boost visibility and career opportunities. As a platform, LinkedIn is particularly valuable for researching companies, team structures, and the career paths of potential interviewers and colleagues, offering key insights before applying. It also serves as an excellent networking tool, allowing individuals to connect with peers and industry leaders who inspire them.

The way you approach social media can vary. It can be by ensuring you have a professional approach to your online presence and that you utilize it to connect with people in the industry via messaging or following up after meeting in person. Alternatively, as we will hear in chapter 12 on working in art content creation, some arts professionals have used social media in ways that have completely redefined their careers.

## LET'S TALK ABOUT MONEY

I haven't had the best experience when negotiating for higher pay. In the past, I have not really known my worth and, as a result, did not negotiate what I deserved, both in relation to salary as well as in position and responsibilities. I have also attempted to negotiate non-pecuniary benefits in the past (asking to travel and for young patron's membership at an arts organization are two good examples — it's good to keep in mind not all benefits are strictly related to monetary salary), but was unsuccessful. As much as I like to admit where I could have improved how I approached negotiations, it is worth noting that sometimes, when salary negotiations go south, it's not the employee's failings but instead due to lack of cooperation by the company—so if it hasn't gone well for you in the past, don't be afraid to give it another try!

To help you properly prepare for salary negotiations in an art world job, SML shared with me that

It's important to have a clear understanding of your ideal number—what you would be happy with—and the minimum you would realistically accept. This helps set a strong foundation for the conversation. Beyond the base salary, consider additional benefits that can enhance your overall compensation package, such as bonuses, commission, healthcare, pension, or professional-development opportunities. It's also beneficial to ask about future salary reviews and opportunities for raises early in the discussion to understand your long-term earning potential within the company.

In terms of what to look out for and potentially circumvent, they add:

While negotiation is key, maintaining a balanced and realistic approach is essential. Avoid excessive back-and-forth and be mindful of the company's initial salary banding. Consistency in your messaging is crucial—if you state a minimum salary expectation early on, drastically changing it later in the process can be off-putting to the employer.

Of course, salaries and the approach to negotiations will look very different depending on the country you are seeking employment in, and I asked the SML team to expand on those potential differences. In the USA, "base salaries are generally higher, but this is offset by higher living costs, the need for employer-sponsored health insurance in the absence of free state healthcare, and less annual leave." However, in the UK, "while salaries may be slightly lower, access to the NHS means healthcare is less of a key negotiation factor. Instead, candidates focus on securing a competitive base salary, generous annual leave (typically 22–25 days plus public holidays), and flexible working arrangements, such as remote or hybrid schedules." In mainland Europe, SML found "work–life balance to be a major priority. Generous parental leave, annual leave policies, and employee assistance programs (EAPs) for mental health are a growing priority among benefits. Retirement plans are also a core focus, particularly as the aging population grows." Understanding those regional priorities is key to salary negotiations in the cultural sector of the city and country you want to work in.

I stated earlier in this chapter that I made the mistake of underestimating my professional value in the past. So, I asked SML what advice they'd give when it comes to knowing your worth, but also ensuring you enter into negotiations well-informed about the current market:

> Candidates should feel confident advocating for a salary that reflects their skills and experience, but it's equally important to be informed about industry standards and market rates. Researching average salaries for similar roles helps ensure expectations are realistic and aligned with current hiring trends, as asking for an unrealistic range could raise concerns with employers. By staying aware of market trends and benchmarking their worth, professionals can negotiate effectively and secure a fair compensation package.

It would be of detriment to you if you ask for a starting salary of £60k as a gallery assistant in London in 2026, as that is not a realistic expectation. Later in your career, a salary of £100k is not implausible. However, it will take time to get to that point. There are a few reports, such as the SML x ArtTactic Talent Report, that show industry standards for salaries, which you can use to prepare for your future negotiations. By staying up to date with art news, speaking to recruiters (who can recommend relevant reports to read, as they will be reading them, too), and speaking to your friends, peers, and colleagues, you will be able to gain invaluable insights into salaries in the industry. I truly believe that you should open the conversation about salaries with your colleagues. It is still considered to be taboo in many places — but it's incredibly important. A friend of mine told me she found out her male colleague, in the same role, was earning almost £7,000 per annum more than her. She discovered this during a casual conversation, because he assumed she was on the same salary. This is just one example of many which goes to show that speaking up and being transparent with one another is a way that we can change the rhetoric (and contribute to closing the gender pay gap in many of these cases).

In order to get to that point, though, there needs to be a path of potential career progression offered by the employers. Without that, why would an emerging professional be incentivized to work at the company — and stay working at the company? Often within the arts, unfortunately, the real potential for progression is seldom a reality when in an entry-level position. SML shared how a candidate can assess whether there is room for progression within a role, and what advice they would give those who are concerned about this:

It's always a good idea to research the company history prior to an interview. Look at the company retention rates as well as the career trajectories of their employees to gauge their typical promotion timelines. You can also ask about growth opportunities in your interviews, demonstrating that you envisage a long-term career with the company and, in turn, you can get a sense as to whether they are committed to your career development and growth. However, be mindful of how you frame this question to avoid appearing impatient or unwilling to invest time in the role you're applying for.

Once in a role, it is important to continue developing your skill set and network. Explore different areas of a company, show curiosity about how other departments operate, and engage with other industry professionals. Understanding how your role fits into the wider art world will make you a stronger candidate for advancement.

When embarking on a career in the arts, it is essential to create a solid foundation. While formal education is essential in specialized roles, other diverse pathways, including internships, volunteer work, and independent initiatives, can also be incredibly valuable in building relevant skills and connections. Combining the two approaches, as many did in the interviews you will read in the following chapters, is a recipe for success. From the varied experiences of established arts professionals shared throughout this book, there is no single formula that leads to a flourishing career. Your journey will be uniquely defined by your choices, experiences, and the relationships you cultivate. In the upcoming chapters, you will gain further perspectives on navigating the complexities of the art world. The early stages of your career can positively shape its trajectory, and with determination, adaptability, and curiosity to learn, a rewarding future in the arts awaits you.

CHAPTER 2

# WORKING IN MUSEUMS

Museums are large organizations, with many different departments including curating and art handling, which will be covered in subsequent chapters. Just as it is not possible to cover the full scope of the art world in this book, the same goes for museum jobs. In this chapter, you will read insights from Sally Tallant, Director of the Queens Museum at the time of writing, about working in a large organization that aims to serve the community it's in. Salome Asega was another great interviewee, as the director of NEW INC, the first museum-led incubator for art, design, and technology founded by the New Museum. Crossing over the Atlantic to the coast of the Adriatic, I also spoke to Maria Rita Cerilli, Manager for Communications and Marketing at the Peggy Guggenheim Collection, about her role in activating audiences for a world-renowned museum, especially during the Venice Biennale.

In this first interview, conducted in her apartment in New York on a sunny day in May, Sally Tallant describes the way a museum functions as a machine with many different moving parts coming together, along with how she as director steers that ship.

---

*Sally Tallant is the Director of the Hayward Gallery in London. She served as President and Executive Director of the Queens Museum, New York, for seven years, and was previously the Director of Liverpool Biennial from 2011 to 2019. From 2001 to 2011 she was Head of Programmes at the Serpentine Gallery, London.*

*She has curated exhibitions in a wide range of contexts including galleries, museums, public spaces, and non-arts contexts. In 2018 she was awarded an OBE for services to the Arts in the Queen's Birthday Honours List.*

---

***Alexandra Steinacker-Clark: It's hard to know where to start with your expansive career, but to begin, can you tell me briefly about your education and career path? What led you to the position you're in today as President and Executive Director of the Queens Museum?***

**Sally Tallant:** From a very young age, I made art. I didn't imagine I would be anything other than an artist, honestly, because I didn't know that you could. I didn't really understand what the art world was. I did a foundation, then I did a degree, but I had a lot of questions in my mind about who art was for. I then did quite a radical degree course in Devon at a place called Dartington College of Arts, which was called "Art and Social Context." Right from the beginning, I was asking questions around who was this for? Who were we making art for? Whose culture was being reflected? I became a curator accidentally because I was in a group of four artists all doing performance art. We called ourselves an affiliation of artists because we didn't want to be the same as a "collective." I was the only one that had a car and a driving license, and I was also good at writing grant applications. So I automatically became the curator of the group. I would raise the money, I would go pick up the materials, I would drive us everywhere, and so on.

During that time, I was still making work, but I was very distracted by other artists, and I was very interested in community-based work. I couldn't do the thing that artists absolutely have to do, which is focus 100 percent on my work and not be distracted by everyone else. I started a course at the Royal College of Art, which was called "Curating Contemporary Art" or "Arts Administration" or something along those lines. One of the main reasons I was interested in that course was that I did not see women, I did not see time-based practices, I did not see artists from diverse backgrounds represented in institutions. I thought, "How do I change that? How do I change what institutions are for?"

When I left the Royal College, I worked freelance for a while, but during that time I think it's important to note that I also did things like telesales, waitressing, and bartending. And all of those things gave me important transferable skills. I always say that everything I did helped to build the experience to do the job I do today.

I ended up getting a job at the Hayward Gallery as an assistant curator, which I loved. From there I went to the Serpentine Gallery. I was the Head of Programmes, so I managed exhibitions, education, public programming, and I had a team of around twelve curators working for me. It was really great, but London is very monopolized by the market, in a way. The job came up to direct the Liverpool Biennial, and I thought that would be interesting. I'm a Northerner from Leeds, and I think that it'd be harder for someone who's intimidated by that very working-class culture. Liverpool is a working-class city with a massive investment in culture and it has more museums than most other cities in the UK, with the Biennial being the largest visual arts project in the UK.

I was able to ask the question "What does art do in people's everyday lived experience?" which from the beginning was my question. Revisiting "Who is this for? And who is this for in a place like Liverpool?" I did that for eight years, and then this job came up in New York. I had an eye on the Queens Museum because there are few places in the world doing what I view as engaging with social justice, thinking about community-based and participatory practice, asking questions around education and really centering that in the work.

***ASC: Can you describe some of the responsibilities you have in your position as executive director?***

**ST:** I'm responsible for everything that happens at the museum, and that includes managing a team. They have their responsibilities, but they report to me. If something goes wrong, my neck is on the line. I have to make sure I hire the right people, I manage the right people. I have fiscal responsibility, so I manage the finances and the fundraising. I manage development, press, communications, exhibitions, education, facilities, everything. If there's a hole in the roof, which there actually is at the Queens Museum right now, that's my responsibility to get it fixed. I also report to the board of trustees, who have fiscal responsibility for the institution. They are the ones who hire an executive director to do that job, and I hire everyone else. I have quarterly meetings with them where I present everything I'm doing and get their sign-off. If I'm doing a bad job, I'm accountable to the board, and they can intervene in my work if they so wish.

It is different in the US than it is in the UK. A big difference is that here in the United States, the board makes a financial contribution. In my organization, the board dues are $10,000 a year plus a gala table. It's something called "give or get," which means you either give that amount of money a year or you get it from somewhere else. For example, one of my amazing trustees has a really great relationship with Marshall Headphones and they've sponsored our Queens Teens Institute for Art and Social Justice, which covered that trustee's dues. In the UK, though, there isn't a financial "give and get" because the tax situation is very different in the UK, but they still have the same legal responsibilities.

My museum's board fees are comparatively low. The Brooklyn Museum's fees are $100,000 a year. At MoMA, it's $1,000,000 a year. When you start having opinions about who should and shouldn't be on a board, you have to understand what it means to be on a board.

In Queens, which is a very working-class, diverse community, the reason I keep my board dues low is not to exclude people from the board, but it makes it hard for me to fundraise at times.

***ASC: If you could pluck out one work day, a typical work day, what would that look like for you?***

**ST:** I have a lot of meetings, because I manage people. I meet with my director of exhibitions, my director of development, my director of finance, and so on . . . every week. I meet with my board chair every two weeks. I have committee meetings pretty much every week. And then in the evenings, like this week, I have a gala tonight, a gala tomorrow, and a gala the night after. At the weekend, I've got two events. It's a very busy season. The only respite, I would say, in the summer in New York, it's so hot that people leave town.

***ASC: You have experience in various organizations, having served as Director of the Liverpool Biennial and as Head of Programmes at the Serpentine Gallery, as you mentioned. How do your past experiences define how you approach your work today?***

**ST:** Recruiting and managing people is key. I've always had great people work for me, a lot of previous staff are now directors themselves. I focus on training people, which makes sense as I was an educator to start with. The way I manage is about training them, giving them an opportunity to grow. I follow a model of distributed leadership in which we take decisions together. If I have a problem, I take it to that group and ask, "What shall we do?" And then we make a decision. There's age diversity and people from different cultural backgrounds, so when we discuss something, we have a good balanced view on it.

*ASC: And speaking of the team, what other roles are there in your organization, and how does your position intersect with them?*

**ST:** We have a facilities team, who look after the building, and I meet with the Director of Facilities every week at least. (Although we've got a leak in our roof right now, as I said earlier, so lately we've been meeting more often.) I have a Director of Front of House, who manages their team which includes security and visitor-services assistance. They're very important, as we really need friendly, welcoming people staffing the front desk and wonderful security who understand how to deal with people.

*ASC: Like how to say "don't get near the artwork" but in a really nice way?*

**ST:** Yes, but also for example if you have a protest, to be able to manage that and respect people's right to protest and freedom of speech without it going wrong for our other visitors. I have a Director of Communications and Digital Strategy who is in charge of the website, content creation, and press communications. She is also in charge of all of the signage in the museum, all of the didactics which we do in multiple languages. Then I have a Director of Exhibitions who is in charge of our exhibitions and curatorial team, which also includes an archivist, collections manager, registrar, and exhibitions designer. I have a Director of Education and Community Engagement who is in charge of a team that delivers our work with schools. We have hundreds of kids every morning coming into the museum and we also do projects off-site in schools. We have the Queens Teens Institute for Art and Social Justice. We do work with older adults. We do a lot of work with people with disabilities and their families and carers. We do family workshops every week.

I have a Deputy Director, who focuses on the front of house and the buildings while helping with all of our fiscal and financial responsibilities and board governance. She assembles the board papers and gets all the board packs together. Then there is the development team, which is incredibly important as it involves fundraising. There is someone who manages the rentals (like if someone wants to hold an event at the museum), someone who manages individual giving, including our gala and events, someone who is responsible for government funding, and then someone who writes trust and foundation applications. So . . . in summary: facilities, communications, exhibitions, education, deputy director, development, H R, and me. Those are the departments and all the people I work with.

*ASC: That is a lot of people and there is so much that goes into managing a museum which is quite small in comparison to other museums.*

**ST:** We're about $6.5 million on annual budget. Comparatively, the annual budget of the Brooklyn Museum is $64 million, or for MoM A PS1, which is actually physically smaller than my museum, the budget is $13 million.

*ASC: If you were hiring someone to follow in your footsteps, what are some personality traits or strengths that you would look for in an ideal candidate?*

**ST:** Being Director of the Queens Museum is not my first directorship. I believe the person that comes into the role after me should absolutely have been a director somewhere before. I don't believe you can walk into a job with this level of responsibility without having had some proven management experience of a team bigger than 30 people. Experience with fundraising and board governance management are very important. And, of course, a good track record of exhibition making. It's important to have developed the resilience from at least eight to ten years of the ups and downs of running an organization, which include the daily curveballs that knock you off your feet. And they come every day.

***ASC: If someone wanted to do what you do, what advice or even warnings would you give them?***

**ST:** If somebody wants to do the job I do, it's important to know why. It's not just to want power. You need a vision, to understand what your values are and why you want to do this job, because it's really hard work. If you know that you're changing what's possible for people in the world, then it's worth it. Work hard on your values. I'm mission driven and focused on people, so although I have a collection at the Queens Museum, I wouldn't be right for the V&A, for example. I don't want to run an encyclopedic collecting institution. I wanted to go to an institution that's really focused on people. I think you have to know your values and why you're in this game, because everyone's different, and that will help you make decisions in the future.

*

Listening to Sally speak, I felt like I finally got an idea of what being a museum director really means. I always viewed it as a glamorous role that meant you choose what exhibitions happen and when—which is part of it, sure—but I now recognize how a museum director must carry the responsibility of the entire museum, all the while reporting to a board. You need to be able to manage people, handle the high pressure, juggle anything thrown your way at any given time, and not be afraid to make decisions. It takes time to work up to it. It was also interesting to learn about all of the teams Sally manages, giving deeper insights into how many different key players there are within a museum for people to contribute— along with the potential entry points for anyone wanting to find a job in a museum.

Taking the train from Queens to Manhattan, I made my way over to NEW INC, the first museum-led cultural incubator, which was conceived as a non-profit platform and professional resource as a part of the New Museum. The New Museum was under construction at the time of writing this book (but by the time it is published, the museum will be open to the public again), so I met NEW INC Director Salome Asega at their temporary offices between Greenwich Village and Lower Manhattan.

---

*Salome Asega is the Director of NEW INC, the New Museum's cultural incubator for creative practitioners working across art, design, and technology. Asega is also an artist, researcher, and educator working between participatory design and emerging technologies. She was the inaugural New Media Art Research Fellow for Creativity and Free Expression at the Ford Foundation, is a cofounder of POWRPLNT, a digital art collaboratory based in Brooklyn that offers free and sliding-scale workshops run by established media artists, and since 2015 has been teaching studio and design methodology courses in the MFA Design and Technology program at Parsons School of Design.*

---

***Alexandra Steinacker-Clark: Can you tell me briefly about your education and career path, and what led you to the position you are in today as Director of NEW INC?***

**Salome Asega:** That story is a winding road. I grew up with computer-engineer uncles who were like guardian angels around me, and they really wanted me to pursue a career in technology or science. So, for fun, they would have me take apart computers and put them back together again. It was their version of a thousand-piece puzzle, in a way. As I got older, I knew I wanted to pursue something in the humanities, but I had set up a kind of false binary between the arts and technology. In this role, I completely dissolved that and see now that there's so much overlap. But at the time, I was still fighting that binary mindset. Still, I pursued an undergraduate degree in 'Socially Engaged Art and Social Practice'. Through that, I became more interested in what I fundamentally understood as a process of design, and exploring how we design community. That, combined with my experiences growing up, led me to an MFA in Design and Technology where the door was fully bust wide open and I was seeing all the ways that people were experimenting with software and hardware as artistic mediums, and I completely fell in love. In a way, my uncles' dreams were fulfilled, and I started to experiment more with technology while falling into incredible creative communities in New York, including ones like NEW INC. I've been around NEW INC since its founding, I'm an alumna of the program, have mentored in the program, and returned as director in 2021.

*ASC: Can you describe just very briefly what NEW INC is and what it does?*

**SA:** NEW INC was founded a little over ten years ago and is the New Museum's cultural incubator that supports creative practitioners working across art, design, technology, science, architecture, and more. I often say we're a home for the misfits, for people who don't neatly fit into any one discipline or category. The people of our program deeply resist boxes in the best ways. I think we're one of the best expressions of the museum's mission, which is to support new art and ideas. There are a lot of things in the program that are so emergent that they don't even have names quite yet, and we're not afraid to invest in and learn about them. We support people through four core areas: professional development, mentorship, community programs, and a shared workspace.

**ASC: *In your position now as Director of NEW INC, can you describe some of the responsibilities that you have?***

**SA:** Primarily, my focus is to design this wonderful, far-reaching community of people. Eleven years into the program, we have over 650 alumni, and my role is thinking about how we engage these people and support them even beyond their year or two at NEW INC. I'm also managing a team of seven people and invested in their own autonomous journeys running and stewarding this community. I'm thinking not only about our public programs, but how the work happens behind the scenes. So, thinking about how we can be just as creative operationally as we are programmatically, and making sure those things are aligned. Oh, and fundraising. Definitely fundraising.

**ASC: *What does a typical work day look like for you from start to finish?***

**SA:** My work day starts during my commute. It's important to start my mornings reading the news. It's important for me to let what is happening in the world inform some decision I'll make that day. I also read publications that are relevant to our work, including, for example, the Substacks our members are writing. After I arrive at the office, the bulk of my day is meeting with people—with staff members, other members of the Museum team, NEW INC members, or alumni and mentors. In between meetings, I answer emails and do any other things that need to get done. There are days of the week, especially towards the end of the week, that I really minimize meetings so that I have headspace to get the things that require more of my attention done.

**ASC: *You are also an artist, researcher, and educator working between participatory design and emerging technologies. You joined NEW INC as director in 2021, but prior to that you were the New***

*Media Art Research Fellow for Creativity and Free Expression at the Ford Foundation, you've taught courses at Parsons, and you have an active artistic practice. I would love to know how all of these past experiences define how you approach your work today?*

**SA:** I'm naturally curious and maybe borderline nosy. When I see something is bubbling and it's exciting, I need to learn more about it. I think that's why there's been a slippage in my career path where I have gone from being an educator at a university, to working in foundations as a researcher and launching grant initiatives, to now leading a team at a museum. I think there are a lot of "pinch me" moments when I'm working at NEW INC where I think to myself . . . there was nothing that was set up in my trajectory for me to be here. There was nothing that I intentionally planned for myself along my route to be here, to have this role. I never thought this could be possible, but I just followed my curiosity and I moved with my heart. I know that sounds a little corny, but I honestly think that's what brings you to the best opportunities, that kind of openness, you know?

*ASC: At NEW INC, what other roles are there and how does your position intersect with them?*

**SA:** There are a few roles on the team that straddle programming and operations. We have a Department Coordinator who functions as a studio manager and is thinking about the design of our workspace, and ways to make it more inviting for members to feel like they can take over and initiate programming. We have a Marketing and Communications Assistant who's thinking deeply about how to tell the story of not only NEW INC but all members, mentors, and alumni. That storytelling can happen through social posts, website, newsletter, video series . . . That role can be pretty playful. We have a Production Coordinator who is the brain of all of our public and internal programming, keeping us aligned by identifying milestones, and solving creative challenges like "How will we host a hundred-person dinner on this rooftop, in October where it might rain?" We also have a Head of Community who is thinking about the active NEW INC members, of which there are around a hundred, and the mentors, of which there are over 20 who join us each year. They are responsible for community design and how all these people get to know each other and stay in an intentional relationship with each other over the course of a year. I think about him in particular as a "vibes counselor," making sure people are active, happy, and engaged.

*ASC: What is a difficult aspect of the job? Something that is particularly challenging?*

**SA:** Saying no is hard. I can run on impulse, I want to have fun, but as a director it's my responsibility to find the edges of our work to protect the team. No one wants to be the person that deflates the balloon, but that is sometimes my job. I have to say no, or maybe not right now, or maybe let's breadcrumb our way to that in the future. Someone gave me good advice when I first started. It was to make sure to find someone you can talk about your work with, that doesn't know anybody on the team and isn't a family member or a partner. Someone who could give you "objective advice" in a way. In having someone to talk with about some of these difficult decisions, I have also had it reflected back to me the moments where there's room for growth for myself. That's been, I think, the most important part about taking on a leadership role like this.

*ASC: If you were hiring someone to follow in your footsteps, what are some personality traits or strengths that you would look for in an ideal candidate?*

**SA:** Eddie [Edwin] Torres who leads Grantmakers in the Arts recently said to me that there are people who fall into a spectrum from risk managers to entrepreneurial. Risk managers think about how to protect the organization rightfully, but they feel most comfortable sitting in the box of "this is how it's always been done and this is how it traditionally happens." People who are entrepreneurial start with the vision and idea and think "How can I use existing structures to get to that idea or vision?" I lean more towards the entrepreneurial. I see the rules but what's the thing I want to achieve, and how can I bend the rules to get there? I would look for someone who is more entrepreneurial, curious, and a little bit of a rule breaker.

**ASC: My final question is if someone wanted to do what you do, what advice or even warnings would you give them?**

**SA:** I would probably give the advice someone gave me when I started this role. Golan Levin, who at the time was at Carnegie Mellon University, said, "Keep it weird, kid," and I think about that often. When I feel stuck or I'm overthinking, I remind myself to just keep it weird, to have fun with it. We're here to bring people together, to ask questions, to find some sense of understanding between our perspectives on the world of society. Otherwise, what are we doing?

*

Keeping it weird will be how I approach my career going forward. We can take ourselves very seriously in the art world and it's important to humanize our work as much as we can, especially when managing teams. A lesson I took away from Salome's interview was how she leads. When you are the director of a team, or of an organization, with people who don't necessarily fit into boxes, and who may actively be fighting against that categorization, it is important to give people the space to be themselves. Sally said something similar when speaking about hiring staff who went on to direct other institutions. I can imagine that they were employees who valued their autonomy, and so their biggest strengths could also prove challenging to a manager who isn't open to investing in their staff's journeys at work.

It was great speaking to both a director of a museum and a director of a cultural incubator as a part of a museum, both based in the USA — but a different perspective of working in a museum was needed. I got on a plane to Italy, first to interview another person for a separate chapter, Caitlin Southwick, who you will hear from in chapter 4 on working in responsible culture, and from there I hopped on a train to Venice to the renowned Peggy Guggenheim Collection, a personal happy place of mine and the one institution I will always pay a visit to when I am in the city of canals.

---

*Maria Rita Cerilli is the Communications Manager at the Peggy Guggenheim Collection in Venice, a role she has held for over three years. She has extensive experience in press relations, social-media management, and public communication, having worked at the museum since 2008. Her responsibilities include managing media relations with national and international press, developing media campaigns, and overseeing all social-media platforms through storytelling and visual content creation. Maria Rita's expertise lies in enhancing the museum's visibility, promoting exhibitions, and engaging audiences through dynamic communication strategies.*

---

**Alexandra Steinacker-Clark: Tell me briefly about your education and professional experiences — can you take me through your career path thus far?**

**Maria Rita Cerilli:** I studied Foreign Language and Literature at the University of Pisa, with a specialization in Art History, driven by a strong interest in modern, contemporary visual culture. This allowed me to nurture what has always been a true passion of mine since high school—art!—while also deepening my interest in languages, especially English. After graduating, I worked for a period at a small publishing house specializing in art history books. Shortly after, I was awarded a scholarship for a three-month internship at the Peggy Guggenheim Collection. I started out in the publications department, and after a few months I moved to the museum's communications and public relations office, where I worked alongside the department head at the time. I've been lucky to grow professionally over the years, taking on increasing responsibilities until becoming Communications Manager.

*ASC: What does a typical work day look like for you, from start to finish?*

**MRC:** No two days are exactly alike, which is something I enjoy. I usually start by reviewing press coverage and media alerts, then move on to team meetings or calls with other colleagues and journalists. My afternoons are often dedicated to writing and editing content, preparing press kits or press releases, or brainstorming with the digital team. If there's an event or a preview happening, I'm onsite to manage interviews and ensure everything runs smoothly.

*ASC: Tell me something I wouldn't expect to hear about your job. What is something many would be surprised to know?*

**MRC:** People are often surprised to learn how much of my job is about diplomacy. Communication in a museum is not just about "getting the word out"—it's about negotiating tone, timing, expectations. It involves a lot of coordination across departments, and often requires a very subtle understanding of both internal and external dynamics.

*ASC: Can you tell me about a difficult aspect of the job, something that you find particularly challenging?*

**MRC:** Balancing institutional identity with the need to innovate. In a museum like the Peggy Guggenheim Collection, which is rich in history and legacy, every communication choice is meaningful. I constantly have to ask myself: how can we speak to today's audiences, which is constantly changing, while staying true to who we are?

*ASC: What are some ways you make efforts to do just that, i.e. speaking to today's audiences while staying true to the values of the organization without drifting due to trends or other influences?*

**MRC:** We constantly work to ensure that our communication strategies remain rooted in the museum's identity, history, and core values, while evolving to resonate with contemporary audiences. We listen carefully to shifts in society, to the language of younger generations, and to the expectations of a more diverse public, but we do so without compromising the integrity of the institution. I'm thinking, for example, about the podcast we produced together with Chora Media about Peggy Guggenheim, titled *Volevo essere libera* ("I Wanted to be Free"). It's a clear example of how we wanted to make her story resonate with contemporary audiences by portraying her as a still-relevant icon while remaining absolutely faithful to her life and legacy. Peggy Guggenheim herself was a forward-thinking, independent voice in the art world, and we try to uphold that same spirit of curiosity and courage. We always stay true to our mission by anchoring each communication initiative—whether a digital campaign, podcast, or onsite activities—in the museum's unique story and collection. Trends may shape how we present content or which channels we use, but the content itself always reflects who we are. Relevance and authenticity are not mutually exclusive!

*ASC: What is a way that people can set boundaries, especially when I feel that working in communications involves so much networking and ensuring to build social–professional relationships in order to strive for visibility?*

**MRC:** Yes, communication work does often blur the line between the professional and the personal, especially in a field where visibility and networking are so deeply intertwined. Setting boundaries starts with clarity: knowing your role, your objectives, and your values. It's about understanding that not every opportunity has to be seized, and not every connection needs to be cultivated beyond what feels right. For me, boundaries are also about being intentional by choosing when to be "on" and when to step back, protecting time for deep work, and valuing quality over quantity in relationships. In a hyperconnected world, true connection and authentic communication stand out even more. It's not about being everywhere, but about being present where it truly matters.

*ASC: If someone wanted to do what you do, where do you think they could start?*

**MRC:** Start by being curious. Read widely, and not just about art, but about how ideas spread and how culture is shaped. Volunteer, intern, join a team even in a small role. Asking questions is also key, because I believe that good communicators are good listeners first.

*ASC: What is specific about your job in your geographical region in particular? Especially when it comes to thinking about communications during the Venice Biennale, for example.*

**MRC:** Being based in Venice, we operate in a city that is at once hyper-local and hyper-global. During the Biennale, the whole world looks at the city, and we become part of a much larger conversation. Communication during that time must reflect both the museum's own voice and the energy of the international art scene.

***ASC: If someone wanted to do what you do, what advice or even warnings would you give them?***

**MRC:** Be prepared to work with care and patience. Communication isn't always fast or flashy. It's about consistency, trust, and attention to detail. My advice? Be humble, be curious, and remember that words carry weight.

*

After hearing from Sally, Salome, and Maria Rita, a museum feels like an enriching, collaborative, inspiring place to work. When I was starting out, I wasn't aware of the various jobs within museums, not to mention the different types of museums there are. Queens Museum, NEW INC, and the Peggy Guggenheim Collection are all vastly different in their mission, exhibitions, programming, and all-around general structure. Maybe if I had known about these institutions earlier on in my career, I might have been more inclined to apply to them—but hey, then this book wouldn't exist (or maybe someone else would have written it).

Learning from two leaders of organizations was invaluable: Sally, who has worked at institutions internationally, bringing insights from both the US and the UK, and Salome, within her position at an impressively young age, showing us how our generation can shake things up and "keep it weird." Maria Rita enlightened me on an incredibly important part of a functioning museum, as communications spans from press releases to wall texts to social-media engagement, and more. It's integral to audience engagement while keeping the image of the museum clear to the public with every piece of information that goes out. There are a lot of other jobs you can have within a museum which I haven't included in this chapter, but you will find them dispersed amongst other chapters in this book.

In chapter 5 on art handling and framing, we will hear from an art handler who has worked at Tate (mostly Tate Britain, with a brief stint at Tate Modern) for over 35 years, and in the next chapter, on curating, we will hear from a curator from the Peggy Guggenheim Collection who has worked at the museum since she was an intern over 15 years ago. Other paths include fundraising, which as Sally mentioned sets a good base for growing into a leadership role, as well as facilities, education, HR, and so much more, depending on the museum and its structure.

## KEY TAKEAWAYS IF YOU ARE THINKING OF EMBARKING ON YOUR OWN CAREER IN MUSEUMS

### Three Practical Tips

- Remember that transferable skills are invaluable, so try to build your experience by working in various roles such as management, fundraising, programming, or communication in whichever organization you can to develop a well-rounded understanding.
- If you envision yourself running a museum one day, cultivate leadership qualities by focusing on managing teams, staying calm in a crisis, and making decisions confidently. Look out for positions as departmental leads, or smaller organizations to build your way up to running a larger organization, because that experience will be invaluable later down the line.
- If you have a role in a museum, no matter what department you are in, network across other departments to understand their functions and foster collaboration, which is vital for career growth.

## Next Steps

- Reflect on why you want to work in museums and what impact you want to have long term. This will align your career choices—where you want to work and what kind of work you want to be doing—with your core values (and it will make a positive impact in interviews and applications going forward!). Make a list of these values and write down your "why."

- Seek mentorship opportunities by connecting with experienced professionals to learn and get advice from. Don't just seek out mentorship from someone in your field, be open to other industries as well! Reach out to a few professionals for a coffee meeting to hear their thoughts.

- Focus on opportunities to lead projects, manage teams, and refine skills like fundraising and strategic planning—think about where you can get these skills, even if it's organizing projects independently or consuming resources (like podcasts or books) on the topics.

# CHAPTER 3

# WORKING IN CURATING

The term "curator," as defined by the American Cambridge Dictionary, is: a person in charge of a department of a museum or other place where objects of art, science, or from the past are collected, or a person who organizes and arranges a showing of art or other objects of interest. However, as we will see in the following interviews, that definition is not all-encompassing. In Karen Love's *Curator Toolkit*, which was published in 2010 (and which is free to access online as a PDF if you are interested), the table of contents lists sections on researching a concept, finding a venue, writing the concept, finding the artists, budgeting, fundraising, loan agreements, public programming, media relations, mounting the exhibition, and post-exhibition tasks. This means that a curator is an organizer, leader, budgeter, planner, communicator, interpreter . . . And in my experience, a curator can do only one or two of these tasks or all of them depending on the institution or situation they're working in.

In my search for a more extensive answer, I started speaking to curators from institutions as well as those who work independently, to get a deeper insight into what it means to be a curator in the 21st century. In this chapter, you will hear from institutional curators of both contemporary and more historic art, and curators who have experience in doing their job independently as well as for museums. I started off in Vienna, Austria, to speak to Jasper Sharp, meeting at the Phileas office on the Opernring and heading up the stairs to his office.

---

*Jasper Sharp is a British curator and art historian. He began his career as an intern at the Peggy Guggenheim Collection, Venice, in 1999, and went on to become Head of Exhibitions and Collections at the museum until 2005. After moving to Vienna, he was appointed Curator for Modern and Contemporary Art at the Kunsthistorisches Museum. He curated more than 20 exhibitions between 2011 and 2021, from major retrospectives and smaller focused projects to presentations of the museum's historical collections. He was the Commissioner of the Austrian Pavilion at the 55th Venice Biennale, founding curator of the talks programme at Frieze Masters, London, and most recently the founder and Director of Phileas, a philanthropic organization based in Vienna that seeks to strengthen the voice of Austrian and Austria-based artists on the international landscape. This interview was conducted before Jasper left Phileas, in May 2025.*

---

**Alexandra Steinacker-Clark: What was your very first experience as a curator when you were just starting out?**

**Jasper Sharp:** My very first experience was actually with a young Korean artist friend in London who I thought was just incredible. I organized an exhibition of her work in my bedroom in London. My grandfather gave me a case of wine, I printed an invitation, we invited friends over and had an opening. I was 22 at the time. I had red wine over everything afterwards, which I took to be a sign that we'd done well. When I was at the Guggenheim in Venice, they didn't have a curator on staff at the time—the Chief Curator of Guggenheim New York also held the title of Curator of the Peggy Guggenheim Collection. That's now changed, but when I was there, I was basically the assistant curator to every single one of the guest curators, including the commissioners of the American Pavilion at the Venice Biennale (which is owned and operated by the Guggenheim). It was an incredible learning process, being exposed to many different curatorial styles and approaches. Then of course Venice, with its churches, *scuole*, museums and biennials, was where I really learned about art.

***ASC: What does a typical work day look like for you from start to finish?***

**JS:** I'm usually the first person in the office, shortly before 8am. I need a bit of quiet time at the beginning of the day. It helps having a young daughter who leaves early for school, gets me up and going. Then the team begins to arrive. I have a chef in the family, and at a certain point when you're a chef, you're not really cooking yourself so much. You're charting a course with the menu, motivating people, dealing with issues in the kitchen, and checking each dish before it leaves the kitchen. It's not dissimilar here at the office, in the sense that I need to be able to screw the lens back and look at this organization, where it's going, and where it maybe could be going and how it could be going along differently. Occasionally I need to hit the brakes on certain projects if it feels like they're distractions from more important things. Hiring people, bringing them on board, keeping people going, helping each one of them with their projects, managing their workloads. So, each day is quite different.

***ASC: How would you classify your business? Would you say it's akin to a cultural agency for Austrian creatives and bringing their work to a global stage? Because this is quite a new business model.***

**JS:** Three of us set up Phileas ten years ago, around 2014. Today I run the ship, or rather, the balloon. We borrowed the name from Phileas Fogg, the explorer from *Around the World in 80 Days* by Jules Verne. The origin of the word "Phileas" is philanthropy, *philos*, the love of one's fellow man. We took those two twin spirits of philanthropy and adventure to create this link. There's nothing business-related about it, though, it's a non-profit organization. We began as a purely privately funded organization, for our first years, deliberately, so as to unhinge ourselves from the public funding mechanism in Austria. It is an extremely generous system, but there are too many institutions here who are fully dependent on it, and we didn't want to be. In recent years, once we had fully established ourselves, we've entered into a partnership with the Ministry of Culture and we are now co-funded. We work purely within the visual arts. Our job is to help the extraordinary artists that live and work here, whether they're Austrian or not, to get out into the world and to be seen in biennials and museums. And at the same time, we help the galleries, museums, curators, and critics who are here, the whole ecosystem.

***ASC: How did your experience as a curator define what you have built with Phileas over the last ten years?***

**JS:** I don't do a great deal of curatorial work at Phileas *per se*. People often think that curators spend their time installing art, writing texts, and traveling around the world. But there's a ton of administration involved in curating, if you're doing it properly. You're doing hours of research, dealing with insurance, writing loan requests, dealing with exhibition designers, architects, lighting technicians, all the rest of it. You're proofreading books. I think the fact that I've understood that the curatorial — and I probably refer to myself as and foremost as a curator still — that there is a lot of very unglamorous, administrative, organizational work and logistics that go into curating that have equipped me very well for doing something like this. If I'd been the type of curator that was never involved in fundraising, that didn't care about events, didn't care about how dinners were produced, I would find it very hard to be doing what I'm doing now.

*ASC: You curated the Austrian Pavilion at the 55th Venice Biennale. What a dream. What was that experience like? And how did the process differ from other exhibitions that you've curated?*

**JS:** Venice is a completely unique thing. It cannot be compared with curating any exhibition anywhere else. I received a phone call from the then-Minister of Culture, inviting me to be the curator. I was allowed to choose the artist myself as there was no jury system at the time.

*ASC: Is there a jury system now?*

**JS:** There is now, yes. There's an open call and teams of artists and curators apply together. Back in 2013, I could choose any Austrian artist. The first question that I asked was, "Could I see the archive of all the photographs of all the exhibitions that have happened here over the last 100 and something years?" and they said, "We don't have anything. There is no archive." So before I even chose an artist, I set in motion a process to build that archive and publish what turned out to be a 500-page book documenting the entire history of Austria's participation at the Venice Biennale since 1895. It has helped every curator since, because you can actually see how the Austrian Pavilion building has shed its skin repeatedly, year on year. For the pavilion itself we produced a 1930s-style hand-drawn animated movie by the artist Mathias Poledna. It was produced in five editions, which are now at the Tate, the Whitney, the Art Institute of Chicago, the Los Angeles County Museum of Art, and with Francesca Habsburg, so we all feel proud about what was achieved. And what's more, Phileas probably wouldn't exist without that project because the group of funders that we put together for the Austrian Pavilion became the nucleus of what created Phileas ten years ago and still exists today.

*

I left the interview with Jasper feeling inspired by Austria's creative scene. His extensive career showed me a lot of different ways someone can curate. Independently, for private collections, for museums, paving the way with new ideas for how to activate museum programming, as well as growing into new business models after developing a deeper understanding of how the ecosystem works. I was excited to head to my next interview with someone at a world-renowned museum, Elsy Lahner, the Deputy Chief Curator for Contemporary Art at Albertina Modern, to hear more about what her job entails.

---

*Elsy Lahner has been a curator for contemporary art at the Albertina in Vienna since 2011. Prior to this, she worked as an independent curator and, from 2007 to 2011, cofounded and directed the exhibition space das weisse haus. She serves on the jury for Visual Arts Prizes in Vienna (since 2023). She has previously served on the advisory board for visual arts of the Austrian Federal Chancellery (2014–16) and was a jury member for the Strabag Art Award, for Drawing Now Paris, and for the Klocker Stiftung in Innsbruck (2013–20). From 2009 to 2010, she was curator in residence at the Academy of Fine Arts Vienna.*

---

**Alexandra Steinacker-Clark: Can you tell me about your education and career path, Elsy? What led you to the Albertina Museum?**

**Elsy Lahner:** It's not a straight career path, to be honest. I don't have what one may consider as the "typical career" for a curator. I studied psychology and worked at Salzburger Kunstverein for an internship, which is how I got into art. I moved to Vienna and worked in a gallery there for four years, then I started to produce my own exhibitions as a curator. In 2007, I founded an art space in the city together with Alexandra Grausam, which is called "das weisse haus." Since 2011, I have been at the Albertina Museum.

***ASC: Tell me more about founding das weisse haus.***

**EL:** When I started as a curator, I was working a lot with artists my age, with a younger generation. At the time, there were a lot of artist-run spaces or independent art spaces that are called "off spaces" in German (which is not German at all, nor is it really English—so it's a funny term). We wanted to have a platform for artists to be discovered, not dissimilar to a Kunstverein, and we wanted to provide an open space for artists to work on exhibitions, to try out what they wanted to do, to show what they wanted to show. We didn't want das weisse house to be the typical "white cube" exhibition space, but location-wise we had to move after its first year. It started in the 7th district in Vienna, and then we moved to the 1st district, then the 5th and the 4th . . . So it's traveled as a semi-permanent exhibition space. Neither I nor Alexandra are involved in the leadership of it anymore, although Alexandra ran it up until 2023. We founded it as a place that was meant for artists to discover their own art and find out how to present works, how to react to the audience and to the visitors. On the other hand, of course, it was a lot about art education and telling people what the art was about by providing text, video interviews, and giving visitors the opportunity to learn about contemporary art.

***ASC: How has that experience impacted your approach to curating now? I am thinking about anyone who is interested in one day curating at a museum and who could try and carve their own way, like you did.***

**EL:** My role as a curator here is a different one than that of a director at a small art space. When I was at das weisse haus, I was responsible for public relations and having to figure out how to get funding. In my *Space Invasions*, which I did before das weisse haus, I painted the walls and handed out flyers. That was all part of the job. Being a curator in a bigger institution, it's somehow slower, but you have a huge network with your colleagues, and you can all have your own experiences you bring when working together. When I started at the Albertina Museum, because of my experience in supporting younger artists, I initiated interventions featuring younger positions which was strongly supported by our director back then. This is still something I keep in mind when I curate group shows, for example: I try to include younger artists as well, even though now it's not my generation anymore. Being a curator at the museum is different from being a curator in an art space. As a curator for contemporary art, I do exhibitions, but I also work on publications for almost all the exhibitions I'm curating. I care for the collection, I manage acquisitions and donations, and ensure all the data in our database is correct and operational.

**ASC: *And a typical work day for you, what does that look like?***

**EL:** I start with emails, maybe even reading them on the way to work. When I do that, I try to figure out what the most important things are to do right straight away. It would be nice to read a lot and conduct a lot of research about the exhibitions every day, but in reality there is a lot of organization and having conversations with the artists and their studios. Today, for example, I had a meeting with my colleague in the publications department, another meeting with my colleague who is preparing the merchandising, and I wrote an article for one of our next shows. We also received a donation to the collection and are assessing the insurance value for that, which was another meeting I attended. I am currently working on three exhibitions while always developing ideas for the next ones—so it is quite varied.

*ASC: Very varied indeed! I am intrigued to hear that there is a lot of needing to have an overview of all the different pieces that come together to form exhibitions and collections in an institution.*

**EL:** I consider myself a switchboard, in a way. I have to ensure everybody has the right information. Our conservators need a list of works that we are planning to show so they can allocate how they will do their condition reports. I have to inform the press department so they can start their public relations and work together with the artist studio, for instance. My colleague in the exhibition-management department is waiting for a list of works so she can ask the shipping companies for estimates.

*ASC: What is a difficult aspect of the job, something that you find particularly challenging about it?*

**EL:** We think about the whole museum when curating and usually we have one exhibition with contemporary art, but then, of course, also historic exhibitions or photography exhibitions. Each exhibition attracts a different kind of audience. We want people who are coming to see a photography exhibition to also feel enticed to see the other exhibitions. When I curate, I have to think for the whole museum, how it works together, and what kind of story we want to tell in total, not just for the particular exhibition on its own. The hard part is to always consider what is important for the museum, what is important for the artist, what is important for the visitors, and create something that fits into all of that. Sometimes it's also challenging to manage multiple projects at the same time. However, I genuinely love working on several projects simultaneously. What I personally find difficult is carving out the right moment—and especially a calm moment, which rarely exists—to write my catalog and exhibition texts.

*ASC: What is specific about your job here in Vienna as a city, in Austria as a country?*

**EL:** When I compare my role to those of curators in Germany, the UK, or maybe in the United States, I think the difference is in the way we think about funding. In other countries, curators have to seek financial support for exhibitions, accompanying publications, and more—it's incredibly time-consuming. In the United States, the job of a curator is heavily involved with fundraising, thinking about how to get works in the collection, and how to get money for the exhibitions. Although, I have to admit it has changed here in recent years as well, because making an exhibition has become quite expensive with shipping costs increasing, for example. We have to think about these costs in advance, and then we have to see whether we can make an exhibition possible. We ask galleries, artists, and collectors for support, so this has definitely become a bigger part of our job than it was before. I am happy that there are a lot of grants and funding for publications and exhibitions in Austria.

*ASC: If someone wanted to follow in your footsteps and do what you do, what advice, or maybe even warnings, would you give them?*

**EL:** Don't wait until there is a perfect opportunity. If you don't have a "white cube" space, think about the possibilities of how to use whatever space you have access to. Think outside institutions, maybe even in public spaces, and find your opportunities there. You can do things on a low budget. I raised funds for my first project by getting donations for providing drinks because I wasn't established enough to request funding straight away. The next time around, though, I was able to secure funding. It's important to have your longer-term goals in mind, but still, you can start being a curator with just a room for three days. Hans Ulrich Obrist started with curating exhibitions in his kitchen, for example. Get creative to make things possible.

*

Elsy's advice made me think about all of the exhibitions in weird spaces I had seen and loved in the past. My friend, art critic, and curator Sophie Nowakowska curated an exhibition in an abandoned butcher's shop in London. Betty Leung, an amazing artist working with AI-generated imagery on fabric with sewing and sculpture, exhibited one of her intertwining soft sculpture works in a kitchen in an apartment in Vauxhall, with the formations jutting in and out of cupboards and bursting from the oven (obviously cleaned and turned off). What I learned from Elsy is that you may not be presented with the perfect opportunities to curate at the beginning of your career—so you should go and create them wherever you can, because that can make for a really interesting exhibition.

I first interviewed Gražina Subelytė, a curator at the Peggy Guggenheim Collection in Venice, for my podcast in 2022, during the Venice Biennale. Fast-forward to 2025, after staying in touch throughout those years, I had the delight of sitting down with her again for this book. Navigating through Venice alleyways and crossing what felt like 50 bridges by the time I found my way there, I walked through the gates in Dorsoduro to enter the 18th-century Palazzo Venier dei Leoni, where Peggy lived for over 30 years alongside her extensive personal collection of modern art. Heading up the stairs to the private offices of the PGC staff where I had interviewed her three years prior, I sat down across from Gražina to interview her for a second time.

---

*Gražina Subelytė is the curator at the Peggy Guggenheim Collection. She has been at the PGC for over 15 years, starting as an intern and working in different departments before taking on a role in the curatorial department. She has a PhD from the Courtauld Institute of Art, specializing in the work of the Swiss–American Surrealist artist and scholar Kurt Seligmann.*

---

*Alexandra Steinacker-Clark: Gražina, it's lovely to be here with you today in Venice. Tell me briefly about your education and professional experiences. Can you take me through your career path thus far?*

**Gražina Subelytė:** I studied for my BA in Germany at the Jacobs University Bremen, and I did a double major in Social and Political Sciences and History and Theory of Arts and Literature. I then went on to do my master's at Christie's Education in London in Modern and Contemporary Art in collaboration with the University of Glasgow. Later on, while I was at the Guggenheim, I did my PhD at the Courtauld Institute of Art in London. I specialized in the Swiss artist Kurt Seligmann, who was a specialist in magic in the Surrealist movement. In terms of professional experiences, I've tried out many internships, including at Christie's Auction House in Berlin, at the ZKM (Center for Art and Media) in Karlsruhe, worked in a private art gallery in London, and did an internship in a company researching looted art in London as well. I eventually came to the Guggenheim in Venice to do an internship about seventeen and a half years ago, and I basically never left.

*ASC: Within your role now, can you describe some of the responsibilities you have as Curator for the Peggy Guggenheim Collection?*

**GS:** In certain museums, there are curators that just take care of modern art, for example, or somebody who is specifically dedicated to photography or video. Here at the Peggy Guggenheim Collection Venice, I deal with all kinds of art related to the period during which Peggy Guggenheim lived and collected. More specifically, mainly European and North American modernism. There are two main areas of my work. First of all, together with our team here, I curate the permanent collection of the museum, which entails the presentation and interpretation of the collection. It is all about creating dialogues and affinities between the artworks within our collection displays. We change those displays several times per year because certain artworks, like drawings, are quite fragile, so they have to be swapped out every three or four months. We also lend quite a few artworks to other institutions, so when artworks travel, we have to replace them with others. In some cases, it might be an easy replacement—one painting replaced with another. In other cases, it means that we have to change the entire room. As a curator, I think of a vision for that room and also write the interpretative materials. In some museums, it's the education department, for instance, that carries this responsibility, but at the PGC it is the curators that write the interpretative materials.

The second area of my work consists of curating exhibitions. We met last time when I curated the exhibition *Surrealism and Magic* in summer 2022. And at the moment I'm working on at least three exhibitions for the future. We start working on them a long time in advance, at least three or four years. There are many steps in the process, from selecting the artworks for your dream checklist and thinking of a potential exhibition layout, often starting on a 3D maquette. Then comes writing the loan requests and working on the exhibition catalog. Authors need to be identified and, as a curator, it is my responsibility to provide the vision for that exhibition and also the publication alongside it. In addition to those two areas, there are many collaborations that happen with other departments in a museum because it's like an organism. We in the curatorial department sometimes assist with certain texts for the social-media department. We work very closely with the membership department and we give tours and travel with museum patrons. We also work with the education department when brainstorming public programs. These are just some of the examples that show how the curatorial department is not by itself, but we very truly collaborate with everybody.

***ASC: What does your day-to-day look like from start to finish?***

**GS:** Every single day differs. One day might be spent researching, going to the libraries around town, trying to find information about the artists whose exhibitions I'm working on, or sometimes even chasing a specific date because maybe there are three publications that all mention a very different date. It is up to the curator to leave no stone unturned, almost going on a scavenger hunt. You're the person who's going to be presenting this information to the public, so you have to make sure that all your facts are accurate. We're constantly researching our permanent collection, too. We have a *catalogue raisonné* that was written in 1985. We've realized that, even when the author interviewed Peggy Guggenheim back in the day, some of the dates and details she remembered were not accurate, so it is up to us to research and redress that.

Other days, I could be giving tours, or I might be going on trips accompanying our patrons. We recently ventured to Naples and Mexico, for instance. Of course, on other days I could be dealing with a lot of emails that come in, as there is a lot of administration in curatorial work. I meet with our exhibitions manager to look at the budget together and see, with all the loans that we have confirmed, if we are still within the agreed-upon budget. Transportation costs are constantly rising, so I check if we are already stretching our limits, or can we still add a work that I'm very interested in? I also have meetings with the corporate department to talk about future exhibitions because they plan fundraising strategies for them. I devote other days to writing texts. Of course, when we are reinstalling the permanent collection or temporary exhibitions, then my

---

* A *catalogue raisonné* is an annotated comprehensive, scholarly publication of the works of an artist or group of artists and can contain all works or a selection of works categorized by different parameters such as medium or period — often referred to in the industry as a "cat res."

entire day is usually spent in the exhibition spaces. There are many other tasks/meetings that come up otherwise—I noted only some examples.

*ASC: Your title is Associate Curator at the time of interviewing you* — can you explain the nuance there? What is the difference between a curatorial assistant, an assistant curator, an associate curator, a curator, a senior curator, and so on?*

**GS:** I'm currently Associate Curator, yes. We also have a curatorial assistant and a curatorial-conservation intern. The curatorial assistant supports the curator of the permanent collection and of exhibitions with administrative tasks and research, accompanying them and learning. It is an assistant role. As an assistant curator, you take on more curatorial responsibilities and may start leading on your projects. Often, an assistant curator starts by working on collection-based exhibitions (but it really depends on the institution), while also assisting the curator. Then, as an associate curator or curator, you are the curator whose responsibility it is to shape the vision of the museum's permanent collection while proposing exhibitions and executing them. Here, I always first discuss any ideas I have with our director, and she makes the final decisions. The exact curatorial duties can vary by institution, but these titles generally reflect a progression from support roles to leadership in content and strategy.

*ASC: If someone wanted to do what you do, where do you think they could start?*

**GS:** First and foremost, I think doing studies in art history is extremely important. I am speaking from the perspective of a curator of classical modern art, so 20th-century art that has already been historicized. When it comes to contemporary art, there are so many curatorial courses where

---

*   Since this interview took place, Gražina's title has changed to Curator.

you're thinking about new ways of curating, which is more relevant when it comes to working with contemporary artists. When it comes to historicized art, you really have to know the material. Beyond that, try to get work experience if you can. Apply for internships, or even see if you can shadow somebody at work.

***ASC: What is specific about curating in Venice, especially when programming during the Venice Biennale?***

**GS:** We don't necessarily align our exhibitions with the Biennale's programming. We have our programming planned out until 2030 and we don't know what the topics of the upcoming Biennales are going to be. We were very lucky that *Surrealism and Magic* was programmed at the time when Cecilia Alemani curated the 2022 Biennale Arte inspired by Surrealism. I was working on my show about seven years in advance, but sometimes the stars just align.

***ASC: Have you ever made a step in your career that you regretted? And if you have, how did you navigate that situation?***

**GS:** I think that one thing leads you to another and you end up being exactly where you are meant to be. Something that might seem like a detour eventually ends up being the exact thing that you need. In the beginning when I came here, I was an intern, and then intern coordinator for a couple of years—slightly closer to human resources, if you will. Then I became a registrar and exhibition manager for a year, on maternity cover for one of my colleagues. I wasn't even sure if I would be able to stay here, but our former director created a new position for me to be his curatorial assistant, and then I grew into my role as curator. I didn't know during that time that this was going to happen, but what I did is I fully trusted the process. I trusted that if you work hard, if you're devoted, the right people will notice. And they did.

***ASC: What advice or even warnings would you give to someone who wants to do what you do?***

**GS:** Showing commitment is important in any job, so don't be afraid to show your passion. Have patience because it will take some time, nothing really comes to you immediately. I do very much understand that there is so much more competition now than 17 years ago when I was starting out. Always be yourself, and I do believe, sometimes when you least expect it, amazing things will happen.

*

After hearing from Jasper, Elsy, and Gražina, I finally felt like I understood the role of a curator in both art by living artists today as well as historical art. The role extends beyond the organization of exhibitions or choosing where an artwork will hang. A curator needs to wear many hats—they are organizers, researchers, communicators, leaders, and sometimes even diplomats, navigating the complex relationships between artists, institutions, and the public. One thing I learned from these interviews is that aspiring curators should not feel confined to traditional education and career paths. It is positive to try different curatorial methods and styles before stepping into an institutional position.

## KEY TAKEAWAYS IF YOU ARE THINKING OF EMBARKING ON YOUR OWN CAREER IN CURATING

### Three Practical Tips

- Gain diverse experiences by seeking opportunities in both established institutions and independent projects. Each setting offers unique insights and skill-building experiences. Check out initiatives like New Curators (which is a paid year-long curatorial training programme for London-based aspiring curators of contemporary art from lower socio-economic backgrounds) or curatorial residencies on callforcurators.com.

- Fostering relationships through networking is vital in order to build connections with artists, other curators, and industry professionals, which could lead to collaborative opportunities.
- If you stay informed of contemporary art trends as well as historical contexts to enhance the depth of your curatorial practice, it will show in your curatorial approach.

## Next Steps

- Start curating small exhibitions or projects in available spaces to build a portfolio—don't limit yourself to a "white-cube" space! Think about spaces you can access and how you can activate them creatively.
- Attend art exhibitions with two goals in mind—to network and build your address book with arts professionals and artists, as well as to train your eye and see how others approach curating various spaces.
- Consider further education—both art historical and curatorially practical—to refine your approach and understanding of the arts, depending on what area of the arts you want to pursue a curatorial career in. (For contemporary, think about creative curatorial courses, but for historic curators researching the art-historical material is key.)

# CHAPTER 4
# WORKING IN RESPONSIBLE CULTURE

What is restitution? How do you conduct provenance research? How can the art world be sustainable, beyond recycling the unused press releases from a past exhibition? Responsible culture encompasses a range of sub-disciplines. In this chapter, I speak to professionals from two different areas of responsible culture. The first is sustainability, exploring how the art world can do better by our planet and what sort of work can be done to ensure that. The second is restitution, cultural property, and provenance, and in this case, specifically within an auction-house context. Other areas within responsible culture can include Diversity, Equity and Inclusion, philanthropy, or other socially engaged and ethical practices. I believe a lot of the lessons shared in the subsequent interviews will be transferable to these areas as well, so I urge you to keep this in mind as you read on if you have interest in any of these categories falling under the "responsible-culture" umbrella.

I first met Caitlin Southwick when she came on the *All About Art* podcast in 2023 to speak about her work with Ki Culture, an international non-profit working to unite culture and sustainability by providing programs and tools to make culture sustainable and position the sector as leaders for sustainability. We met at the podcast studio in London. Caitlin had traveled from the Netherlands, where she was living at the time, and we had an enlightening discussion on the ways that the sector could be more sustainable. In 2025, I was the one traveling to meet Caitlin, in Rome, Italy. She picked me up from the train station with her dog Max, and we strolled to her apartment where we sat down in the afternoon Italian sun and conducted the interview.

*Caitlin Southwick is the Founder of Ki Culture and Ki Futures. She holds a Professional Doctorate in Conservation and Restoration of Cultural Heritage from the University of Amsterdam. Caitlin has worked in the conservation field and in museums around the world, including the Vatican Museums, the Getty Conservation Institute, and Rapa Nui. She was a Professional Member of the American Institute of Conservation's Sustainability Committee, the Secretary for the Working Group on Sustainability for the International Council of Museums (ICOM) and is a Climate Reality Leader.*

**Alexandra Steinacker-Clark: *What did you do before you started Ki?***

**Caitlin Southwick:** I got my undergraduate degree at Boston University, studying ancient history. Afterwards, I decided to move abroad to Florence, Italy, to study art conservation, because I had heard it was the best place for it. I fell in love with it, continued my studies and ended up getting degrees in Italy, the UK, and the Netherlands. I have a Professional Doctorate, a Master's of Science, and a few more qualifications. The idea, of course, was to become an art conservator, but during my studies and my practical experience working on-site, I started making the connection between sustainability and conservation, and realizing how unbelievably unsustainable art conservation is. Eventually, I couldn't really align my moral and ethical compass with what I was doing in the lab and on-site. Standing on the beaches of Rapa Nui dumping toxic chemicals over the Moai* just churned my stomach. I thought there's got to be a better way to do this.

---

*    Moai, or mo'ai, are monolithic human figures carved by the Rapa Nui people on Rapa Nui (Easter Island) in eastern Polynesia between the years 1250 and 1500.

***ASC: Can you describe some of the responsibilities you have as the director of a company that focuses on sustainability in the cultural sector?***

**CS:** I started out thinking sustainability work needed a "how-to" manual, so I created the Ki Books, which were comprehensive guidebooks full of step-by-step instructions. However, I quickly realized that just having the information wasn't enough. People would download the books and then never look at them again. They'd sit on desks unread, or people would start them but get stuck at some point. Sustainability isn't passive, it's really an active movement that needs community and ongoing support. This led to Ki Futures, which combined coaching, training, and community support. It sounded great in theory, but it ended up being way too broad and too education-focused. I was covering everything from decolonization to energy audits to green banking—fascinating stuff, but people were still asking "okay, but what do we actually *do*?" The need for action ended up morphing Ki Futures into my Climate Control Program. Instead of trying to cover everything, I focused on one specific goal: updating climate conditions and reviewing energy efficiency. I made it time-bound (18 months) with tangible action and results (and no room for procrastination!). The whole journey took six years of experimenting and iterating. Sustainability is ultimately about helping people, and that means figuring out not just what information they need, but how to actually support them in taking action. You can't just expect to create the resources and hope they take action on their own. Impact needs encouragement.

An interesting part of working in sustainability is the difference in requirements of expertise. A lot of the jobs that we have these days are incredibly niche. I'm an art conservator—but I'm not just an art conservator, I'm a stone conservator. But I'm not just a stone conservator, I'm a marble conservator—specializing in Carrara marble. That's about as niche as it gets! But when it comes to my work in sustainability, I don't have a specialization. I have a wide knowledge base—a little bit of everything — encompassing decolonization, repatriation, energy efficiency, waste and materials, green banking, etc . . . It's vital to take a step back to see the bigger picture. It involves critical thinking and questioning the status quo. Why do we do what we do? Is there a better way? I may not know the answer, but I know someone in my community who does. Sustainability isn't something you can do alone.

In terms of running a business, there's an interesting distinction here — being the director of a company and focusing on sustainability in the cultural sector. I learned very quickly that those were two different things, and I was really good at one of them. Being the director of a company is the same no matter what type of company it is — non-profit, for-profit — it doesn't matter. A business is a business. I would have had a very similar role if I had started a company that made and sold reusable coffee cups. It involves making sure that the company is functioning and financially viable. It's also managing people, delegating, and growing the company. Running a business was taking away too much focus from what I really wanted to be doing, to be honest.

***ASC: By the time this book comes out, your company will have finalized its transition with Articheck. What does that next step entail?***

**CS:** Yes! I am very excited, Ki Futures is combining forces with the company Articheck, which is a leading technology platform transforming how the cultural sector manages and protects its assets. They work with digital condition reporting, standardized workflows, collaborative tools, and data capture that make art handling more secure, efficient, *and sustainable*. It all happened very organically, because I've been working with Articheck for years and I love what they do. Throughout my entire experience with running Ki, Annika has been there for me as a fellow female founder and CEO, as a fellow conservator turned entrepreneur, and as a fellow expat living in a foreign country. We have so many parallels, including our personal passion for sustainability. Articheck is a tech company, but they believe in technology supporting sustainability and implement this thinking into the design of their software. While Ki will remain a separate company to the main Articheck company, the collaboration and support of the Articheck team enables me to focus on what I do best, and for Ki to thrive.

As I mentioned earlier, I had come to a realization that my strengths did not lie in being a CEO, but instead they are in creating programming to help people make a difference, and that's where I can have my biggest impact and where I have the most joy. I didn't want to run a company anymore and Articheck gave me the opportunity to step away from that while continuing to do what I love. It's a win–win–win!

*ASC: If someone wanted to work in sustainability but wasn't ready to actually launch a company like you did, where do you think they could start, or what sort of options are there to work in that area within the cultural sector?*

**CS:** In a lot of cases, it's a matter of creating opportunities. Being honest here, there are so few jobs that are sustainability and culture specific. For example, there may be around ten curators of sustainability in the entire world. I know of five sustainability leads at museums. Those jobs are few and far between, and often they are given to people who do not have a cultural background, but instead to people who have a sustainability background. If you have a cultural background and you want to combine that with sustainability, a lot of people assume you have to go and study sustainability. Which of course you can — and I always support more education on the topic! And sustainability is a fabulous way to stand out as a candidate for any job in the cultural sector.

In any cultural role, you can find ways to insert sustainability into your job. I do an exercise with various cultural professionals where we rewrite their job description to include additional sustainability tasks, or reframe current ones to incorporate sustainability. For example, in one job description for a curator the responsibilities include "Ensure collections are properly preserved." Let's make that sustainable! Update that task to read "Ensure collections are properly preserved *in the most energy efficient way.*" All of a sudden, it is literally your job to help reduce energy consumption. You might add a sustainability policy to your procurement contracts or make sure that you're working with the artists who have sustainability as part of either the materiality of their work or the subject of their work. It can be challenging because it may feel like extra work, but it's so important that we incorporate sustainability into what we are already doing and into our working hours rather than continuing to make it a task that is in our free time or an "eventual want."

*ASC: Having an "intrapreneurial" spirit!*

**CS:** Anyone who is employed can be an intrapreneur because they have a job that they can add value to, expand, and make it more their own. Sustainability is all about problem solving—it's about being creative. And that's why I feel so strongly that the cultural sector is the right fit for sustainability leadership! Because we are creative! It all ties together.

*ASC: What is a piece of advice you would give someone who wants to break into the realm of sustainability in the arts?*

**CS:** Persistence is key, especially when it comes to sustainability. You don't have to start your own company, but no matter what, I think that the same rules apply, persistence and courage. If you want to bring sustainability into your job, don't take no for an answer. Figure out a way to do it. If you're really passionate about it, you really want to do it, then you can 1,000 percent make it happen.

*

On King Street, near Green Park in central London, I made my way to Christie's Auction House to speak to someone else working in responsible culture, but in a completely different area. Lauren Farrington is not only a dear friend, but an incredibly skilled art historian and provenance researcher. If you have ever wondered about what happens when the provenance of an artwork raises questions or red flags about having been looted by the Nazis between 1933 and 1945 (and how you can be the one discovering it), Lauren has the answers.

---

*Lauren Farrington is a German–American art historian specializing in provenance research and its due diligence. Her research on Nazi-era restitution and art crime has been featured on the BBC1's* Fake or Fortune *and published on various media outlets, such as BBC News, ITV News, and the* Independent. *Before joining Christie's as Restitution Researcher in 2024, she worked at the Art Loss Register.*

---

**Alexandra Steinacker-Clark: Can you take me through your career path thus far, and what led you to what you do today?**

**Lauren Farrington:** I did my undergraduate degree in California, majoring in German studies and art history. During that time, I spent a semester in Berlin and took a course titled 'Art and Dictatorship' on the intersection of art and politics under dictatorships in the 20th century— Francisco Franco in Spain and the cultural policies they introduced, Benito Mussolini in Italy and the interest in Futurism, Soviet Russia where modernism was initially championed but shifted to social realism, and then, of course, Nazi Germany and their cultural policies which were very anti-modernism. This ignited my interest in the field. I went back to the US and wrote my bachelor's thesis on Nazi-era cultural policy and degenerate art specifically. After graduation, I moved to Germany full time on a Fulbright Scholarship. I knew I wanted to work in the art sector, so I applied for a master's degree in the history of art at UCL.

I specialized again in 20th-century art and politics in Germany. My thesis focused on the *Erinnerungskultur* (memory culture) surrounding "degenerate" and Nazi-looted artworks. I was looking into the memory these objects carry; beyond their physical displacement, they are intertwined with very deeply personal histories. This is something that I then was able to eventually turn into a career, but directly after my master's it wasn't that simple a journey. Before my master's, I hadn't even realized provenance research existed as a job. I worked in education in museums for a few years whilst applying to jobs closer to my interest. My first job in provenance research came three years after I finished my MA when I joined the Art Loss Register (ALR). I stayed there for about four years, mostly working in provenance research for their restitution team. During that time, I had worked with my now manager at Christie's, as Christie's is also a client of the ALR. That connection eventually led me to my current role here at Christie's restitution team.

***ASC: What are your responsibilities as a restitution researcher for one of the biggest auction houses in the world?***

**LF:** My main responsibility is to investigate the ownership histories of art objects with a focus between 1933 and 1945. This spans all categories across the auction house for any art object that was created prior to 1945. This could be a manuscript, an antique Roman bust, a Louis XV soup tureen, an Old Master's painting, or something more modern. My work is to research and identify any objects that may have been subject to looting, dispossession, or forced sale during the Nazi era. I do that by conducting in-depth provenance research, consulting a wide range of specialized internal and external databases, as well as dealer records and historic auction records, to fully trace a painting's ownership history. Many of these key resources are now publicly accessible online; however, this has only been the case for the last 15 years or so. The digitization of wartime inventories, post-war restitution claims, and other historical records has transformed the way we do our research today. However, there are still plenty of materials not digitized or accessible online, so I will often reach out to an archive or travel there myself to conduct this research.

***ASC: What does a typical work day look like for you? How has that changed throughout your career as you gained experience in different organizations?***

**LF:** I might review works planned to be offered for sale in an upcoming auction sale and their cataloging, and start with a risk analysis. I start by looking at the provenance, or in other words the ownership history of these works. I look for names that might be problematic, if the work changed hands between 1933 and 1945, or a suspicious gap in provenance. If I identify something that looks sensitive, that becomes the starting point for my research. I'll check specialized databases and search for potential matches for wartime losses.

Due to the nature of our work, where these objects were dispossessed under persecution, documentation is often scarce. Database registrations for missing artworks may lack images, dimensions, or medium, and titles and attributions can change over time. I will cross-reference as much archival material, such as sale records or exhibition catalogs, to see if I can construct a bigger picture of the work that we have consigned for sale. This is a core part of the work, when I have a potential match, doing as much research as possible to analyze whether a work is likely to be the one in question.

I think all provenance researchers say that we tend to look much more closely at the back of an artwork for physical traces of the artwork's history. These reverses can offer really important clues like labels, stamps, gallery stickers, signatures, stock numbers, handwritten notes. For example, works that were processed by the Monuments Men and Women* will often have a blue number that's been written in chalk on the back of the picture or on the bottom of an object. These things can also help identify an artwork's history.

At the Art Loss Register, my previous job, I was doing Nazi-era provenance research, but they conduct due diligence for the art market which includes research into stolen works beyond 1933–45, and it is done across the art market as a whole. The Art Loss Register has over 140 auction houses as clients, along with the major art fairs like Art Basel, Frieze, and TEFAF as well. It's much more broad in terms of who they serve at the Art Loss Register.

***ASC: Can you tell me something that I wouldn't expect to hear about your job? What is something that many would be surprised to know?***

**LF:** People are often surprised by how much remains unresolved in terms of Nazi-era looting. It's very difficult to know how many artworks were displaced, but estimates generally range in excess of 650,000 objects having been looted from Nazi-occupied territories in Europe. Today it is estimated that anywhere between tens of thousands to more than 100,000 works remain missing. The world was not as sensitized to the issues of art displaced during World War II as it is today and there were few, if any, resources available to researchers in the field. It was only in the late 1990s, with the signing of the Washington Principles in 1998—a set of 11 guidelines co-signed by 44 governments to guide the research,

---

* The "Monuments Men and Women" refers to the Monuments, Fine Arts, and Archives (MFAA) Section, a wartime unit composed of museum curators, historians, and other specialists tasked with protecting and recovering works of art looted by the Nazis during World War II.

identification, and restitution of Nazi-confiscated art to rightful owners or their heirs—that a more tangible framework was put in place. Since then, the digitization of provenance research resources and increased access to wartime archives have made research more feasible.

**ASC: What is something you find difficult about the work that you do?**

**LF:** It can be very heavy because provenance research focusing on the years 1933 to 1945 often means confronting histories of persecution, forced displacement, and systematic dispossession of property. It involves more than merely identifying a chain of ownership. You are also looking at the broader structures that enabled such losses, including antisemitic laws, forced sales, state-sanctioned confiscations. In this context, these artworks take on a significance that extends beyond their cultural or aesthetic significance as art objects. Every object has the potential to reveal an individual story and it's important to remember that there is very real human suffering behind these names.

**ASC: If someone wants to work in provenance research and restitution, where do you think that they could start?**

**LF:** I would recommend starting with some of the seminal literature. There are many publications in most European languages, but I will give some English recommendations. Firstly, Lynn H. Nicholas's book *The Rape of Europa*, which is considered the definitive account of Nazi art-looting across Europe and the Allied efforts sent to recover property. It's a great overview and was also turned into a documentary film in 2009. Then there is Hector Feliciano's book *The Lost Museum*, which focuses on looting in France, particularly collections like those from the Rothschild or Schloss families. The third one that I would recommend is Rose Valland's memoir *The Art Front: The Defense of French Collections*

*1939–1945*, which was recently translated into English. It's an extraordinary firsthand account from the curator of the Jeu du Paume (which was used by the Nazis as their looted-art storage facility) who secretly tracked Nazi art looting in occupied Paris and became one of the most important figures in post-war restitution. In addition to reading materials, sign up to the Arthist.net and International Art Market Studies Association newsletters as they send through job postings, conferences, and other resources. Specifically for provenance research of the 1933 to 1945 era, sign up to the lootedart.com newsletter, which is run by the Commission for Looted Art in Europe.

In terms of job opportunities, auction houses, museums, and other institutes all offer internships or work experience, which is a great entry point into the field. I don't know if these things get widely advertised, though, so it might be worth reaching out to people who work at the place where you'd like to gain experience and inviting them for a coffee. For students, there is also the opportunity to apply to the Christie's Grant for Nazi-era Provenance Research. The grant is offered annually to fund applicants researching Nazi-era and restitution-related topics. You can find out more information on the Christie's Restitution website.

***ASC: If someone wanted to do what you do, what advice would you give them?***

**LF:** My job is quite specific in that it requires curiosity but simultaneously a tolerance for ambiguity, because you might not be able to solve every question you have. I would also say hone your language skills because it's important to be able to read primary documentation in German, French, and Dutch. Read the relevant literature, attend conferences, and stay up to date on news relating to the topic; the field is ever-evolving. Be prepared for the learning curve because there is a gap between the theoretical knowledge and the day-to-day practice of provenance research—particularly the nuances of each individual object and its story. There is also a learning curve in knowing where to find what information, as it's not always found on Google. In this job, you build up your skills object by object. You never stop learning.

*

A takeaway from speaking to Lauren is how much has changed during the last decade in the arts. When Lauren was thinking about what to do for her career, there were no specific university programs or summer schools on art restitution, and the same goes for master's degrees in curating or a more recently emerging one, arts administration and art business. Lauren's role seems to combine both a passion for art history as well as a passion for investigation, all leading to either a sale contributing to the successful running of the auction house or to a family receiving their due. Lauren and Caitlin work in different areas within responsible culture, but they both paved their way by thinking outside the box to secure the knowledge needed to make a difference to the sector through the specific work that they do.

## KEY TAKEAWAYS IF YOU ARE THINKING OF EMBARKING ON YOUR OWN CAREER IN RESPONSIBLE CULTURE

### Three Practical Tips

- Educate yourself continuously by seeking internships or volunteer roles, finding courses on the subject that interests you, and consuming informational online resources.
- Building analytical and problem-solving skills can help you throughout your career (not just in responsible culture, but in general!). Prepare for this by researching deeply and remaining curious throughout your professional endeavors. Ask yourself what you could do to expand whatever role you take on and how that can be meaningful to you.

- Whether it be in sustainability, restitution, or other areas, cultivating emotional resilience is vital. Prepare for emotionally demanding work, advocating for yourself and your beliefs, and seek support from other industry professionals to navigate these situations.

## Next Steps

- Choose one book, whether it be on Nazi-looted art, sustainability in business, or something else, to read to jumpstart your self-education in the area of responsible culture you are interested in.
- Reach out to someone from the industry to have a coffee with them and start cultivating your network. Look at teams in auction houses or museums, as well as specialized companies like Ki Culture or the Art Loss Register.
- Engage with the latest research by looking into conferences you can attend, newsletters you can subscribe to, or articles you can read on what has been happening in the field you are most interested in — some resources are listed at the back of this book.

# CHAPTER 5

# WORKING IN FRAMING AND ART HANDLING

When I first started working at Sotheby's, I kept seeing staff walking around the exhibition rooms (also referred to as the galleries, but not meaning commercial art gallery—in this case, it just means the rooms in which the art is hanging) wearing dark-blue Sotheby's aprons and sometimes sporting white cotton gloves. I asked another colleague who they were, and made a comment about how I also wanted one of those aprons (I have always been a sucker for branded merchandise). I was told that these were the "techs," short for technicians, which is another term used for the role of an art handler. Intrigued, I wanted to know more, and down at the pub later that week, I met a few of them, including Gregory Baker, who is now a close friend.

In this chapter, you will hear from Greg about his experiences in commercial art companies, but he also shares his knowledge on art framing. Subsequently, you will read interviews with the incredible Mikei Hall, who has been at the Tate for over three decades and who has worked with world-renowned artists that have become household names, and Keisha Prioleau-Martin, who gives insights on working as a freelance art handler in New York City while continuing an artistic practice as a painter and sculptor.

---

*Gregory Baker studied Fine Art at Central Saint Martins and has since worked as a fine-art picture framer, including running his own independent framing business, an art handling technician at Sotheby's, and is currently the Gallery and Studio Manager for artist and art dealer David Breuer-Weil.*

---

*Alexandra Steinacker-Clark: What led you to working in the arts, and furthermore into framing and art handling?*

**Greg Baker:** I did foundation-level Art and Design at Reading College and applied to Central Saint Martins (CSM) for their Fine Art degree in the 4D pathway (time-based media). After I graduated, I began my first job at conservation framer Stewart Heslop Frames in Battersea, where I was thrilled to work closely with artworks in the process of learning how to frame them. In the years following, I worked for Michael Harding Artist Oil Colours in Whitechapel and later at John Davies Framing, who specialized in antique reproduction framing, at that time based in St James's, Mayfair. John Davies Framing gave me my first exposure to the secondary art market world as we were within walking distance from a great number of galleries and, in particular, just around the corner from Christie's Auction House on King Street. Measuring up works by Matisse, Brueghel, and Dalí rank as early head-spinning moments! Later on, I worked as an art-handling technician for the Sotheby's warehouse and eventually their New Bond Street location. During all of this, especially due to my early experience with picture framing, I initiated my own practice as a framer, which I continue today. I currently work with David Breuer-Weil, artist and art dealer, as his Gallery and Studio Manager. Suffice to say, the consistent streak that runs throughout my career is my proximity to the materials and physical artwork this industry orbits.

*ASC: Can you describe some of the responsibilities you have as an art handler as well as your work as a framer? They are very much two separate things, but sometimes there are crossovers, right?*

**GB:** The two are very fundamentally linked—framing can be seen as a more specialized refinement of the broad school of art handling. From my time at Stewart Heslop's through to my time at Sotheby's, art handling is an ever-ongoing education in correct procedure. The great challenge with handling any artwork is to do so without damage to yourself (correct lifting technique, communication with your colleagues, awareness of your surroundings) or damage to the work (using suitable gloves, holding a work appropriately, correct installation methods). For example, this might be unpacking a large canvas from a travel-frame/crate, or moving an 80-kg marble bust from one gallery to another, or installing a neon-light sculpture (something we'd always have specialist installers complete, as 40,000 volts would be more than enough to bring an early end to your career). Knowing what your limits are is also vitally important. Physical capability is an aspect of the job, but there is no need to "hero-lift" something when it'll either damage your back or damage the work. There's a reason there are procedures and equipment to help.

Much of this attitude carries over to picture framing. Concentrating more specifically on "flat" artwork—painting, drawing, photography—I find it useful to consider the picture frame as a gallery environment in and of itself. There is a deep cultural history on the role of framing relating to exhibition displays within a gallery context, but turning our attention to the practical concerns begs questions along the lines of conservation techniques: is the glazing sufficiently UV filtering? Should we use glass or clear acrylic if a framed work of art is to travel overseas? Will the materials used in the construction of the frame or mount negatively affect the condition of the artwork? Is the frame constructed in such a way as to allow re-opening or re-fitting? Many questions, but all of these are born out of practical necessity. The curious aspect of framing is that these practical concerns are also met with aesthetic ones—what is suitable for the artwork from a historical context, for example. A contemporary work on canvas might look very inappropriate in a carved and gilded Louis XIV frame, and by comparison an Old Master painting might look utterly peculiar in a sprayed-white contemporary frame.

*ASC: What does a typical work day look like for you, from start to finish, if you are spending the day framing?*

**GB:** It might be useful to consider the whole process of building a frame as if it were structured like a day. I would begin by deciding the style of frame or mount required in consultation with the client. This is primarily a question of aesthetic preference, something which I would verify with the client either in person using frame corner samples or by using Photoshop to generate a digital mockup of how their artwork could look in advance. Depending on whether a work is on paper or on canvas, for example, the work's physicality will determine how big or deep a frame needs to be to accommodate it. If given the go-ahead based on what we have agreed, I'll take accurate measurements of the artwork and determine the dimensions of all other elements of the frame required. From that point, the process of construction begins: cutting wooden lengths to size, pinning/gluing the frame together, filling, sanding, staining, or finishing the frame to match requirements. In addition to that, I will cut the mount and glass, cut the backboard, and mount the work.

Eventually, when the frame is in a suitably complete state, the process of "fitting-up" begins—literally fitting all the elements prepared together into the frame. Once complete, I'll take a photo of the finished frame, send it on to the client, and then wrap the frame ready for collection. Such efficiency of workflow rarely ever happens over the course of one day, though. Tasks from one day are sometimes necessary to complete later or other tasks will jump up as higher priority. Also, it can be easier to complete one part of the process for a number of frames, such as sanding, at the same time. And of course, in between all of this, you have to stop for a tea break or three at some point!

*ASC: What are the most important considerations when choosing framing materials for different types of artwork?*

**GB:** Again, this is a meeting point between practicality and aesthetics. Fundamentally no material should be chosen that will have an adverse or damaging effect on the artwork. This is the essence of conservation framing. A frame should offer layers of protection to ensure its safe housing for continuing enjoyment over the years. Framing something to last an eternity is obviously a rather large benchmark to aim for, but the ambition should be to take whatever measures are required to enjoy a picture for a long time while minimizing any potentially damaging environmental conditions to the work. One concern might be to consider the glazing required. Works on paper will be particularly sensitive to the damaging effects of ultra-violet light from the sun. Although not necessarily something we can witness over the course of minutes, a work on paper will slowly "burn" over months and years if exposed to direct sunlight. To help prevent this, specialist ultra-violet filtering glass is used to block damaging UV light, much like SPF in sunscreen.

***ASC: Can you tell me something you love about art handling and framing?***

**GB:** One of the most enjoyable aspects is having had the opportunity to combine my experience as a picture framer with my position as a technician at Sotheby's, specifically making frames for the Contemporary department for a number of works offered up for auctions. It was a moment of great pride to see a frame I made for a Cy Twombly work on paper hanging on a wall in the sale room. It's been extremely gratifying to find a form of creative work that has a direct place in the world. Also, my current position as Studio Manager for David Breuer-Weil means I enjoy a very rewarding working relationship with David. As an ex-employee of Sotheby's himself, there is a great kinship in our dealings with the auction houses but also on a practical level — David's prolific studio output and idea-generation complements my abilities in methodological problem solving.

***ASC: If someone wanted to do what you do, where do you think they could start?***

**GB:** I've had many jobs that came from word-of-mouth recommendation for either installing works in someone's house or for framing, so it may just be a matter of making contact with art handlers or framers to gain an insight into their respective disciplines. With framing, I would thoroughly recommend applying to work for picture framers — so much experience and instruction can be gained by directly working for a framer. Alternatively, one could look to educational courses such as those run at West Dean College near Chichester or City & Guilds of London Art School — such establishments can provide anything from short courses introducing the basics of picture framing, or more specific skills such as gilding or frame restoration. Art-handling wise, I wish I had known that working as an art technician is a job I could've considered after graduating. Of course, not everyone will have the inclination or interest, and perhaps my starting at Sotheby's came as a result of my experience working at a number of picture framers before, but the auction house gave me a very broad and grounded education in many aspects of art handling. One observation I will offer is that, as gratifying as art handling can be, the salaries offered can be frustratingly low compared to the level of skill required for the role. For me, this proved the inception of beginning my own practice as a framer as a supplementary income.

***ASC: What advice or even warnings would you give to someone who wanted to do what you do?***

**GB:** I can't offer any greater advice other than to be pleasant, make friends, and, when concerning jobs, turn up on time! The world of operations and logistics with the art industry can be quite a small bubble, so it is always best to foster pleasant professional working relationships through your career — you'll undoubtedly bump into your colleagues time and time again. Consistency, dependability, and punctuality are some of the greatest strengths when working in the art world. If you are pleasant to work with, your network of contacts will grow in a very organic way—people will want to work with you again. Of course, there will be days that are disheartening or when things don't go correctly, but I've been able to draw upon the wisdom of a number of my friends if I've reached an impasse. This might be asking for help in moving studios or consulting colleagues on the best way to hang a picture, or asking friends of friends how to go about writing up terms and conditions for invoices. Perhaps the nicest description came from one of my colleagues at Sotheby's, who described our teams as friends who just happen to work together. Perhaps this is due to the unique trauma-bonding experience that comes with working at the speed required of an auction house . . . but it remains true.

*

Greg's sentiment of building friendships rings true. I met him through the auction house, when we both worked there at the same time, but I have learned so much from him since. He taught me how to make a frame, but he also stayed up with me until 3am hanging an exhibition I was curating independently (in exchange for pizza, which definitely doesn't equate to the value of his art-hanging expertise!). He has a keen eye for detail and likes the physical nature of art handling. This seems to be a through-line in all of the interviews with art handlers I spoke to for this chapter: They all love working with their hands.

On a warm but cloudy day in London (so . . . nearly every day of the summer), I hopped on the Victoria line to one of the most reputable art museums in the UK, Tate Britain, to speak to someone who has been there longer than I have been alive. Walking up the stairs to the entrance always leaves me with a feeling of awe. Designed by architect Sidney R. J. Smith in the late 1800s, when you walk in you are greeted by a large, breathtaking atrium crowned by a windowed dome and a circular balcony which you can ascend for a magnificent view of the black and white scallop-pattern terrazzo floor. I met Mikei Hall downstairs on the lower ground floor, and he took me to his office in an adjacent building so we could have a quiet space for him to answer all of my burning questions.

*Mikei Hall is a Senior Art Handling Technician at Tate Britain and has spent over 30 years at the museum. He has become a beloved and highly respected figure, working on numerous exhibitions, including more Turner Prize exhibitions than any other technician. He has worked with artists such as Tracey Emin, Damien Hirst, Matthew Barney, and Monster Chetwynd, to name a few. In 2024, he was nominated for the Sky Arts Hero Award for his work in mentoring the next generation of art handlers and curators.*

***Alexandra Steinacker-Clark: What led you to your role at Tate?***

**Mikei Hall:** Going back in the time machine, I remember leaving school with my A levels, and the one that was probably the most important for me was Art. I've always been what we now regard as a creative person. I didn't quite know what I wanted to do, but I enjoyed making things. I ended up attending the London College of Furniture, which no longer exists today. Once I completed that course, I spent about eight or nine months trying to find a job. Getting a bit frustrated, I found a career center in London, which doesn't exist anymore, which specialized in finding jobs for people in the arts.

***ASC: Well, I guess that could now be akin to recruiters like Sophie MacPherson, Lacey West, or DRAW Recruitment!***

**MH:** At that time, it was quite rare. After a long process of interviewing for various roles—and not getting any—I ended up finding a job at a furniture company. I worked there for about three years, but this was in the 80s when we had a bit of a recession, and my job was affected, which I am sure a lot of people today can relate to. When I was asking around for other work opportunities, someone said, "Oh, I know someone who runs an art studio—you're pretty hands on, you'd be perfect."

I ended up fabricating a glass shelf for an artist and we became friends. I did an install or two with him in smaller art galleries, and it was him that told me Tate was looking for people at the time. I thought "Me? Tate? No way." What needs to be mentioned is the fact that being a man of color, it wasn't easy to get into art and design, so I was very apprehensive about going for the interview, but this artist friend of mine persuaded me. I filled out the application form, and got invited for an interview. I thought it went well . . . but I didn't hear anything for about six weeks. At around week four, I had given up hope. My mum came home one day and said, "Someone's rung up from a place called the Tate Gallery asking why you haven't replied to a letter." Turns out that the Tate had replied, but the letter had gone to the wrong address. Not really possible today, with email and social media and everything else! Thank goodness we eventually got the letter. Thirty-five years later, here I am.

***ASC: What are some of the responsibilities that you have as an art-handling technician?***

**MH:** Firstly, you have responsibilities to the artwork itself. It has to be handled and installed in a particular way, and you have to be aware of best practices in a museum such as the right lighting and climate control. Your responsibility is to think about what equipment to use when handling and any extra preparations for the work so that it's not at risk. You're responsible to curators, artists, and a whole project team. We will do risk assessments on larger installations, because you're responsible for your team members and you have to make sure no one gets hurt. We're very stringent with health and safety. We all make sure that everybody is certified if they're going to use special lifting equipment. It takes a lot of training and it can take a good couple of years before an art handler can say they're qualified to do everything. It's an ongoing process because art installation is, like art itself, an evolving industry. Artists come up with new ideas, we have to come up with new techniques. One minute I'm installing something made of chocolate or Vaseline, like in the case of Matthew Barney. Never done that before, it was quite tricky, let me tell you. It can be a fighter jet hanging from the ceiling, or someone wants to put a shark in a tank, which we did. Someone asked me once "What is the most challenging thing you've ever done?" And I always have the same answer: "The next thing I'm asked to do, because I don't know what the next thing might be."

*ASC: How do you define success in your job as an art handler?*

**MH:** Success is being able to undergo the task to a high standard. If an artist says to me, "This looks amazing. I'm really happy with this," and for me to know that I've done the best possible job I can do.

*ASC: What does a typical work day look like for you from start to finish? Because I can imagine that it looks different depending on if you're in the middle of installing an exhibition or not.*

**MH:** The reason why I've been here 35 years is that no two days are the same! It's a wonderful challenge. There isn't what I would call a typical day, but I'll outline what a day can be. I come in at 8.30am. Sometimes we have display changes. Sometimes I do some prep for an exhibition that's coming up. Within the day, I might have project meetings because a lot of what I do is forward planning. We look at how we can break an exhibition down into a workable schedule. When will we do the lighting? When will we need the artist? What are the artist's or curator's requirements? Some days I have to be on-site to make sure that artworks are being maintained, or some days we have to change the display because of public visitor interference resulting in an object needing to be taken to our conservation team, for example. It really varies on the day-to-day!

*ASC: Tell me something I wouldn't expect to hear about your job. What is something that many would be surprised to know about your role?*

**MH:** That there is a lot of trust involved when it comes to working with the artists. They're sharing their visions and their dreams with you. If an artist shows their work at a museum like Tate, it's a big thing for their career. If every detail isn't perfect, it's understandable that they worry about what that could do for their career. I've worked with so many artists who I've managed to build up a lot of trust with because they know that I try and share the vision with them. It's not just me thinking "Oh, I get paid to do this, and I can go home at a certain time." You do get really engrossed in what you do, and it becomes very personal.

*ASC: If someone wanted to do what you do in today's art world, where do you think they could start?*

**MH:** The way I started was a bit more random, but now there are websites you can go to, such as arttechspace.com. They're like an organization that gives training and advice to people who want to be art handlers. Most of the major institutions like Tate, the V&A, and the British Museum have a section on their websites where they list job opportunities. If you come from an art-school background, a lot of art schools have affiliations with different organizations that give training. For example, across the road from Tate Britain is Chelsea School of Art, where they do an art-handling course so people can get some basic training. It has now definitely become a more recognized profession. When I started, it didn't even have a name, but it's evolved because art has become more technical. Even just going on YouTube can be a great place to start, because there are institutions and groups that put out content and show techniques so you can see what art handling is about.

*ASC: We said earlier on that you boast over three decades at Tate Britain, which is phenomenal. Can you give early career professionals a tip on 1. Knowing if their place of work is one that they can stay in long term; and also 2. How can they play their part in being able to stay, grow, and enjoy their job for decades to come?*

**MH:** I come from a very different generation. Nowadays, it's important to get as much experience in as many places as possible to have more variety. I am lucky because I work in an environment that gives me variety, which makes the job interesting. I can be installing sculpture one day, paintings the next. I can be working with an artist like Richard Long, where we're doing a mud painting on the wall, and I can be covered head to toe in mud. What I'd say to younger people who want to find an institution where they could work for a long time is to do your homework and find out if people stay in the long term. Find out what the workload is like, what skills and knowledge the people in the institution have, are they transferable skills that you'll benefit from? Do they have structures for professional development in place for their employees? It's important to be in an environment where you can keep learning.

*

Over 30 years of experience, having installed more Turner Prize[*] exhibitions than any other art technician, it was insightful to speak to Mikei and hear his input on what today's generation needs to think about in comparison to what the sector was like in the 1980s.

---

[*] The Turner Prize, named after the English painter J. M. W. Turner, is an annual prize presented to a British visual artist. Between 1991 and 2016, only artists under the age of 50 were eligible (this restriction was removed for the 2017 award). The prize is awarded at Tate Britain every other year, with various venues outside London being used in alternate years. Since its beginnings in 1984 it has become the UK's most publicized art award. The award represents all media.

Fast-forwarding to today, I wanted to speak to someone who works as a freelance art handler in New York City, home to some of the greatest galleries and museums in the world. My connections in New York were extremely limited before traveling there to interview people for this book, so before I got on a plane, I made some calls. The advice I received from professionals in the New York art world was invaluable, and the Brooklyn-based painter Liz Ainslie pointed me towards a few potential interviewees, including Keisha Prioleau-Martin. I walked through the East Village to her art studio, microphones in tow, looking forward to not only speaking to her about her professional experiences, but also seeing her art. Keisha is a practicing artist, working in painting, drawing, and sculpture, as well as an art handler.

---

*Keisha Prioleau-Martin is an artist and art handler with a history of working in world-class institutions such as the New Museum, the Guggenheim, MoMA, and the Museum of Arts and Design. She holds a Bachelor of Fine Arts (BFA) focused on Painting and Drawing with a minor in Art History from Purchase College, State University of New York.*

---

*Alexandra Steinacker-Clark: Can you take me through your education and career path thus far?*

**Keisha Prioleau-Martin:** I got my Bachelor of Fine Arts from Purchase College in New York for painting and drawing. While I was there, I did an internship at the Neuberger Museum of Art, where I learned how to do some art handling. It wasn't a lot, but it was enough for me to start as a freelancer by moving people out of their studios, packing up their artwork, working as a studio assistant, and setting up shows at galleries.

*ASC: Is that kind of how you got your foot in the door, would you say?*

**KPM:** It was a combination of meeting a lot of artists at art shows and telling them about my different skills as an art assistant, a painter, or an art handler. I just kept going around finding work like that at smaller galleries . . . until I got to larger places like the Guggenheim. I then went from the Guggenheim to the Museum of Art and Design to MoMA to the Queens Museum, and more.

*ASC: Can you describe some of the responsibilities you have as an art handler and maybe how they might differ when you're employed by one organization versus freelance work for various organizations?*

**KPM:** When you're freelancing, you could be driving freight around, moving and unpacking crates, and installing the art, be it painting, sculpture, or a room installation. You could arrange the furniture or do the finishing touches. If the museum has less delineation between roles, you could also be painting or building walls. If you work for one organization, you will most likely have more project-management responsibilities. You could be responsible for locating objects in storage, organizing deliveries, and working between departments. Whereas when you're freelance you're focusing on just one task or project at a time. You might come in just to pack sculptures that week, or load a truck, or to do every part of one show before moving on.

*ASC: If you had a full day of art handling planned, what does a typical work day look like for you?*

**KPM:** There is often a formal meeting in the morning that outlines all your tasks for the day. It could be anything. If you're installing, for example, you get your instructions to install, then you get all your supplies, which museums mostly provide. There are some things in art handling where, when you show up for work, you just carry them with you on your person because you know that you'll need one. Those things are a knife, a pencil, a Sharpie, a tape measure, and some people like to carry their own tape or tape dispenser. You never really know what the task is going to be, because depending on the institution and exhibition, we will have different things to install, different walls to install them on, and different tools. You have to be quite flexible with how you do things.

***ASC: Can you tell me about a difficult aspect of the job, something that you find particularly challenging about it?***

**KPM:** The pace of the work is something we call *stop and go*. There might be 30 minutes or an hour where there's nothing to do because we're waiting for something like a truck to deliver or a curator to make a final decision about where to put a piece. It can be odd because then the other side of the *stop and go* is when we have so much work once that decision is made and we have to get it finished before the end of the day, so we're running at top speed to get it all done. It can throw you off in your workflow. In some instances, a project is so ambitious that safety concerns get ignored. I've worked in places where certain jobs were not done safely, meaning people were in danger of getting their head hit or things falling on them, which is absolutely unacceptable.

***ASC: Can you tell me an aspect that you love about the job? Something that you find particularly enjoyable.***

**KPM:** I love seeing different art all the time. Every time I open up a crate, it feels like I'm opening up my very own Christmas present.

***ASC: If someone wants to handle art, where do you think that they could start?***

**KPM:** The advice I hear a lot of people give, but I didn't follow this myself, is to start in an art-handling company that has their own warehouse. They install the art at their clients' houses or, nowadays, some institutions like hotels or commercial galleries. Crozier is a good example. If you work there, you will be doing so much every day and you will have the opportunity to learn quickly. Whereas freelance, it might take a little longer to learn the ropes.

*ASC: Do art handlers need to specialize in a certain type of art like installing sculpture, installing painting or, for example, installing pre-17th century art due to the fragility of the works? Is that a thing?*

**KPM:** Sort of. To work in a museum, I would say you have to have around two years of art-handling experience. To work on certain shows, though, you need to have at least five years of art handling experience because the work that you're dealing with is by Piet Mondrian or Vincent van Gogh or something else of big historical significance. If you are new, you won't be handling work like that.

*ASC: What other roles are there connecting to your role and who do art handlers typically deal with?*

**KPM:** I consider all these people part of the team for installing a show or maintaining a collection of art. A lot of this work is in tandem and overlapping, so we are all looking out for each other. You have the registrars, whose job varies, but they keep track of all the art objects. There's conservators who look at the condition of a work. Sometimes they need to repair something that, through time, weathering, or sometimes an incident, has affected the condition of the work. There's mount makers, who produce customized displays for objects, ranging from a plinth to a stand to some other kind of support.* The displays have to be strong enough to hold the weight of heavy objects and secure them over a long period of time, and they also have to aesthetically disappear so you concentrate on the object and are not distracted by the support. It's cool!

***ASC: If someone wanted to do what you do, what advice or even warnings would you give them?***

**KPM:** I received this advice when I was first starting out, but I had to grow into it. Never, ever think that you know everything. When you're art handling, a painting or sculpture might look straightforward, and the task at hand might look like something you've seen before, and you think you know how to do it. However, always double-check and be prepared for anything. Another piece of advice is to stand up for yourself. I don't know if it's like this everywhere, but in the art world people can be demanding, entitled, and want magic to happen. You are allowed to tell them that their idea is impossible. There have been so many unsafe situations because of someone's desire or suggestion, so learn how to advocate for yourself and articulate why you believe a certain approach is not the right path forward—and this goes for whatever role you are in, not just as an art handler.

*

Freelancing, no matter what area of the arts you may be in, can be hard to do straight out of university. Keisha mentioned to me that she freelanced while still living with family in the beginning, because she wasn't making enough to sustain an independent life in New York City in the early days. Although starting while she was still at university, gaining some of those skills and then speaking to peers propelled her

---

*    If you are interested in learning more about mount making, there is an *All About Art* podcast episode with mount maker Alex Abbott, director of Dauphin.

forward in not only gaining even more experience, but also in getting her name out there as a reliable art handler. Mikei's story goes back decades. One lesson we all can take from him is the importance of finding something that will allow you to learn. Finding areas to grow within your career is incredibly valuable. Asking clear questions in the interview process, and potentially talking to current and past employees of that organization, will help you find the right fit—whether it be as an art handler or something else. Greg's story shows that different areas in the arts inform each other. Experience in framing, art handling, and studio and gallery management can bring knowledge and valuable expertise for various scenarios that come your way in these professions. Starting out can be tough, but asking peers to hang works or helping out art-handler friends can be a great way to get your foot in the door and learn a thing or two about the profession.

## KEY TAKEAWAYS IF YOU ARE THINKING OF EMBARKING ON YOUR OWN CAREER IN ART HANDLING

### Three Practical Tips

- Start with hands-on courses and apprenticeships, or try to learn from experienced professionals. Look for specialized training programs like art-handling courses or workshops to build foundational skills and credibility. Volunteer or seek mentorship opportunities at museums, galleries, or art fairs to see best practices in action.
- Building a diverse skill set can aid you in finding more opportunities, so gaining experience in framing, packing, logistics, and conservation, to name just a few examples, increases your versatility and, as a result, your employability.

- Network within the art-handling community, because that is a primary source to find professional opportunities in the industry.

## Next Steps

- Go to your favorite gallery, museum, or auction house and see how the works are installed. Maybe even ask a staff member to tell you more, as if they have an in-house technician they can give you a lot of insights right then and there!
- Develop relationships with your peers who are artists, and see if you can help them out with their installation needs. Working with them, gaining their trust while developing your skills, is something you will be doing for the rest of your career in art handling.
- If you are at the stage where you know this is the career you want to pursue, invest in some equipment, starting with a tape measure.

# CHAPTER 6

# WORKING IN COMMERCIAL GALLERIES

Most of my professional experience has been in commercial galleries, one of my internships having been at the gallery of one of the interviewees in this chapter, Thaddaeus Ropac. I interned during the summer in 2018, the busiest season at the Salzburg gallery. After that, I was a sales assistant to the Senior Director at Skarstedt Gallery for a while, and moved on to be the Gallery and Exhibitions Manager at Galerie Max Hetzler, a German gallery with a location on Dover Street in Mayfair, London. I have been a part of teams in smaller galleries and larger ones. Some of my friends own galleries. It's an intense business that straddles relationships with artists while building their careers and cultivating relationships on their behalf with both art collectors and institutions.

Galleries work to support the artists they represent by, of course, facilitating sales but also by facilitating institutional shows, or supporting the production of publications of the artist's work. They organize events, tours, and dinners to celebrate the artist. They support international exhibitions and collaborations where appropriate (which was briefly mentioned by Elsy Lahner in the chapter on curating, as she spoke about raising funds for museum shows). It's a commercial endeavor but, when done correctly, it centers around the relationship to the artists and their positioning within the art world.

In this chapter, you will hear Thaddaeus Ropac echo that exact sentiment, and more, as he shares insights into running one of the largest galleries in the world. You will also hear from Millie Jason Foster, Director of Gillian Jason Gallery, about leading a mid-sized gallery in today's economic environment, which is harder on younger galleries and other art-world businesses. In the final section, I include my own insights from personal experiences working in galleries, sharing my perspective not as a founder or director, but as a junior-level employee.

One of the most respected blue-chip* galleries is Galerie Thaddaeus Ropac, with international locations in Austria, France, Italy, South Korea, and the United Kingdom. It was a surreal moment to arrive at the Ely House location late on a Wednesday as the sun was setting in London. I was supposed to have my interview with Thaddaeus the next afternoon, but at around 6pm, his team got hold of me to say it was no longer going to be possible. They asked if I would be able to come by the gallery that evening, and I had a feeling that it would be the only time I would get the chance to interview him in person, so, of course, I took it. At 8pm on Dover Street, he opened the gallery doors and we took the elevator up to his office for our interview.

---

*Thaddaeus Ropac is an Austrian gallerist who founded his first art gallery in 1981 and has since expanded to multiple locations globally. He is known for representing both established and emerging artists, including some of the most influential names in contemporary art.*

---

***Alexandra Steinacker-Clark: Can you tell me briefly about your education and your career path? What led you to found your gallery, and what experience did you have in art beforehand?***

---

* A blue-chip gallery is a gallery that sells high-value artworks. They are distinguished by their representation of established, internationally renowned artists whose works command substantial prices.

**Thaddaeus Ropac:** I come from a rather middle-class background in Austria and art did not play a real role in my upbringing, the focus was more on literature. For me, art was not contemporary. Education in Austria at the time—we're talking about the seventies—somehow ended with Klimt, Schiele, Kokoschka. I only found out about the existence of contemporary art when I went on a school trip to Vienna where we visited the modern art museum and saw an installation by Joseph Beuys. It was irritating, it made me ask so many questions . . . It almost angered me, this inability to understand what I was seeing. That was the start of everything. I became a big fan of Joseph Beuys's work and I looked up to him, in a way. Beuys would always say, "Everyone is an artist," which I tried to be, but I figured out very soon that I didn't have any talent for it. However, because of my attempt at becoming an artist, I ended up interning with Beuys as he was preparing for Documenta 7 in 1982. I was there planting the trees [for the artwork *7000 Oaks—City Forestation Instead of City Administration*] and also helping with an epic exhibition called *Zeitgeist* at the Gropius Bau in Berlin. I was able to be close to this incredible, larger-than-life artist, had the opportunity to meet other artists and totally immersed myself in this incredible world of the arts. I knew then that this would dominate my life, and every path I thought of pursuing had to do something with that.

*ASC: You started your gallery in Salzburg over 40 years ago, and so much has changed, including the emergence of the internet, globalization through multiple art fairs around the world, along with wider access to international artists and an international collector base. If you were in the position now that you were in back in 1983, on the cusp of starting a gallery, would you still proceed with a traditional gallery model?*

**TR:** Definitely. I always say that, in these 40 years, I've seen the art world move from the ivory tower to the center of life. Back then it was very exclusive, in an intellectual sense. It was difficult to get into the art world. All of this has changed. The art world has become quite inclusive, everybody is invited to participate and I think we are having a very exciting period now. Communication has changed, and I think social media has influenced the way we can look at art and be informed. At the time, when I started my gallery, they had just invented the fax machine and that was the biggest tool of communication. Otherwise, there were only letters to be sent by mail.

I would still do it all exactly the way I did it back then — of course, maybe I would try to avoid a few mistakes, but really making mistakes is how you learn. I still believe very strongly in bricks and mortar, in the physical experience of looking at art. We have to create the best possible space for an artist to truly host their artworks. We see art in books, and it still isn't the same sensation as to be in front of it. People come to Paris by the millions wanting to see the 'Mona Lisa' even though they have seen it thousands of times in prints and books. The physical experience is still what really drives people's emotion and more than any print of it or, I believe, any artificial space. One of my strongest beliefs is fighting for this, to give artists the best possible physical space, and I would still proceed with that if I were starting my gallery again today.

***ASC: You just spoke about how you might have wanted to avoid a few mistakes, but also that it's a part of the learning process... What would you do differently, and how would you approach founding a gallery now, knowing everything that you do?***

**TR:** I believe that learning by doing is an important experience. To be young and to work with young artists, growing together. It is important to experience this incredible process of gaining the trust of an artist while working on exhibitions. Sometimes, when people want to start their own gallery I hear them say, "I want to learn everything—and then I will do it." In these cases, I think that sometimes people try to learn for too long.

It can be good to jump into the cold water and try it yourself because this "do it yourself" is what makes the difference. If you do it that way, then you're not copying somebody else's experience, you're inventing it for yourself. Every artist has to invent the language they use, and I also think every gallery has to invent the model again.

*ASC: What really resonates with me is this idea of "don't wait until you feel like it's perfect to dive in" because there will always be something else that will need to be perfected, and you run the risk of never actually starting.*

**TR:** Exactly.

*ASC: What was specific about founding a gallery in the geographical region of Salzburg? Why not start a gallery in Vienna or Munich, two much bigger cities?*

**TR:** I always say I love Salzburg, and I'm happy that I went to Salzburg because if I had gone to Vienna or Berlin, maybe I would have stayed. What I mean by this is Salzburg made it necessary for me to move on, to expand, and that's the reason I ended up in Paris. In all honesty, Salzburg is not the ideal place to run a contemporary gallery, in part because of the lack of artists who live there.

*ASC: It's interesting to frame it in that way—I would have thought the question would be "where are the collectors?"*

**TR:** No, that's not the question I ask myself when thinking about location. The reason we didn't open the gallery in Hong Kong, but instead chose Seoul, is because in Hong Kong you hardly have any artists. In Seoul, you have many.

***ASC: You now have gallery locations in London, Paris, Seoul, Milan, and Salzburg. What else does someone need to take into consideration when they're thinking about scaling internationally?***

**TR:** First of all, I think it is not a necessity. It is a possibility. Instead, I would say that a gallery is about relevance. Ensure you work with the right artists and you gain the respect of the art world, of the critics and curators and collectors. You can do it from anywhere, and you also only need one location. To really be a part of the art world, it needs to be a place where artists live and work. That's the reason, after Salzburg, I chose every place very carefully, looking at the artistic productivity and activity. After I had been in Salzburg for a couple of years, I wanted to go to Paris because I felt Paris was the great host for artists in the 20th century. I didn't realize that Paris, by that time, had already lost some of this gravitas to New York or to London. But I'm still very thankful that I was able to come to Paris and that I was accepted and embraced by the art world there. It was important to grow within Paris by opening another space, our very large space in Pantin, because I felt after a while that I was limiting our artists by not offering them enough physical space. We needed one space where there is no limit of size and there's no limit of weight, where the art transport truck could basically drive into the building. London was another step, as we show many artists who live and work in London. In addition, Asia is definitely part of the future. I was drawn more to opening something in Asia than in another part of the world and Seoul was, for me, the ideal place because of all the movement in the art scene there. Milan is our newest development and I always felt Italy was missing from our European activity. We have done so much in Italy over the years, at almost every Venice Biennale — but I reiterate, I would not have opened a gallery in Venice because of the lack of artists. Milan has been the city, throughout the last 40 years, where art was produced. We have

[Lucio] Fontana, all of Arte Povera*, which really developed around Milan, and even the very contemporary arts, artists like Maurizio Cattelan, live in Milan. Milan is the heartbeat of artistic production in Italy, which was the reason we decided to open there.

**ASC: *Why not New York?***

**TR:** New York is too important to run with a long arm. If you are going to be there, you need to make New York your center, and I was never ready to move to New York. I've seen European galleries doing it at an arm's length, and New York doesn't work like that. Either you're there and you make it your headquarters, or you should leave it. Maybe I'm too European . . .

**ASC: *Can you describe some of the responsibilities you have as the owner of one of the world's most renowned galleries?***

**TR:** My responsibility is to represent the artists at the level they deserve, respecting the trust they built with us by supporting their careers in the most professional way. Artists deserve an infrastructure to build on, but really what makes the difference is that you have an intellectual understanding of what the artist is doing and are able to communicate that to the wider world—to the critics, the curators, the collectors, and to an audience.

**ASC: *What does a typical day look like for you, from start to finish?***

**TR:** There's not much of a pattern because every day is really different. I'm traveling constantly to our seven locations where we put on between 30 and 35 exhibitions per year. There are certain patterns, of course, in

---

*   Arte Povera is a radical Italian art movement from the late 1960s to 1970s whose artists explored a range of unconventional processes and non-traditional "everyday" materials.

the way things work. We are a big team of almost 150 people with an infrastructure that works well. That means that part of my time is dealing with ensuring all of these galleries are working professionally within the infrastructure. The best part of my job is spending time with artists, discussing their work and planning for exhibitions. Then there are the meetings with curators, with collectors, with museum directors, with aspiring directors, the list goes on. Every day is full of surprises, which is what makes this work so exciting, because just as every exhibition, and as every work of art, is unique and different, the challenges are also different. But there are certain patterns in how things work in making sure that everything is running smoothly.

*ASC: Can you tell me something that I wouldn't expect to hear about your job? What's something that many people would be surprised to learn?*

**TR:** People sometimes have this image of a gallery in their minds as basically hanging out and discussing art. There is sometimes a naïveté involved in the way people expect the business to work. One of the things that people tend to be surprised to know is that we do a lot of work in fundraising for non-commercial exhibitions if our artists are exhibiting at institutions. We have to spend a lot of time making sure a project is feasible and can be done, making sure things are able to move on as planned. Often, when we have interns, I feel like they have a specific image of how a gallery works and think that it's something very cool and glamorous. I do really like the idea that people have about galleries, but at the end of the day, it's really hard work. It is not just exhibition openings with nice wine and discussing artworks every day.

*ASC: Can you share a difficult aspect of your work?*

**TR:** It can be challenging to combat the misconception that we're just here to sell art. It is so much more complex than this, you know? I always say we are trying to "place" the works of art, meaning we want to find the best possible homes for them when they are entrusted into our hands, not just sell it for profit. Nowadays, we have a lot of speculation* because art prices have gone up rapidly for certain artists. It is important for us to protect the artist and the longevity of their career by making sure that we identify the real collector trying to build a collection.

***ASC: What would you define as a good placement versus a bad placement?***

**TR:** A good placement is a collector who is serious, who knows about the intellectual and emotional value of the artwork—not only the monetary value. It's a level of engagement with the art which is defined by a respect for the artist and therefore also for the piece of art. There is a certain understanding necessary alongside an ability to create the right context of how different artists may fit together within a collection.

***ASC: If you were hiring someone to follow in your footsteps, what are some of the personality traits or strengths that you would look for in an ideal candidate?***

**TR:** I would look for someone who has a talent in identifying the quality of a work of art. I would also look for someone who is really hard-working, because this is definitely one of the biggest components of what I do. A combination of those two things would be ideal, because I've seen people who worked very hard but lacked the eye to understand quality. In addition, I would look for honesty. It's sometimes missing in this business, and it is so important because you have to earn the trust of the artist and not misuse it. To be successful in the long run, in order to gain the trust of

---

* Speculation is the practice of buying art with the primary intention of reselling it at a higher price for profit, rather than for its aesthetic or intrinsic value.

the artist, you need that base I just mentioned. The eye to understand the quality and the ability to work really hard. All in all, when you believe in the important power that art holds for human beings, then I think you can create a very serious space to make it a success.

*ASC: If someone wanted to do what you do, what piece of advice—or maybe even a warning—would you give them?*

**TR:** You need to have a trained eye, which you can develop and improve, but you have to build it on a very serious basis. It is important to understand the context within which all this art created today is based. A lot of art we're looking at is about the human condition, so it goes into the deepest of our feelings, the most honest of our feelings. I think an artist gives everything they are able to give and can only be successful if it's truthful—it's not enough to have a clever idea. There are many artists who are clever and they can create something stunning, sure, but if it doesn't have the truthfulness which art requires, it will not go very far. In the same vein, but in a very different coding, this also applies to galleries. You have to find this truthfulness and develop an openness and honesty to be able to create partnerships that are instrumental for the successful development of both a gallery and the artists.

*ASC: What have you learned in your approach to having relationships with artists? I'm asking this on behalf of any budding gallerists out there who want to develop relationships with artists, who want to do what you have done, which is foster decades-long relationships with artists.*

**TR:** Going back to appreciating truthfulness, what I learned—and I'm really thankful for this—is that artists have often helped me to correct the way I (we) live, because of their honesty and the way they describe what life is about. It has been an incredible privilege for me to be so close to artists and, of course, for my professional life, to be stimulated by works of art. I feel privileged to be consistently inspired by artists who think differently, who have different ideas about art and have developed an incredible creative language to describe these ideas. To have that so close to you over such a long time, you learn an enormous amount about your own life and what is truly important. I think artists show us life in a different way, and not to have pursued this professional path in my life would have been a big loss.

*

In hearing Thaddaeus speak about how he has built his gallery over the last 40 years, I realized that he was never deterred from his underlying values of centering the artist and their practice. I think we often wonder what "magic touch" a lot of large gallerists have in how they built their art empires. Of course, there are a lot of factors, including privileges relating to socioeconomic circumstances of a different time, for example—but he was candid with what he views as valuable attributes of a gallerist: having an artistic eye (which you can develop by immersing yourself in the arts community, seeing art, meeting artists, and maybe even some reading) and being able to graft.

Interviewing one of the greatest gallerists of our time was an honor, but at the same time, Thaddaeus started his gallery a decade before I was even born. Times were very different, giving more benefit socioeconomically and geopolitically to a young gallerist, but less benefit to anyone coming from outside of the art world. Things have changed a lot, as Thaddaeus stated, in that the art world has come down from its ivory tower. It led me to thinking I needed to speak to someone working to build their gallery in today's art world. I interviewed Millie Jason Foster on the *All About Art* Podcast and within the episode, Millie was not only incredibly transparent about the work that she does, but she came prepared with advice and strategic tips for artists and arts professionals alike—so I knew she would be the best person to include in this chapter, especially reflecting the positioning of her still quite young, mid-tier gallery in central London.

---

*Millie Jason Foster is the Founding Director of Gillian Jason Gallery (GJG). In 2019, GJG became the first commercial space in the UK to solely champion female-identifying artists. GJG opened its London space in 2021 and since then has showcased over 100 artists both within the Gallery and at international fairs. Foster has been a patron to Studio Voltaire, Serpentine Gallery, Hayward Gallery, and the Tate. She has also founded her own young patrons' group "New Vanguard," which provides access and insights into the arts for young collectors. In 2024, GJG sponsored Tate Britain's first ever all-female exhibition,* Women in Revolt!

---

***Alexandra Steinacker-Clark: Millie, tell me briefly about your career path. What are some formative moments in your education and career that got you where you are today?***

**Millie Jason Foster:** I never thought I would get into art, despite growing up around my grandmother, Gillian Jason, who was an art dealer. I studied Human, Social, and Political Science at Cambridge because I didn't know exactly what I wanted to do and that was casting a broad enough net. In my second year, I did an internship at J. P. Morgan which turned into a job, and in my final year, I switched my speciality to Management Studies, so I have a joint degree in that and HSPS. It defines what I do today, because I learned how to build a business, how to assess cash flow, how to look at finances, all in preparation for working for this big corporation, which I loved. I worked at J. P. Morgan for two years, but found that I wasn't passionate enough about building businesses for other people. I wasn't interested in being a small cog in a big wheel. Around that time, my grandmother developed Alzheimer's. My mother, Elli, and I decided that we didn't want her legacy, namely Gillian Jason Gallery, to lapse. We decided to reopen her gallery with an ethos of championing art by women. It snowballed with its popularity and we opened a space in December 2021. I decided to do a master's course in Art Business at Sotheby's Institute during the pandemic, as well, because I thought "How are people going to take me seriously if I don't have any grounding at all in the art world?" In 2023, my mother retired so I've been running the gallery ever since.

***ASC: Can you delve into the history of Gillian Jason Gallery (GJG) and its mission now?***

**MJF:** My grandmother, a ballet dancer, lived with my grandfather, an actor, in Camden Town among a lot of other Jewish emigrés. Having a love for the arts, my grandmother retired from ballet after having children and opened up a space on the ground floor of her home and started presenting what then became modern British art. Frank Auerbach, David Bomberg, but also the wives of the male artists. Lillian Holt was David Bomberg's wife, and my grandmother would put on duo exhibitions. When you look at archives like the Tate today and what they have in their collection, the Lillian Holt pieces have my grandmother's provenance. I don't necessarily think it was a straightforward vision to show women and to champion them in this way, but it was something that was important to her. When it came to reopening the gallery, we wanted to do something that fitted with my grandmother's legacy that was important to her, but also was a passion for me and my mother at the time, and that was championing women. The mission of the gallery is to show the best of art by women, whatever that might be, and to provide a platform for their voices while supporting them through the social hurdles that women face (like the fear of losing gallery representation if a woman artist decides to have a child). We also work with artist estates, to create the recognition for the women artists from the 60s, 70s, 80s who deserve that spotlight. My vision is to help create parity in the art world, to provide a platform for voices that have historically been marginalized.

***ASC: Can you tell me more about the positioning of GJG in the art world, as a mid-sized gallery in London?***

**MJF:** Our positioning as a mid-tier gallery is threefold. Number one, having a good curatorial reputation. Number two is an unrivaled service for artist management and also helping clients grow their collections. Number three is institutional recognition. When you look at commercial galleries today, a lot of them don't have catalogs or curatorial texts written in-house. The way that the market environment is at the moment, a lot of galleries are trying to turn over sales just to keep going, so what often falls to the wayside is that these artists need to be written about, and their legacy needs to be solidified. We write a curatorial text and a catalog for every single artist that we show. Our catalogs are collected and recognized by the Metropolitan Museum of Art in New York in the Watson Library's digital archive. I look at a lot of other galleries, and I understand the need to just keep running, not having enough staff, not having enough time, so the curatorial contextualization doesn't really happen. We also are philanthropic with institutions because that is how women artists can create a true legacy in the art world, being recognized and collected by these institutions. We sponsored exhibitions at the Tate and the Hayward Gallery, for example.

***ASC: Can you describe some of the responsibilities you have as the Director of GJG? And what does a typical work day look like for you?***

**MJF:** My aim for the business is for my team to not need me on a daily basis. As a director, I talk to clients, conduct institutional outreach, and focus on exhibition generation, finding and building relationships with new artists. In terms of my day-to-day, I sit in the gallery, front of house with the rest of the team. I always keep the morning to myself, with my coffee (a need, not a want), so until around 1pm I am answering client and artist emails and doing institutional outreach, all from my desk. I then enact it in the afternoons. I either do studio visits with artists, follow new business leads, or welcome curators to the gallery for a conversation.

*ASC: What have you learned in your approach to your relationship with artists? Am I correct in stating that having a gallery means building an artist roster and supporting their careers alongside the growth of the gallery?*

**MJF:** My approach is artist first, every time. Don't get me wrong, I've made mistakes where I realized that I haven't put the artist first, and that's cost me a lot. I try to bend over backwards to make sure that the artist's vision is achieved. This means that we take on everything—the admin, shipping costs, logistics, curation, marketing, and anything else that is needed. Ultimately, I want the name of the artist to be known before the name of the gallery. If they're in the best exhibitions and they get paid fairly, I'm happy. People don't need to know my name.

*ASC: Can you tell me about a difficult aspect of the job, something that you find particularly challenging about it?*

**MJF:** I'd have to say cash-flow management. I do my books and check numbers every day. When you look at the number of galleries closing, a lot of them say cash-flow management was their problem.

*ASC: Is there a tip you can give on managing cash flow well? It's a useful skill, whether running a gallery or another art business, or even for your own freelance or personal finances, I find.*

**MJF:** I have a cash-flow spreadsheet. You can find templates for them online. I include cash at the beginning of month, outgoing subscriptions, then money we owe to artists and money we owe to suppliers. Then, I add sales. In the business of art, sometimes it takes a while for a client to pay an invoice, which also means that a payment to an artist may stall. You have to juggle that. When we make a sale, I have to ask myself: do I put it in this month's cash flow, or do I put it in next month's cash flow? When can I pay the artist for this piece? The cash flow also then helps determine our monthly goals. Otherwise, we don't know how much we need to sell to make it through the month. That's a prevalent problem with galleries who don't keep an eye on their cash flow or directors who don't understand it.

***ASC: What other roles are there at the gallery, and how does your position intersect with them?***

**MJF:** We have our Gallery Manager and Artist Liaison. They have a dual role, managing the team as my "second in command" while managing relationships to artists, giving them deadlines for shipping, for example, but also supporting them in making sure they are happy with what they are creating. In addition, this role involves writing the curatorial texts, speaking with the artists, and researching deeply to contribute to the literature we produce. We have a Head of Operations, who we found through an advert we put out on the Sotheby's Institute careers platform. Their responsibility is to manage logistics and shipping, invoicing, and VAT returns. We also have a Head of Marketing who deals with our mailing list, social media, and CRM system. We had a research assistant for six months, who started off as an intern and grew into the role. I met them because they came up to me after a panel discussion and asked if they could work for us. It was impressive to see someone take that initiative! We do our best to train interns so well that they go on to get gallery-assistant jobs in other big galleries in London. I want to be really transparent about the next thing I say. We can't really afford to pay our interns a salary, and that causes me a lot of heartache because I'm a big believer in equal opportunity. It may change in the future, but so far we haven't been able to. We fully cover weekly travel and food costs so the intern doesn't lose any money by working with us. I train them within an inch of their life, because if they're going to spend their time not earning money with us, they must be able to walk away with invaluable skills and be employable elsewhere. It's a daily battle I have with myself, but I decided either I can provide someone with an opportunity and make sure I cover their costs at a minimum, or I don't pay and I don't have an internship program. I decided it was better to offer the opportunity than none at all.

**ASC: *What do you envision for the gallery in the future? As someone building an art business in today's economic climate.***

**MJF:** I'd like to be international, so the next step for Gillian Jason Gallery is a secondary space elsewhere in the world, and I have my sights set on a few different locations. I'm interested in frontier markets, in places where the art market is growing and where women, once again, have been historically marginalized and need a platform. I'm not interested in going to overcrowded markets, I want to be in new markets.

**ASC: *If someone wanted to do what you do, what advice or even warnings would you give them?***

**MJF:** When I came into the art world from finance, I found it really opaque. Everyone sells the same artist for a different price. No one will tell you who their clients are. Everything is smoke and mirrors. In the traditional art world, no one really trusts each other. If I am giving advice to someone in the art world today, I would say become a person who fosters collaboration and openness. Surround yourself with people who you enjoy spending time with. Never do the business deals that make you feel bad because they will come back to bite you.

*

Throughout my time working in the commercial art world, in auction houses as well as galleries, I have seen different team structures, different positions, and witnessed the way different galleries work with artists and artworks (especially if one is dealing in more secondary-market works, versus primary, and working directly with an artist and their studio). Most smaller and younger galleries work with early career artists, and, to take a page from Thaddaeus Ropac's book (or, better said, a line out of his interview), one of the most valuable actions you can take is to develop deeper relationships with artists, their studios, and/or their estates. Younger galleries, like Gillian Jason Gallery, are in such a special position to do just that with the next generation of talented artists.

My experience in galleries is not as extensive as someone who has worked in the gallery world for decades. However, I may be in a similar position to you, the reader, so my insights may be relevant to the "here and now." My role as Gallery and Exhibitions Manager probably looked different from a role with the same title at a different gallery, because each team is structured differently and the role will differ depending on the size of the team, the art being shown, and the type of gallery it is. Please take note here: it is important to get a clear job description before you say yes to a role, and make sure that you advocate for that when you first start. Based on stories I have heard from my peers, a difficulty in the commercial art world is that directors are trained as salespeople, *not* as team leaders, but they are still the ones responsible for managing teams. The work culture in galleries is often criticized for this reason. Who you hire, who you fire, and who you promote sends a clear message about company culture in any industry, and in the arts it is often directly associated with your client book, not necessarily your work ethic, management skills, or other values. This is mostly relevant to the higher positions within a gallery, such as senior sales directors. Although one of their main job responsibilities is sales, they also have to think about all the other moving parts within a gallery—including how all other members of the team function well with each other to work towards the shared goal of keeping the gallery going.

Other roles in galleries include research, which involves liaising with an artist or their studio, writing the exhibition texts and press releases for the gallery, keeping the databases of artwork and artist information up to date, and contributing to the production of publications, if the gallery is large enough to be producing (or co-producing) them. If you come from a finance background and want to pivot into the arts, working within accounting at a gallery is a great opportunity to capitalize on your transferable skills. Although we all love to engage with culture, working in the sector means we all ultimately need to be somewhat business-minded and having clear accounting makes everyone's lives easier, including the artists who are represented by the gallery. If you studied Fine Art or you love working with your hands, every gallery needs an art handler, as we learned in chapter 5. If you are at the beginning of your career, and you want to work your way into sales, becoming a sales assistant is one of the best ways to learn the ropes. You can even start as a gallery assistant and express your interest in assisting with sales if given the chance. Something to keep in mind is that if you are a sales assistant at a larger gallery dealing in works that are on the upper end of the market, it could be difficult to make sales. If you are given the opportunity to sell, if the art is priced above a certain level for your existing client base (who may not be wanting to purchase art for millions, but who may have the budget for works in the thousands, which is also valuable), you won't be able to reach your quota. Think about this progression strategically. Are there works offered at different price points in the gallery you want to work at? Is there opportunity for growth in that regard? Will you get the chance to attend art fairs and other important events where you can meet new clients? From experience, working for a gallery that deals at the higher end of the market and also represents younger artists selling at (relatively) more affordable prices could be an indicator that there is an opportunity to grow within a sales role in a more natural way.

Galleries like Galerie Thaddaeus Ropac function on a completely different scale compared to a young gallery within its first decade of existing. For example, when it comes to developing a client base, art fairs are an integral part of the strategy, but they are a point of contention amongst smaller galleries because of the high participation costs and no guarantee that sales will actually happen. Younger galleries tend to be more hands-on, with smaller teams that have many roles all wrapped into one person. In some cases, the gallery founder is a strong team of one. Even in big teams, working overtime happens all the time. Galleries typically have a six-week exhibition cycle, with one week in between for de-installation of the previous exhibition and installation of the upcoming one. In London, it's typical that exhibition openings happen on Thursdays, with a rare Tuesday or Wednesday opening here or there. In Paris, however, it seems that Fridays and Saturdays are the typical days for exhibition openings. No matter where you are, there will most likely be a general consensus as to when exhibitions will open and it would be good for you to find that out.

I have often heard people comment on how unfair it is that galleries who represent artists take 50 percent (sometimes 40 percent, sometimes 60 percent) of the sale price. I strongly disagree with this statement, if the gallery is fulfilling their role. I have witnessed good gallery teams work themselves to the bone to make their artists happy, to make their clients happy, to keep their business running. A gallery is not just a space for artists to exhibit their work. What I learned from working in extremely reputable galleries is that they can be career-long partners with artists. Galerie Max Hetzler, for example, has been working with Albert Oehlen since 1981, for over 40 years.

# KEY TAKEAWAYS IF YOU ARE THINKING OF EMBARKING ON YOUR OWN CAREER IN COMMERCIAL GALLERIES

## Three Practical Tips

- Start with internships or think about your transferable skills. You can gain hands-on experience early by interning at galleries to learn the practical aspects of gallery work and build industry connections. Big names on your resumé are great, but if you are starting out and want a full overview, the smaller the gallery, the more pies you will be able to stick your fingers into.

- Reflect on whether a fast pace and late working hours are something you are willing to accept. Non-profits are slower and you generally don't do much work outside normal working hours. It's a very different story in commercial galleries. For example, in October in London during Frieze week, it's 10–12 hours a day for 8 days straight, at least.

- Define your interests and values before applying for jobs, to ensure you are applying to the places that are the right fit for you. You will then be able to demonstrate genuine enthusiasm for art and prioritize honesty and respect in all professional interactions, which will in turn build your confidence and credibility within the industry.

## Next Steps

- Build relationships as early as possible by networking with gallery professionals, artists, and collectors. You can do this by attending exhibitions, art fairs, and industry events every chance you get. As mentioned, exhibition openings happen on Thursdays in London. Check out when they happen in your local art scene and do an evening gallery hop!

- Identify your focus and decide whether you want to pursue sales, curatorial, or management roles within galleries. It may be hard to do in the beginning, so just focus on gaining experience when starting out, but do keep this in the back of your mind going forward.
- Learn about the business while developing an "eye" for the kind of art that galleries show. See exhibitions at galleries you respect, think about how they put it together and what their approach might be to the art they choose to show and the artists they choose to represent. Not only will you develop a more critical eye for these things, but you will know the business of the galleries really well when the time comes to interview for roles there.

# CHAPTER 7

# WORKING IN ARTIST AND STUDIO MANAGEMENT

When I first started out in the arts, I wasn't really aware of any artist-management agencies. Maybe it was just because I was quite new to the sector at the time, but it looks like there has been quite a boom in the last decade.* Now more than ever there are new business models and structures that exist to manage artists outside of the traditional gallery model of representation. There are a lot of different ways this can look, and depending on the country an artist manager or artist agency is in, the day-to-day tasks and project management can differ greatly. In this chapter, you will read insights from Paula Marschalek, an Austrian artist manager who began her journey in the arts in galleries, museums, and PR, but saw a niche in her local art scene and grew her own business from there, as well as from Valeria Szabó Facchin, founder of Studio Expanded and cofounder of Aster, working in areas of strategic investment, artist management, and philanthropic commissioning. Although artist management agencies seem to be on the rise, another role included in this chapter is that of studio manager. It's another job that involves working directly with artists, but instead of working with multiple artists, being a studio manager involves working closely with one specific artist. Thus, alongside Paula and Valeria, you will read the insights shared by Marie von Ribbentrop, who was the studio manager for artist Alicja Kwade for four years.

When I first met Paula, we were both interning at the Kunsthistorisches Museum in Vienna. She was in the press department, and I was in the

---

* Laura Gomez, "How Talent Agencies Are Reshaping the Art World", ArtTactic, 10 March 2025.

director's office. We both have wavy brunette hair and big smiles, and, maybe for that reason, the team couldn't stop mixing us up. We bonded over being mistaken for one another, and over our mutual love for art. Becoming friends, then professional collaborators, we went on to form a creative partnership for a while called C/20 Association for International Curatorial Practice, where we worked together on exhibitions during the Parallel Art Fair and the FOTOWIEN Festival, both in Vienna, Austria. During the COVID-19 pandemic, Paula started leading on projects and developed communication strategies with artists. Now, Paula has made a name for herself in the Austrian art landscape with her artist-management company, Marschalek Art Management.

---

*Paula Marschalek is an Austrian art historian and cultural manager. She studied Art History at the University of Vienna and continued her education at the University of Applied Arts where she obtained her Masters in Arts and Cultural Management. She has worked with renowned art institutions such as the Dorotheum, the Kunsthistorisches Museum, and the MAK (Museum für Angewandte Kunst), and gained experience in the art market as a communication manager for galleries. With the communication agency Marschalek Art Management, she develops individually tailored communication strategies for artists and cultural workers.*

---

*Alexandra Steinacker-Clark: Tell me about your education and career path thus far—what led you to your current position?*

**Paula Marschalek:** I studied Art History at the University of Vienna and Arts and Cultural Management at the University of Applied

Arts. During my studies, I had the opportunity to gain my first work experience in major cultural institutions such as the auction house Dorotheum, the Kunsthistorisches Museum, and the Museum of Applied Arts, also known as MAK. At the same time, I started working in the independent art scene and was responsible for press and social media at a young gallery. Additionally, since 2018, I have been working as a freelancer in different projects and responsibilities, because I enjoyed it so much, but didn't initially think that this work had a sustainable and long-term future. In 2019, I received a cultural scholarship from BMKOES (Federal Ministry for Arts, Culture, Civil Service, and Sport), which took me to Los Angeles. There, I worked at the MAK Center for Art & Architecture and had the opportunity to immerse myself even more deeply in the inner workings of a cultural institution. Los Angeles, with its dynamic and vibrant art scene, was exactly the right place for me. After several inspiring conversations with art professionals from the industry, I made the decision to officially start my own business.

Upon returning to Vienna, I founded the communications agency Marschalek Art Management in November 2020, right in the middle of the pandemic. What started as a side business with a few projects quickly turned into a real success story. In my first year, I was working 80 to 90 hours per week, which led me to the decision to leave my safe employment and fully pursue my dream. Since 2021, I have been 100 percent self-employed with Marschalek Art Management, developing communication strategies for artists and cultural professionals, curating exhibitions, writing texts, and continuously creating new projects. Being self-employed is not easy and often quite literally means working by yourself and all the time. It comes with financial risks and challenges but also offers immense learning opportunities, about yourself, about others, about the value of work, and what truly makes you happy. Personally, I can no longer imagine working a regular 9-to-5 job, as it wouldn't provide me with the freedom I need in my life.

*ASC: How would you classify your business Marschalek Art Management? Can you tell me more about the art-management business model that you have?*

**PM:** The business model is based on providing specialized services such as press & PR, social media, and consulting. Close collaboration with clients allows me to understand their needs and develop customized solutions. Depending on the type of client, budget, planning timeline, and other parameters, there are different pricing structures (they vary between corporate rates, association rates, and rates for artists). For certain services, such as opening speeches, artist talks, or written texts, I have fixed rates. For art-management consultations, I offer individual packages — mostly annual consultations with milestones as well as estimates of hours worked. The reason for this is that these individual packages usually span a longer period of time and cover various topics, for example self-presentation, portfolio development, press & PR, writing, securing media coverage, exhibition organization . . . you name it.

*ASC: What does a typical work day look like for you, from start to finish? What sort of responsibilities and tasks do you juggle?*

**PM:** A typical work day varies greatly and depends heavily on the current workload and upcoming projects. My tasks are highly diverse, ranging from organizational and administrative duties to creative and strategic work. As a self-employed professional, I truly value the freedom to structure my day flexibly. I usually start my day with exercise, which is an essential balance for me and something I consciously make time for. At the same time, this flexibility also means that I sometimes must complete certain tasks in the evening or on weekends when projects require it. On office days, my schedule includes computer work, email correspondence, financial management, invoicing, tax matters, and annual planning. Additionally, I focus on strategy development, client acquisition, concept and content creation, communication, maintaining my social-media channels, and writing newsletters. A significant portion of my time is also dedicated to working directly on client projects.

Beyond office work, I frequently have external appointments, ranging from meetings with the artists I support in art management and discussions with clients about ongoing projects to regular networking events. Business trips are also a recurring part of my professional life.

*ASC: Tell me something I wouldn't expect to hear about your job. What is something many would be surprised to know?*

**PM:** One thing that many wouldn't expect when thinking about my profession is the constant companion: self-doubt. As an entrepreneur, especially in the arts and culture sector, there is no straight path to success, and regular questioning is simply part of the process. You come up with many ideas, write countless estimates and concept papers, but in the end, only a small portion of them actually come to fruition. Many would also be surprised by how much invisible work happens behind the scenes. In addition to creative projects and strategic work, administrative tasks like accounting, contracts, grant applications, and handling tax and legal matters take up a significant part of the work day. For freelancers, these bureaucratic hurdles are often a challenge that is barely noticed from the outside. Despite these challenges, however, the freedom and the opportunity to realize my vision outweigh it all.

*ASC: Can you tell me about a difficult aspect of the job, something that you find particularly challenging about it?*

**PM:** One of the most challenging aspects of my work is maintaining a healthy work–life balance. The boundaries between work and personal life often blur.

*ASC: That's so understandable! Our friendship, for example, is such an exemplification of that. We worked together for years and I attended your wedding—it's something quite typical in the art world, I am finding out!*

**PM:** Exactly. It takes a lot of discipline to consciously take breaks and not be available around the clock. By now, I've found a routine that works for me, but in the beginning it was a real struggle. Another major challenge is negotiating fees. Unfortunately, the belief still prevails in the art and culture sector that creative work is done purely out of passion and should therefore be provided for free or for very low compensation. What is often overlooked is that artistic and creative services require time, expertise, and professional experience, and should be paid accordingly. Setting clear boundaries and confidently asserting one's own value requires a great deal of sensitivity and negotiation skills, which is something I had to work hard to develop.

*ASC: When it comes to gauging success, how do you measure that for yourself, your projects, and your organization?*

**PM:** Success means something different to everyone. For me, success primarily means being happy. Of course, success is also tied to classic metrics and measurable factors, such as feedback on exhibitions, client responses to my work, reviews from joint projects, or recognition and recommendations from colleagues. Financial success, whether through sales at fairs or in receiving funding for specific projects, is also an important confirmation of the sustainability of my work. For me, success is also reflected in people supporting my work, just like with this interview. Visibility plays a crucial role, which is why I consider media coverage of my projects a success. I believe it is essential to consciously acknowledge and celebrate achievements and progress, as these often get lost in the fast pace of today's world.

***ASC: What is specific about your job in your geographical region in particular? I would particularly like to hear more about the public funding aspects that set Austria apart from many other regions and how this plays a part in your business.***

**PM:** In Austria, there are quite a lot of funding opportunities for projects in the art and cultural sector. In 2023, for example, I received project funding for the "Artist's Toolbox," an educational platform that offers hands-on workshops in the form of videos, templates, and guides on a wide range of topics and challenges within the arts and cultural sector, from the Vienna Business Agency. Additionally, artists or associations can apply for support to cover the costs of their projects, residencies, catalog production, and more from the federal government, including funds such as the Otto Mauer Fund or Bildrecht.

***ASC: If someone wanted to follow in your footsteps and do what you do, what advice or even warnings would you give them?***

**PM:** If someone were to follow in my footsteps, the most important advice I would give is to listen to your gut and trust your intuition. You should not fear failure, because only through making mistakes can you learn and grow. Sometimes it's crucial to simply take action and try new things, and it's important to do your best to be bold in embracing new challenges. One more thing . . . Learn to say no, because no one has to do everything. Those who know their own worth and stand confidently in it create space for what truly matters.

*

After speaking to Paula, I was reminded of how alike we are in the way we approach work. Even while we were studying, we were working part time. Even while working, we were developing projects on the side. We both love the juggle. Personally, it has always been hard for me to settle into one thing because I enjoy change and a fast pace, which is why working for myself, or in a role with a lot of autonomy, is ideal. This was echoed in Paula's approach to running her business, with excitement, freedom, and flexibility. It's not ideal for everyone, and the precariousness, especially in the beginning stages, can be incredibly taxing, but her last piece of advice about not fearing mistakes and standing by your worth is what can push someone from being good to being great, in both an entrepreneurial endeavor or a 9-to-5 job in the creative sector.

Paula's business is one model of many to support and manage artists' careers. There is the studio manager, for example, who works for one artist in their studio, who you will hear from later in this chapter. However, I still wanted to find out more about these business models that support artists in an agency model. Marschalek Art Management does this with a varying structure that involves offering services to both artists as well as companies and associations, with packages adjusted to the needs of the client.

In London, however, a new business has emerged. In 2024, Valeria Szabó Facchin launched Studio Expanded. As Founder and CEO, Valeria has built an artist-management agency that is admittedly still in its infancy as I write this chapter, and has expanded into another company, Aster, since. The business structure and approach she takes to the London art scene—a global and incredibly competitive market—are quite unique. When we sat down for the interview, we hit two birds with one stone. We recorded the interview for the book, which you will read in the following pages, but we also spoke on the *All About Art* podcast. The episode has become one of our most popular to date, because these new business models that support artists and contribute to an existing ecosystem of galleries, museums, and other project spaces are a valuable contribution to a growing sector.

*Valeria Szabó Facchin is the Founder and CEO of Studio Expanded, an artist agency dedicated to sustainable practices and the creation of lasting cultural value. Since launching the company in October 2024, she has gone on to cofound Aster, a next-generation cultural-investment platform designed to support the careers of socially impactful and institutionally recognized artists by uniting strategic investment, artist management, and philanthropic commissioning within a single circular ecosystem. Valeria's career includes roles at leading organizations such as Sotheby's, Somerset House, and La Biennale di Venezia. As a founding director of the Nicoletta Fiorucci Foundation in London, Valeria played a pivotal role in establishing the foundation as one of Europe's most prestigious contemporary art collections. Valeria is also a published author and a guest lecturer at several prestigious universities. She holds master's degrees from both the Courtauld Institute of Art and Ca' Foscari University in Venice.*

**Alexandra Steinacker-Clark: Can you tell me more about what you studied and how your career has developed?**

**Valeria Szabó Facchin:** I've been drawn to the arts since childhood, guided by Dostoevsky's belief that art will save the world. For me, beauty is the manifestation of life in its highest form. Living with ADHD, art has always been the way I sensed the world; it gave me comfort. However, I have dyscalculia (a learning disorder that affects my ability to understand number-based information and math) as well as ADHD, so I really struggle to do simple math but I'm very good with spatial and abstract thinking. I did a master's in Italy in art history and then another master's in curatorial studies at the Courtauld Institute in London. Studying art history was the perfect foundation because you need to have the base knowledge. As much as I loved studying, I really needed to work, so I applied for an internship at Sotheby's in Milan while I was studying. That was the first job I've ever had in the arts, and it was like a baptism of fire because that was my first ever work experience. After that, I went to the Peggy Guggenheim Collection as an intern, and then I worked in their educational program. When I was at the Courtauld, I was the curatorial assistant at Somerset House but I was already thinking about what jobs were out there after graduation. I was in that terrible phase in which you start sending out applications for available positions but you already know they are not the right fit for you — but you need to get a job so that you can prove to your parents that they weren't right in thinking you should have never gone into the arts in the first place.

*ASC: That is a common theme I hear when speaking to people in the arts. There is a belief that there are little to no viable career paths in the arts sector . . . I guess everyone I am sitting down to interview for this book is living proof of the opposite! I'm not saying it's an easy sector to find your way, but I do think it's worth it . . .*

**VSF:** Exactly . . . I always knew I wanted to be in the arts, and when you love something, you have to take that chance. So, one evening, I happened to go to the opening event of an exhibition for a private collection. I went straight to the director of the organization and I said, "Do you need an assistant curator?" It was just pure luck that at that point the two former assistant curators were leaving for other jobs, so they really needed somebody. On the same night, I had an interview with Nicoletta [Fiorucci]. It was very surreal.

*ASC: You didn't prepare for the interview? You just showed up, pitched yourself, and got an interview on the same night?*

**VSF:** Yes. Desperate times called for desperate measures.

**ASC:** *You had such bravery in going up to someone at an opening and saying, "Hey! Do you need someone? I'm willing."*

**VSF:** I was never in a place where things just came to me. I ended up staying at the Foundation, growing in my role, and eventually becoming Director and leading the business through the COVID-19 pandemic.

**ASC:** *What made you want to develop a company that manages artists instead of starting your own art gallery, for example?*

**VSF:** It was a matter of necessity again, and about valuable resources. I was on maternity leave as Director of the Nicoletta Fiorucci Foundation at the time. I was nursing and chatting with my artist friends on the other side of the world and they would say, "We're going to do this amazing exhibition. What do you think? How should I be doing this or that, how should I be negotiating on the contract?" While giving my advice, the idea came when I realized I could add value with this. Hence, I launched Studio Expanded, which within just a few months proved successful, giving me both the reassurance and the stamina to expand the ecosystem further. Partnering with art finance expert Francesca Casiraghi, founder of London Trade Art and a pioneer of art fractionalization, we went on to launch Aster the following year, an amplified evolution of Studio Expanded, embedding the investment component directly into artist management.

**ASC:** *What does your role look like at Studio Expanded and Aster?*

**VSF:** I'm the Founder and CEO of Studio Expanded and cofounder of Aster, so in many ways, its lead artist strategist. My role is to build the infrastructure around artists. Ensuring everything is connected, efficient, and that resources are used in the best way possible to support their practice.

With Aster, we are taking this mission further by merging alternative financial-asset strategies with artist management and philanthropic commissioning to create a circular ecosystem where artistic vision and financial sustainability reinforce one another. What we do could be described as a form of impact investing or catalyst finance. We don't simply acquire works and wait for them to appreciate in value; instead, we take an active role in shaping the artist's career, which is why the artist-management component is fundamental.

***ASC: How do you choose the artists that you work with now at Aster?***

**VSF:** Through my work, especially with Nicoletta, I developed a collector's eye. I developed an ability to understand the wider context, to understand where an artist is placed within a specific location. What are the trends there? Where is the world currently going? How do they fit into that? It has become fundamental to both art management and investing. I am drawn only to artists I believe are destined, sooner or later, to enter museums, recognizing the next Turner Prize nominee before everyone else does. It's about sensing the *Zeitgeist.* Some artists have the extraordinary ability to tune into reality in all its dimensions, to capture change, emotion, and atmosphere, and distill it into a single work. My role is to discover that ability before it becomes obvious. I am also naturally drawn to artists who are interdisciplinary, whose practices unfold across mediums rather than being confined to one. I look for cultural makers whose work becomes a vessel for urgent social discussions and carries the power to create lasting impact. But most of all, working with artists is like falling in love. Trust and mutual respect

---

*   *Zeitgeist* refers to the defining spirit or mood of a particular period of history as shown by the ideas and beliefs of the time.

are essential. It is a long-term relationship and, like any relationship, it requires commitment and extra effort to make it thrive.

***ASC: What other roles are there in your organization? I think it's interesting to touch on the other moving parts in your company and what sort of roles contribute to how it all functions!***

**VSF:** There are artist liaisons, who are a crucial part of the entire infrastructure because they function as the spokesperson for the artist. They also act as their studio assistants. There is support for production budgeting, management of their inventory, as well as to bring in leads such as gallery representation and institutional shows. That is probably one of the most important roles that we currently have and it's for people who have strong art-historical backgrounds as well as strong production backgrounds. When we start the onboarding process with an artist, the artist liaison will go into a "due diligence" phase in which they have one-on-one sessions with the artist, looking at the artist's inventory and starting a historical track record of past sales and partnerships. Then we develop a strategy for the artist and prepare a portfolio. I manage all of those moving parts and contribute to the strategy building when the time comes.

***ASC: Can you tell me something that I wouldn't expect to hear about your job? What's something that many would be surprised to know?***

**VSF:** My time is dedicated to thinking strategically, as there is a lot I need to consider when I pitch. If I create a structure, who is benefiting? Where is each party located? What does that mean if the inventory has to be shipped to a gallery that is in the UK and the artist is located in mainland Europe? What is the cost associated with that? There are a lot of tax implications as part of my job which I don't think people expect but, in the end, it is a business.

*ASC: Hypothetically, if you were hiring someone to replace you, what are some personality traits or strengths that you would look for in an ideal candidate?*

**VSF:** Oh my gosh. Well, probably a finance lawyer.

*ASC: No, don't say that!*

**VSF:** I'm just kidding—sort of. You also definitely need the art-historical knowledge. You need to be able to ask yourself, "Is this a good painting? Is this a bad painting?" and be able to judge if a painting is worth it. You need to be a problem solver. Solutions oriented, analytical, creative, and also a good negotiator. Understanding people's needs. Everybody is moved by something, and if you're able to understand what they need, then you can create strategies for them. Otherwise, if what you are creating does not meet their needs, you're just wasting your time.

*ASC: If someone wanted to be an artist manager and do what you do, what advice or even warnings would you give them?*

**VSF:** I would tell them to start working in artist studios. They need to be close to the artist to understand what it actually means, because it can be a very chaotic kind of work. You need to understand all the different partners, such as galleries or institutions, that are involved in the process. You need to understand the artist's needs, but also you need to understand the gallery's needs. Or the institution's needs. You need to be able to mitigate all the different accounts, all the different complexities that might be happening, and you need to be able to compromise.

*

Valeria's business structure allows artists to focus on their practice while she takes on the more analytical, financial aspects of thinking about where an artist functions within an ecosystem. No matter how much the art world would like to distance itself from the art market, one does not exist without the other. Both Paula and Valeria have found ways of putting their analytically creative brains to use in serving artists in ways that sustainably support their careers. Artist agents typically work with multiple artists, but aren't responsible for the everyday admin or operations of an artist's studio. There are some people that choose to work with one artist—overseeing the running of the studio, so that an artist can concentrate on what they are best at: creating their work. Being a studio manager is not for the faint of heart. You are working closely with someone who is baring their soul to the world through their work. No matter how you spin it, working with artists is an incredibly personal endeavor and you need to develop a strong set of boundaries and an ability to know what the artist will want before they want it.

When I was introduced to Marie von Ribbentrop, I knew I had to speak to her for this chapter. Marie now works at Convelio, an international fine-art shipping company (another interesting area of the art industry that sadly I don't have the space to cover in this book!) but she was the studio manager for Alicja Kwade for four years up until 2023. Alicja Kwade is a world-renowned Polish artist, best known for her sculptures and installations that challenge scientific and philosophical concepts in different ways. She uses materials and objects to deconstruct the viewer's perception, making us question both our own realities of what we are seeing, as well as on a deeper level, asking questions about society and the wider universe. I saw one of her works for the first time in 2017: having just moved to London, I was oblivious to the huge public sculpture trail that gets erected in Regent's Park each year for Frieze, so I was pleasantly surprised to discover works by Tony Cragg, John Chamberlain, even KAWS—as well as Alicja Kwade's *Big Be-Hide*. There were two large boulders, one with its natural stone finish and the other painted in an eclectic silver, with a large mirror inbetween the two. It was part optical illusion, part participatory experience, part confusion.

I was enchanted, and out of all the sculptures I saw that day, that is the one that has stayed in my mind all these years later.

---

*Marie von Ribbentrop is the current Head of Sales UK at Convelio Fine Art Shippers after four years as Studio Manager and Head of Operations at the Berlin-based studio of artist Alicja Kwade. Marie has a bachelor's degree in History of Art and Art Theory from Goldsmiths, University of London.*

---

*Alexandra Steinacker-Clark: Tell me briefly about past professional experiences. Can you take me through your education and career path thus far?*

**Marie von Ribbentrop:** I did my BA in Art History at Goldsmiths, University of London. My mother had a gallery and that's how I got into art. For my first job out of university, I took a leap of faith and went to Hong Kong to work for a small start-up that wasn't involved with the art world in any way. It was a stroke of luck for me because that's where I first met Alicja [Kwade]. We met through friends of friends, because although I wasn't in the art world professionally at the time, it was still a huge interest of mine. We got to know each other better during Art Basel Hong Kong at a dinner we both attended . . . and the afterparty following. Quite a typical way to form connections in the art world, I'd say! After two years in Hong Kong, I came back to Berlin and met her for a drink. While we were chatting, she happened to mention that she was looking for a studio manager, so I pitched myself for the role. We always got on quite well and ultimately I think she chose me because we clicked personality-wise. I know she took a chance on me because I didn't have any prior experience at the time.

Back then, there were around 15 people employed at the studio. In the four years that I was there, we grew to 30. I had never managed anyone before, and working for an artist does result in quite a special relationship. In the first six months, I will admit it was quite tough . . . I just kept thinking, "Please don't fire me, I can prove I can do this." I once overheard someone who worked at the studio talking to Alicja and saying that I couldn't do this job, it's too hard, I had no experience. I got so scared. Alicja said, "No. Let her. She will figure it out somehow. I trust her." And that gave me a big push to work my ass off, but it was definitely rough in the beginning. In that first year, I actually dreamed of Alicja almost every night.

*ASC: Oh my gosh, that happens to me, too! When I first start a job, I dream about the workplace and my colleagues quite a bit. Can you expand a bit on the responsibilities that you had as studio manager for Alicja?*

**MvR:** I would say the most important thing is to keep the artist and the team happy and not overworked. Alicja was always super involved with the projects, which is not always the case in other studios—no artist studio functions the same as another. As Studio Manager for an artist who is quite involved, you sort of become "the artist whisperer." Artists are quite solitary, sometimes introverted by nature. It can be overwhelming to have a studio with a large number of staff, so my role was to ease that pressure as much as I could. If someone had a problem, it was my responsibility to try to resolve it without Alicja. I delegated the projects to our project managers, I checked the budgets, I assessed the timelines, and I liaised with all of her galleries for any important communication, including working with Alicja to determine which works would go to which art fair, or which works fitted which gallery. I also was responsible for pricing the works. Sometimes, if she didn't feel inspired, I looked through her old sketches and said, "Hey, why don't you continue this series or maybe this could be nice?" She would either say no, that's too old, but sometimes she would be open to it. In these instances, it could be really positive because the galleries would often ask if we had another edition of certain works, so it could be an opportunity to support the studio financially. Although making art is a creative endeavor, you also have to have a business mindset. In a lot of ways, Alicja is a businesswoman. She doesn't fall into the categorical misconception of the "aloof artist." She knows exactly what she wants, and she is a very strong negotiator.

***ASC: What is something I wouldn't expect to hear about the job, what would be something you think many would be surprised to know?***

**MvR:** A pattern I have noticed is that most of the people who work for artists are also artists. Of course, the accountant wasn't an artist, for example, but the project managers who weren't architects were all artists who had their own practice next to the job. It's quite common in artist studios.

***ASC: Can you tell me a difficult or challenging aspect of the job?***

**MvR:** In the beginning, I'll be honest, I found everything challenging. It was a challenge to work with people who were much older than I was. Most of all, though, the biggest challenge that took the most time was learning how to say no. Alicja and I grew very close, and at one point we even did personal training together. That was the point when I realized I needed to set boundaries in order to maintain a healthy working relationship. However, and this goes for any sort of professional relationship where you approach things with tact and empathy, I always found a different way of saying no. It was never just an outright "No, I am not doing that." It was a matter of thinking deeper about my reasoning for saying no, and explaining it in ways she would agree with. I think this is a skill that is valuable in any profession, and it keeps people from taking things too personally.

*ASC: Did you feel like your personal life seeped into your professional life? How would you suggest someone could set boundaries to prevent fatigue and burnout?*

**MvR:** I didn't set any boundaries in the beginning, because I didn't know what was really urgent and what could wait. In order to make that judgement, I needed to have a little bit of experience in the role. It was important for me, in the beginning, to say yes to everything and then later down the line, work out what needed an immediate response and what didn't. Being her "right hand" meant that she would often come to me first, with things that could be done by others in the team, too. It's about clear communication but also knowing when it's appropriate to delegate.

*ASC: I have heard a lot of people give advice to set boundaries early. You are saying the opposite, that you should be a "yes man" at the start and then figure out the boundaries later down the line?*

**MvR:** It was really helpful for me to do it that way, to gain a better understanding first and then set appropriate boundaries. You have to be careful with burnout, and you also have to know yourself and how much you can take.

*ASC: And now that you're no longer a studio manager, can you shed some light on your current responsibilities as Head of Sales UK for Convelio and how your previous role informs how you approach your current one?*

**MvR:** I'm very happy about my current job because I'm learning new skills in sales, and am learning more about another area of the arts, namely fine-art shipping. In terms of the skills I brought with me, as a studio manager you need to be able to see the big picture and keep an eye on everything going on and where it will all lead. As Head of Sales, you also have to be able to see that big picture. It has also been helpful to know how galleries work. Even if I didn't work at a gallery, I had contact with all of Alicja's galleries, learning how they think, what they want, how they work, and how complicated the buyers can be. Since we ship on behalf of galleries to their end clients, this is great knowledge in order to be able to foresee potential pitfalls or bumps along the road.

***ASC: What are some personality traits or strengths that you would look for in an ideal studio manager?***

**MvR:** You have to thrive in chaos a bit, but you also have to want to bring order to the chaos. You need to be interested in ensuring that there are efficient operations and processes in place. How do you display something on the website? How do you archive it? Who takes over the relationship with a specific person or foundry or gallery, and why is that the best way forward? That sort of thing. I also think you have to be quite a tough cookie. You have to have a thick skin and not take things personally, because artists will make things personal, that's how they work. You have to understand the distinction, and not be too sensitive.

***ASC: If someone wanted to do what you do, what advice would you give them?***

**MvR:** Artist studio-manager jobs are rarely advertised, it feels like. The best way is to get a referral, because this job is based on trust. It could also be beneficial to go to their exhibition openings, try to meet the artist and ask them about their studio. Get to know them and see if you get along in a setting not related to you wanting a job. I feel like that's the best way to gauge if it's a good fit for both of you.

*

As seen through the experiences of professionals like Paula and Valeria, artist management involves strategic thinking paired with a passion for art. It is necessary to understand the multifaceted needs of artists while considering the wider arts ecosystem and how an artist can maneuver within it. It also involves fostering a nurturing environment for their creativity, which is extremely similar to studio management, according to Marie. When working in the studio, getting to know the artist and being able to foresee their needs is one of the most important parts of the job, and teaches you how to think in a future-oriented manner for any positions you will take on later in your career.

## KEY TAKEAWAYS IF YOU ARE THINKING OF EMBARKING ON YOUR OWN CAREER IN ARTIST MANAGEMENT

### Three Practical Tips

- Develop strong communication skills to grasp the personal and professional aspirations of the artists you manage, and understand their vision.
- Learn the business landscape by familiarizing yourself with contracts, pricing structures, and market trends in the arts (and remember—know your worth!).
- If you want to work as a studio manager, it's important to consider if you get along with the artist on a personal level, while also keeping in mind your professional boundaries. It can be a tough line to walk, but a great lesson for any future endeavors.

## Next Steps

- Gain experience by working closely with artists or in studios to understand the way they operate.
- Explore internships in related organizations, such as commercial galleries, to acquire practical knowledge and build connections (shadowing an artist liaison could be beneficial here).
- Make sure you are always developing your art-historical and art-business knowledge—either through education, attending events in your free time, or consuming educational media such as books and podcasts.

CHAPTER 8

# WORKING AS AN ART WRITER

Writing about art can arguably be just as creative as making the art that's being written about. Although, in many ways, art can speak for itself, art writing is not only how we further art-historical and critical discourse, but it's also a means to connect art to its viewers. In Ancient Greece and Rome, writers and philosophers often discussed art, architecture, and society. In the 1500s, during the Renaissance, when there was a renewed interest in art outside of its role within religion, painter, writer, and architect Giorgio Vasari wrote *Lives of the Artists*. Featuring anecdotes and biographical notes, the dialogue surrounding artists as authors of their work and identifying themselves as such was a shift from the Middle Ages and paved a new path towards what we understand as an artist today. A few centuries later, in the early 1700s, English painter Jonathan Richardson coined the term "art criticism" in a treatise titled *An Essay on the Whole Art of Criticism (as it relates to painting)*, which sets out to create a system for ranking works of art. Although it is definitely no longer what we know as art criticism today, which has developed into a plethora of methodologies engaged with aesthetic theories but also anthropology, poetry, philosophy, psychology, and more. In this chapter, I speak to three different kinds of arts writers—an editor, an author, and a journalist—although in reality these categorizations are futile because all of them do all of those things.

Walking through Regent's Park towards Primrose Hill (a great place for a skyline view of London, by the way), I was mentally going through my prepared questions as I strolled towards the art-filled apartment of my interviewee. I had first met Francesca Gavin, editor of *EPOCH* magazine, at a dinner I organized for a gallery I was working for at the time. I rang her doorbell and walked to the top floor, where Francesca was inbetween meetings and offered me a cup of green tea before sitting down to chat with me.

---

*Francesca Gavin is a consultant, writer, editor, and curator based in London. She is the Editor-in-Chief and cofounder of EPOCH, a publication and platform looking at the now in dialogue with history. She is also the Founder of creative consultancy ArtPresentFuture and host of monthly radio show* Rough Version *on NTS Radio, which looks at the relationship between contemporary art and music. She has authored 11 books on visual culture and was formerly the Artistic Director of viennacontemporary and the co-curator of the Manifesta 11 biennial in Zurich, alongside other international curatorial work.*

---

*Alexandra Steinacker-Clark: I would like to start off by asking you to tell me briefly about your education and professional experiences. Can you take me through your career path?*

**Francesca Gavin:** My father is an actor and musician and my mother went to Central Saint Martins. I had inherited her postcard collection, which was a huge influence on me when I was younger, so by the age of around 12, I already had an encyclopaedic knowledge of art history. I went on to study Art History at university in York — Old York, not New York — and loved it. I had no intention of going into the art world afterwards, though.

*ASC: Really? No intention at all?*

**FG:** None. I didn't think I was meant for a gallery and I had no idea what roles there were. When I left university, I worked at a book publisher in the design department. I then went to *Dazed*—I phoned them up and said, "I want your job. How did you get it?" and ended up getting a position as an editorial assistant for about a year. Again, not focused on art. I was looking at fashion projects, random bits of music, some exhibitions, and after some time I ended up becoming their freelance book editor. That's how I broke into journalism. I went to *Time Out* for about a year and a half, again working on non-art things as the international agenda editor, which was a section that covered the best events in every city around the world. I began to freelance full time as a journalist after that, and I haven't had an in-house job since. My writing focused on everything from soul music to books to some visual art and more. Over time, I got more involved with art and curation. I was writing professionally from the beginning but I came into the contemporary art world late in a way that became a total fusion of things that I was interested in.

***ASC: Can you describe some of the responsibilities you have as Editor in Chief at EPOCH?***

**FG:** I cofounded it with Leonard Vernhet, an incredible creative director in Paris who I'd done some copywriting for. He wanted to start a magazine about the wholeness of civilization. It's a completely independent publication and I have utter freedom conceptually in what I do. I come up with the thematics for the issues, I respond to the themes, I commission all the texts, I look at the writing, I get it laid out. I promote the publication and we have a variety of contributors. I commission a lot of women. I've done interviews with Pierre Huyghe, Arthur Jafa, Wolfgang Tillmans, Martine Syms, etc. We're funded by branded partnerships rather than advertising and we come out annually.

***ASC: Can we also briefly talk about the responsibilities that you had as Founding Curator of Soho House, and then also a little bit more about the responsibilities you had in your role as Artistic Director of viennacontemporary?***

**FG:** I was the founding curator of the Soho House Group for seven years. I did it initially in collaboration with Jonathan Yeo, who's an artist, as a one-off project. It went so well that I was invited to continue doing that for when they opened up new Soho Houses. I would get between 150 and 400 artworks from artists in exchange for a tab that they could spend on hotel rooms, food, and drink, which meant we were really responding to the artistic communities in different places. I began with Dean Street Townhouse in London and continued with Soho House Berlin, along with collections in Istanbul, Chicago, Toronto, New York, L A, Miami, and ones all across the U K. I built up a collection of around 3,000 artworks and incredible relationships. My role involved looking at the site, working out how many artworks they needed for the site, deciding what the budget would be, and approaching all the artists with the concept. I would then choose the artworks that would fit conceptually and physically within the space, do all the contracts and paperwork, sort all the transportation of the artworks to a storage base (or a framer), and then be on-site for the day of collection. For viennacontemporary, I was Artistic Director. My role was to give the fair a strong curatorial direction. We had incredible press, everything from *Vogue* to the *Financial Times*, praising the content of the fair, which was one-third Austrian, one-third Eastern European, and one-third Central European. I thought about the architectural layout of the space, the advertising, the partnerships, the PR, and having meetings with gallerists internationally. I also aimed to bring in buyers and collectors and organize the talks program. It was a great experience.

*ASC: And now, what does a typical work day look like for you from start to finish? I bet it's different every single day.*

**FG:** A lot of travel. When I worked for viennacontemporary, I was traveling four times a month. During my time at Soho House, I was constantly on flights and would regularly spend three weeks in a different location. Even editorially, I travel a lot. My typical work day is working at home, checking my emails. In the afternoons, I'm a little bit more meeting based, but it's really project dependent. Consultancy is probably where a large amount of my income comes from, and if I've got an editorial deadline, that's my focus. It's always a balance between writing, doing decks, Zoom calls, emails, and then, of course, seeing exhibitions because I have to see the art. I go to art fairs, I go to biennials, I say yes to a lot of press trips. I must admit, for me, there is no boundary between my social life and my work life. It's one big blob, blending between boundaries. There's a lot of fluidity within the structure.

*ASC: Can you share a difficult aspect of what you do?*

**FG:** Things like buying a flat or having a pension. You get to inhabit the same world as the super-rich, but at the same time inhabit the world of artists, writers, and other creatives. It's this really strange cross-society experience, which is really interesting, but in the long term there are issues around livelihood and precarity that are very much intertwined in the art world but aren't really talked about openly.

*ASC: If someone wanted to do what you do, be an editor, a writer, a consultant, wearing all the hats that you wear, or even wanting to wear one of the hats that you wear, where do you think they could start?*

**FG:** Go out. Be friendly. More than anything, make conversations, meet people. Visit exhibition openings and galleries and talk to whoever's working there. It's about embedding yourself in that world. Those personal relationships are the things that lead to work down the line.

***ASC: Have you ever made a step in your career that you've regretted? And how did you go about navigating that situation?***

**FG:** In general, I would make sure I hire an art lawyer to look at employment contracts, which is something a lot of people don't do. In a broader sense, making sure you have some kind of structural support to what you do as a freelancer is a really difficult thing. I don't regret most things in my career, but I've also made my own opportunities. That probably would be my wider advice: I never got offered the right job, so I made my own. If you want to curate, make exhibitions. If you want to write about art, or talk about art, or produce a podcast about art, do it. At the end of the day, it's about getting things out there and approaching people whenever you can.

*

Francesca started out in the arts sector in quite a non-linear way. She studied art history and engaged with art academically, yes, but the first few positions she held in her career as a journalist were non-art related, although still very much involved with the wider cultural sector. From what I gleaned from speaking to her, these wider cultural experiences not only allowed for her work — be it writing, curating, her radio show, or other aspects — to be created through a multifaceted cross-cultural lens, but it was also a catalyst for developing her network of artists, curators, and other cultural-industry leaders.

In some ways, it can be incredibly difficult to break into the arts sector, as meeting people can prove to be less straightforward than many make it seem. The arts is considered quite an inaccessible and confusing industry, especially to those of us who didn't grow up around museums and galleries. When author Bianca Bosker announced she was releasing a book on the art world where she went "undercover" working in the industry, I knew I had to buy it as soon as it hit the shelves. I also knew that I had to speak to her for this book.

---

*Bianca Bosker is an American journalist and author known for her* New York Times *bestselling books* Cork Dork *and* Get the Picture. *She's also a contributing writer for* The Atlantic. *Her work has appeared in publications like* The New Yorker, The New York Times, *and the* Wall Street Journal. *Bosker's writing explores diverse topics, including technology's influence on culture, the world of wine and sommeliers, and the art world. She previously served as the executive tech editor for the* Huffington Post.

---

*Alexandra Steinacker-Clark: Can you tell me briefly about your education and career path? What led you to becoming an author and, more specifically, writing about the art world?*

**Bianca Bosker:** I'm an only child and I grew up reading a lot of books, so my interest in writing probably started from when I was little and looking for one-player activities. I worked as a journalist and I'd written another book before I wrote *Get the Picture*, which focuses on my journey into the weird, wild, wonderful world of art. Embracing art as a book topic was a bit of a surprise, because I started working on it at a point where art and I were not on speaking terms. Art had been a passion of mine growing up, but when I moved to New York after college, instead of embracing art as I thought I would, I felt totally alienated from it. I hadn't really tried to reconnect with art until a number of years ago, when I was back in my childhood home in Oregon, helping my mom clean out her basement. I came across paintings by my late grandmother, some of which were inspired by her time as a Holocaust survivor in a displaced persons' camp after the war. My grandmother had always treated art as a necessity. It was this thing that she turned to at this moment when life turned itself inside out. The painting of hers that had been inspired by her time after the war, it haunted me. It trailed me back to New York, and it kept spinning my mind round and round, this question of why art had been so essential to her.

I think for me what really pulled me ultimately into the art world is my obsession with obsession. When it came to these art fiends, I'd never met a group of people willing to sacrifice so much for something of so little obvious practical value. I became intrigued with this question of whether I could see art, whether I could see the world the way they did, and what might change if I could. And so I decided that I didn't want to just go and see galleries, but I really wanted to understand how this world works. As a writer, I believe in learning by doing and I ultimately disowned my regular life to sell thousands of dollars' worth of art at galleries, to work as a studio assistant, and to patrol museum wings as a security guard guarding a pile of dust. And I loved it. I started very much from a place of feeling like art was optional and a luxury, and now I feel like it's absolutely essential and fundamental to the human experience. Handing my life over to the art world was grueling in moments, but also one of the best things I've ever done.

*ASC: Going back, what was your foot in the door in the creative sector as a writer? How has it developed, and how do you approach your writing now?*

**BB:** One of my first journalistic experiences was launching a neighborhood newspaper that lasted all of one issue. Like I said, I was always reading and really interested in the power of the word on the page. I was a short-lived editor of my school newspaper, then I interned for some local papers in Portland, Oregon. If you want to become a writer,

I think any writing experience you do matters. Something has to exist, especially if you want to do nonfiction writing or journalism, because you need clips for your writing portfolio. It doesn't matter where you start, but you need to practice stringing sentences together, getting through the agony of staring at the empty page. After graduating, I worked at the *Huffington Post* and helped cofound their tech section. I was eventually the executive tech editor there, and then quit my job to start drinking very heavily when I started the process of training to become a sommelier—which all led to the book *Cork Dork*. Ever since then, I've been writing books and freelancing. I probably write most frequently for *The Atlantic* and just feel really, really lucky to be able to have a job that, as I see it, is finding interesting stories and sharing them with people. It's a lot of learning in a lot of different areas. Many journalists choose to have a beat, and there's a logic to that—you get to know a subject really well, you build up sources. I have not made my life easier by doing what I have done in my career because each time I'm basically starting over from scratch.

***ASC: What are some of the responsibilities that you have in your job? What's the writing process like?***

**BB:** I feel a lot of responsibility to the reader and that manifests in a number of different ways throughout the process. In the research process for the book, I feel the responsibility to keep a very open mind. As a writer, I begin with a question or many questions, but do not seek out a specific answer. It's important to let the reporting and the research guide you rather than having a hypothesis that you're trying to reverse-engineer with evidence when you step out. I want to give the reader the truth, I want to show them how these worlds work, I want to bring them inside the logic. With *Get the Picture* and my journey into the art world, I was really curious to understand how a work of art goes from being the germ of an idea in someone's studio to this "masterpiece" that we "ooh" and "aah" over in museums. I wanted to see that process and be in the room when it was happening because I felt like all the decisions that shape an artwork are ultimately decisions that shape us. I also have a very immersive research process. I believe in learning by doing, as I said, so I didn't want to just sit down and interview people. I wanted to actually be selling artworks, dealing with the irate VIPs during the insanity of Art Basel Miami, stretching canvases for artists in their studios, telling people not to use flashes in a museum. I wanted to be there, and I do believe that oftentimes the miraculous emerges from the mundane. Later, as I'm sifting through all the information I've gathered and trying to translate it from an endless pile of notes to words on a page, I also feel a big responsibility not to bore the reader.

**ASC: Did you also have a sense of responsibility towards the people that you've interviewed?**

**BB:** Oh, hugely. I have enormous gratitude and admiration for people that are willing to let in journalists like myself and be vulnerable. I believe when writing about people it's important to be accurate, which means getting your facts right but also means being fair. For *Get The Picture*, I hired a fact checker who went through all my information. I do hope that when I'm writing about people, if you don't know them, you feel like you're in the room with them. And if you do know them, you recognize them in what I've written. Part of writing a book is also helping it find its way in the world. I feel a responsibility to the work to support it by telling everyone I know (and then some) about it—being that really annoying person who sends a million emails asking people to please write about it, share it, buy it. Anyone who has read my book or listened to it feels like a friend to me, even if I've never met them. It's like we've gone on an adventure together. And I'm so grateful. A book is sort of a pile of paper until someone picks it up and reads it and breathes life into it.

*ASC: Would you ever actually go into the art world full time?*

**BB:** Absolutely. I believe in what artists are doing, I want to support them. There are things that I miss a great deal. Certainly, working with artists day-to-day is one of them. Some of my greatest memories of my adult life are showing up to work with Julie Curtiss at her studio.

*ASC: What was the reception of your book like? How do you think the art world in New York, or even globally, reacted to it?*

**BB:** There was an early reader of the book who told me that he hoped I didn't get assassinated on the book tour. So that was a great vote of confidence.

*ASC: Oh my goodness.*

**BB:** I definitely had my concerns because going into it, getting access to people in that world was so difficult. I had laid out these goals of going and working in the art world—it's an admittedly pushy goal. I got warnings, threats, even a gallerist who told me that if I wrote anything he disagreed with, he would trash my reputation personally, professionally, psychologically. And sure, there are elements of the book that are controversial. But on the whole, the reception has been phenomenal. It's been especially exciting to get great feedback from artists. They tell it like it is. They're the conscience of the art world.

*ASC: Can you tell me something that I wouldn't expect to hear about your job? What is something that many might be surprised to learn?*

**BB:** One thing that may not immediately meet the eye is how much additional research I did that didn't explicitly make it onto the page. There were other art fairs that I worked at that I didn't write about. There were other artists that I worked for. There was a whole week I spent at this art residency that ended up being just a paragraph. Stacks and stacks of books I read that, in the course of the revision, get distilled to maybe a clause in a sentence. I felt like there was so much other research that I had to do in order to have the knowledge and, perhaps more importantly, the confidence to write a sentence, to make a particular assertion.

***ASC: Can you tell me about a difficult aspect of the job?***

**BB:** Dealing with crippling self-doubt and uncertainty. Dealing with one's own shitty writing. Not knowing where it's all going to go. However, and this is something I learned working with Julie [Curtiss], that's all part of the process. It's much less intimidating when you just accept that these difficult feelings will come, and they will also pass.

*

As I edit these interviews, write these sentences, and put this book together, Bianca's words are echoing in my ears. A lot of doubt creeps in, and the lessons she learned about creating are akin to what artists feel when they create a work and put it out in the world. Although Bianca said she will engage with the art world more within her future career, she hasn't built her entire career around the visual arts. It's a good reminder that, no matter where you are at in your career, whether you are in the arts or you want to pivot from another industry, you can engage with the sector by dipping a toe in. I am someone who likes to take plunges into deep ends, and I really dove into my career in visual arts. However, seeing how Bianca approached her professional engagement with art, you don't have to commit your entire career to this industry. You can love it, you can write about it, and enjoy professional commitments within it, while also entertaining a wider career more broadly in different industries.

Although we primarily spoke about Bianca's book, she mentioned that she writes about a plethora of different topics in her capacity as a journalist. But what if you only want to write about art and research the art world? I knew I had to speak to someone at the most well-known art news source: *The Art Newspaper*. Gareth Harris, Chief Contributing Editor at the paper, came on my podcast in 2025 to speak about a book he wrote for the "Hot Topics in the Art World" series, published by Lund Humphries and Sotheby's Institute of Art (another great resource to learn more about the art world, FYI!). Although he shared insights into his work at *TAN* on the podcast, he was more than willing to sit down with me again and delve into his career in more depth for this book, too.

---

*Dr Gareth Harris is a London-based freelance journalist specializing in the art and culture sector. He has contributed to major outlets such as the* Financial Times, The New York Times, Vogue, *and more. Harris is the chief contributing editor at* The Art Newspaper, *where he has worked for the last two decades. He authored* Censored Art Today *(2022) and* Towards the Ethical Art Museum *(2025). With formal education in literature, art history, and poetry, Harris has also taught university courses and offers multilingual skills in Italian, French, German, and Spanish.*

---

**Alexandra Steinacker-Clark: Can you tell me briefly about your education and career path? You are the Chief Contributing Editor at** The Art Newspaper (TAN). **What did you study and how did you end up as an arts writer?**

**Gareth Harris:** I did it in a very roundabout way. I studied languages at Royal Holloway, University of London. When I left university, I did what's called a PGCE, which is a teacher-training certificate in the UK. I taught French and Spanish in a secondary school in South

London — kind of hell on earth, really. After four years of that, I was around 28 or 29 years old and I remember going to the University of London careers service and picking out some sort of weird company directory. I scanned through all the publishers in London and decided to call Art Books International, which is a distribution company for European art books. I rang them and they said they had a job opening. I worked in that role for about two years and during that time I did PR, press, and event planning around the books. After that experience, in 2000 I got a job as Press Officer at the Victoria and Albert Museum, which is pretty amazing when you think about it. I had not really worked in a huge institution before, and it was brilliant. I worked on shows like Art Deco, Vivienne Westwood, Versace, doing the press and communications. I did that for about four years and I was able to meet so many different journalists and editors. That was key to everything, because once you know somebody you can ask, "Who do I send this pitch to? Who could I talk to about an article on X YZ topic?" And you build up relationships. In my spare time, I had written two or three book reviews for *The Art Newspaper*. I emailed the editor one day, asking if there were any staff writing jobs going, and it turned out there was. I had a really weird casual interview and I got the job. I was thinking, "Wow . . . How did that happen?" I'm not a trained journalist, but she [Cristina Ruiz, former editor of *The Art Newspaper*] put faith in me. In 2010, I technically went freelance, and since then I've been on a monthly retainer. I'm on a contract which means I mainly write for *TAN* and can't write for any rivals, but I do write for the *Financial Times* sometimes, for example. I have written for *The New York Times* twice. Now *that* was difficult. A very bruising editing process there.

*ASC: Can you describe some of the responsibilities you have in your job?*

**GH:** I basically get up and try to find exclusive news stories for our daily newsletter, which goes out every day at 12.30pm. It's our "general news" newsletter at *TAN*, where we run five or six stories. It's quite challenging to find content to include every single day. The way I approach finding things is I'm so plugged into other media—podcasts, TV, and so on—and I normally have a good idea every morning about a story I want to cover. I pitch it to my editors and by 9am I know which story they want. My deadline every day is around midday. The afternoon prior, I sometimes look for stories because I can email people for responses and comments. If we're lucky, everything goes out in the newsletter by 12.30 to 1pm and then the cycle starts again for me. I also run the diary section online, which is more gossipy. I try to do a little story for that once or twice a week—I can't lie, it brings in lots of clicks.

***ASC: So that is everything you do with* TAN *online. What about the print version?***

**GH:** I have a different kind of set of responsibilities with the print edition of *TAN*. Every month, I co-edit the book-club section, where we do a little page on new books, and it's meant to be a bit more accessible than traditional book reviews. I also run the diary pages in the print section, similar to online. In addition to all that, I have a column called "Global Briefing," which is a roundup of news worldwide. It's quite full-on and around the clock, you have to learn how to draw boundaries.

***ASC: Yeah, I can understand that. Do you ever feel like you need to balance art-world relationships with honest reporting? Has there ever been a situation where you've been at a crossroads professionally?***

**GH:** That's a really hard question to answer. I don't think I've ever really been compromised in that kind of way. When you run a tricky story that can cover any kind of dilemma from fundraising to geopolitical situations around the world, it's something you have to learn to balance. Ultimately a good professional will know that that's par for the course. Every story feels like a huge responsibility to me because you're putting out your version of something into the world. I'm an impartial journalist, and *The Art Newspaper* is a really important journal of record, but it is still my spin on things and I never really forget that.

***ASC: Do you think that being in such a big city has been beneficial for your career as a journalist?***

**GH:** Definitely. The most obvious thing to say is, at the very least, it's great to build up a network in one of the art-world centers. Also being able to see exhibitions on a regular basis, which feeds the soul.

***ASC: How do you feel the industry has changed throughout the years? What is different for someone entering the field now?***

**GH:** The rise of digital and how social media has totally fragmented the media landscape. It's really interesting how positions and attitudes have changed. With the rise of the internet, we were thinking everyone could be a blogger, everyone could be a journalist, but that's flipped back on its head now. People are realizing the value of art critics and proper news reporters. That's a really strange turnaround I've seen in the past twenty-odd years. I'm not saying bloggers' opinions are invalid, because it's great that everyone has that opportunity, but you have to have the expertise to back you up. We live in a digital world. I'm very conscious that, wherever I look, people are on their phones and this is where they are getting their information. So, taking that into consideration, I do wonder if journalists entering the field now need extra skills. Will they need to be able to video-edit? Will they need to be able to construct clever social-media posts? I'm out of the game in that way.

*ASC: Tell me something I wouldn't expect to hear about your job. What is something many people would be surprised to know?*

**GH:** When I write my news stories every day, the editors always ask me to write the headlines, which is so much harder than you think. It can't be too sensational, but it has to totally distill the story idea. What a skill to be able to encapsulate that narrative! The headlines are then usually changed by the editing team. Sometimes, I think I've done something brilliant and they say, "This is not really quite right," which is their job. Good editors are so rare, and they really help guide. You come to respect them. A golden rule is that I never push back on editors unless I'm totally shocked by what they suggest. Some journalists will really kick back. Either way, you just want to work with good solid people who respect deadlines and file readable, fairly intelligent prose.

*ASC: Can you tell me a difficult aspect of the job?*

**GH:** It's hard when you make mistakes. You try to be as accurate as possible, and that, for me, never gets easier. It's easier online if somebody thinks something is wrong. We can amend it pretty quickly with a correction or clarification if it's appropriate. On a much more serious level, you do worry about being sued. With certain stories you think, "My god, I don't want to be libellous." I've taken out libel insurance every year for about twenty years as a freelancer, since about 2010. In theory, the publication should be covering you, but it differs with every publication. I'm a bit belt and braces with it, as we say.

*ASC: What are some personality traits or strengths that you would look for in a budding arts journalist?*

**GH:** The ability to enjoy talking to people. That, along with the curiosity and hunger to find a good story. I'm not the most officious, hard-nosed interviewer because I lead people into a sense of security . . . And then I ask the nasty question at the end. If you've built up a kind of rapport, most people are really nice.

***ASC: Do you ever send questions in advance?***

**GH:** No, I don't, but this is another area that needs a bit of discretion. Some PR representatives will ask us to send questions. I will check with my editor and if they say it's best not to, what I tend to do in that scenario is say, "I will send you springboard topics for discussion and not set questions." I keep it loose because I don't want people to be totally primed. I understand people want to be prepared and do the research, but you do miss that spontaneity a little bit.

***ASC: What advice or even warnings would you give someone wanting to be an arts journalist?***

**GH:** It would be naïve to say I'm not worried about AI. A lot of observers say it won't match the kind of human intellect or curiosity. However, I believe it is going to come pretty close. I am concerned about how AI is going to impact journalism generally. Students are getting AI to write their essays, for example. As a response to that, print is weirdly becoming more popular and more prestigious. Imagine your own column in print, what a great thing that would be. Even now, if I see my name in the *Financial Times* or something, I'm like, "Wow. It's just so great to have that validation." As a young journalist, perhaps you should imagine you have a column in print. That would be something to aim for on every level. I would also say learn a language, because at least you have a foot in the door when you go to another country and are able to translate things more quickly than via Google Translate. It's good for your brain. Finally, I would also say be prepared for rejection.

***ASC: How do you deal with rejection?***

**GH:** Take half an hour. Go to the loo and cry. Then remind yourself that it's going to be fine.

*

Another important piece of advice Gareth mentioned is: if you are pitching to *The Art Newspaper*, or any other organization, ensure you get the name right. It's not the Art*s* Newspaper—it's just Art. A–R–T. But he sees this faux pas all the time. It's an immediate negative first interaction, and those first impressions are important!

There is no one-size-fits-all way to get into art writing. Hearing from three incredibly established writers, all producing work in various formats, you need to develop the ability to write well, which comes with practice. Start writing, even if no one will see the first few articles or blog entries. Practice and find your voice. However, in addition to that, it's important to develop a thick skin. You are creating something, putting it out into the world. Finding the middle ground between taking on constructive criticism and letting it shape you into a better professional versus taking feedback personally and letting it discourage you or knock your confidence is a hard line to walk, and it's one that arts writers need to straddle at every point in their career.

## KEY TAKEAWAYS IF YOU ARE THINKING OF EMBARKING ON YOUR OWN CAREER IN ART WRITING

### Three Practical Tips

- Develop a multidisciplinary approach—it adds more strings to your bow. Engage with fields like philosophy, psychology, or poetry (or, like Bianca, geology and wine!) to enrich your understanding of art (and the world in general) and diversify your critical approach.

- Cultivating authentic connections and building relationships will be a key cornerstone of your career in art writing—be it with artists and curators, or with PR representatives and other press staff.
- Work on developing your writing voice. Write whenever you can, for blogs or newspapers, to get your name out there or to practice your skills. Engaging in critical discussions such as panels or workshops and staying up to date through various media such as podcasts and the news can ensure you stay relevant and informed with your writing.

## Next Steps

- Create a portfolio by assembling a professional collection of your best writing, including links to published work, clips from newspaper articles, original essays, and critiques. If you don't have those yet, don't worry! Start looking for opportunities to contribute to small online platforms or local publications to gain experience.
- Start connecting with industry professionals. Go to press previews, attend openings, and keep an eye out for industry events. The more events you go to, the more people you can meet and the more topics you have to write about! Two birds with one stone.
- Follow some of your favorite journalists and writers on social media and keep up to date with what they are writing. If you have the chance to meet them and ask for their advice, mention something you loved in their recent published articles. It will leave the best first impression and it will also demonstrate your dedication and professionalism.

# CHAPTER 9

# WORKING FOR AN ART FAIR

Earlier in this book, when we were exploring the world of artist and studio management, I mentioned seeing artist Alicja Kwade's sculpture for the very first time at Frieze sculpture park, and how much that impacted me. That year, though, I never ended up attending the Frieze London art fair. It was only when I began working in galleries that I began attending fairs and recognizing their significance within the commercial art landscape.

As with a lot of things, especially since COVID and a wider economic downturn in recent years, more traditional models of business (galleries, auction houses, and publicly funded bodies like museums are included in this statement) need to find new approaches and structures to better serve not only their clients, but also their community on a wider scale in order for their businesses to survive. Art fairs need to think about how they activate audiences to attend, but once that's done, they also need to devise strategies to nurture client relationships on behalf of the galleries. Tours led by the director of the fair, for example, or specific introductions during the VIP days can go a long way. However, it's also about finding the new generation of collectors, so galleries are not vying for the same top ten collectors. One way some art fairs really alienate the younger clientele is pricing entry tickets over £100. It's too high a barrier for the "Zillennial" generation working as mid-career employees in high-earning industries who might not be familiar with art fairs but, once inside, can be inspired to start their art collection. When I was in Basel in 2025, VOLTA art fair offered free entry for locals on the Friday of fair week, for example.

These approaches foster a more loyal community and give people an incredible experience, while opening up the possibility for galleries to discover new clients or collaborators.

Frieze has one of the strongest community-engagement activations in their program with the public sculpture park. I have interviewed the curator of the sculpture park, Fatoş Üstek, on *All About Art*, and have led groups of emerging arts professionals through the sculptures and to the fair on behalf of NXT GEN. It's one of the biggest events of the year in London, and the global art world flocks to the city during Frieze. Museums plan their strongest programming during this time and the galleries pull out all the stops for their exhibitions and auxiliary events. The London art world is absolutely buzzing in October, and it's all because of Frieze! It is one of the biggest international fairs in the world, so I was excited to speak to Christine Messineo who shared a different perspective of the fair with me, giving insights on the positioning of the fair in the United States, which is a different beast altogether.

---

*Christine Messineo is the Director of Frieze Americas, including Frieze Los Angeles and Frieze New York. Christine has over 15 years of experience working in the arts, having previously been a partner at Bortolami Gallery in New York and a director at the Hannah Hoffman gallery in Los Angeles. Most recently Christine founded Plan Your Vote, an initiative established in 2020 in association with Vote.org that encouraged US citizens to exercise their right to vote. Plan Your Vote was hailed as one of the biggest cultural initiatives in the civic voting sphere since 2008, with over 200 participating artists and organizations.*

---

*Alexandra Steinacker-Clark: What was your first experience in the arts when you were just starting out, i.e. how did you get your "foot in the door"?*

**Christine Messineo:** I worked for the fashion designer Donna Karan directly out of college in her shop on Madison Avenue. The first floor was dedicated to the home: hand-sewn textiles using dark indigo dyes from Japan, thin porcelain ceramics shaped like stones worn by salt and sea, brass and bronze belts and jewelry by Robert Lee Morris. I got to visit the studios of ceramicists, textile makers, and embroidery artists. Donna's vision was always grounded in the artist's unique creative output; and she was generous in allowing me to participate in that process, even though I began working in sales. She saw that I was curious and helped mentor that interest. Looking back, I realize that from the very beginning of my career, I was fascinated by the artistic practice: understanding an artist's motivations and helping shape how the work might connect with a broader audience. That thread remains in my current role as Director of Americas at Frieze.

*ASC: Can you tell me briefly about your education and career path— what led you to the position you're in today as Director of Frieze Art Fair for the Americas?*

**CM:** When I first moved to New York, I worked in styling and retail to support myself while figuring out my career. And "career" kind of belongs in quotation marks, because these other jobs positioned me to understand what was feasible both financially and creatively. My friends worked across fashion, design, publishing, and art. My jobs in fashion and retail allowed me to create savings in an expensive city and ultimately be able to venture into the art world. I interned with Artists Space, Independent Curators International (ICI), and David Zwirner. I was a bit older, more ambitious than the typical intern, and made relationships that I hold today. At Artists Space, traveling to help install the Prague Biennial was especially pivotal—it was my first glimpse into the deep sense of community that can form around exhibition making. At Zwirner, conversations began with the directors (many of whom are now partners), which helped me realize that galleries brought together all the things I was interested in: working closely with artists, building exhibitions, engaging with institutions, and thinking strategically.

My first official role in the art world was working for Leslie Fritz, managing her gallery on Renwick Street. It was a small space that fostered a strong community, with film nights, video installations, and a taco truck out front. After working with Leslie for several years, I joined Stefania Bortolami's gallery in Chelsea, Manhattan, which was a larger, more high-pressure environment where I grew quickly. After almost seven years there, I moved to Los Angeles. I'd only ever lived in New York, and I wanted to be an adult living in a new city. It was exciting to see how my relationships could help shape a new gallery program in a different city. There is an openness to LA, it embraces new voices and new energy. I stayed for over six years.

*ASC: You have been a director of galleries in the past, but you also established Plan Your Vote, which was hailed as one of the biggest cultural initiatives in the civic voting sphere, with over 200 participating artists and organizations. How does this past experience define how you approach your work today?*

CM: I had a child just before the pandemic, and as everything shut down, the 2020 election came into focus. A good friend, Andrea Hailey, was running Vote.org, and I remember thinking, "I know how to help get the message out in a compelling way." Originally, it was just going to be one artist making an image, but the project grew quickly into "Plan Your Vote", a visual campaign encouraging people to prepare for mail-in or early voting. We ended up collaborating with over 150 institutions—including MoMA PS1, the Guggenheim, and the Brooklyn Museum—and artists like Jenny Holzer, Julie Mehretu, Laurie Simmons, and Robert Longo. The initiative demonstrated how artists and institutions can play a powerful role in civic engagement. And to me, it wasn't so different from exhibition-making. We were curating visuals, storytelling, and building audiences, just with a different sense of urgency. That work continues at Frieze. We've partnered with Vote.org at our fairs, offering voter registration and raising awareness through campaigns, like the "BANNED" water bottle which references a law in Georgia preventing the distribution of water at polling stations. Artists are often already engaged in these conversations; and, as an art fair, we can be a connector between artists, institutions, and the public.

*ASC: What is specific about directing fairs in the USA? Especially with you being responsible for Frieze New York and LA, along with Frieze acquiring EXPO Chicago. I would love to hear how your approach to these regions differs.*

**CM:** Each fair distinctly reflects the identity of its city: its artists, institutions, collectors, and energy. New York, Los Angeles, and Chicago are all cultural hubs, but they have distinct personalities. In LA, for example, we have the outdoors, the parks, and we bring programming with Art Production Fund to the public spaces surrounding the fair. Chicago has this incredible multidisciplinary energy through its music, performance, community organizing, and a strong DIY scene with students or recent graduates hosting exhibitions in apartments and storefronts. In New York, the quality and variety of institutions and galleries creates its own rhythm. Education is central across all three cities, from CalArts, UCLA and Otis in LA to SAIC in Chicago and Columbia, SVA, Pratt, and Parsons in New York. These schools feed the arts ecosystem. Each fair is built in dialogue with those communities, which keeps our gallery presentations and programming rooted in place.

***ASC: What does a typical work day look like for you, from start to finish? (And how might that change during the busy fair seasons such as New York in May?)***

**CM:** Most of my day is spent speaking with galleries, artists, curators, and collectors. Zooms, calls, in-person meetings. I've had to be intentional about carving out time to write, research, and look at art. During the fair, the days are longer and more intense. We welcome thousands of visitors, and I'm often focused on conversations and making connections. I've learned to arrive early or stay late, after the fair closes, to actually see the art in person. We are also always thinking about access points to an art fair. We welcome school groups, host public programs, and spotlight nonprofits such as AMBOS [Art Made Between Opposite Sides] in LA, which supports immigrant communities and last year raised their operating budget through Frieze. Another example of this is the Impact Prize, which helps feature artists without gallery representation. In 2024, Gary Tyler (who was wrongfully incarcerated for over 40 years) received the prize. He learned quilting while in prison, and his work is now in major collections. His story is a reminder of why visibility and access matter.

***ASC: If someone wanted to do what you do, what advice, or even warnings, would you give them?***

**CM:** I'm a mother to a very active five-year-old who sometimes pops into Zoom calls in his underwear. This wasn't a version of leadership I saw when I looked at people who had a career, one where work and life bleed into each other. It's sometimes messy and unpredictable. But it's real, and it's possible. This job isn't 9 to 5. It's full of conversations, follow-ups, planning, and relationship-building. If you're energized by dialogue, by shaping ideas with artists, institutions, and collectors, it can be incredibly fulfilling. Not all career paths are linear. I came to this from fashion, from sales, from making mistakes and asking questions. You build your way in by staying curious and showing up.

*

Christine shed a light on the active community aspect of what a fair can bring to their local areas. She doesn't shy away from political engagements, seeing as she brought in Vote.org's mission of raising awareness to increase voter registrations. It was also intriguing to hear that Christine came from a gallery background, but with experience in fashion. I felt a kinship to her when hearing about these experiences, because my professional path was similar in the early years, working in retail before getting my first art-world job. She gave a good tip, which is to come early or stay late to see the artworks at the fair—I used to do that when I was a gallery employee, because during the day it would be far too hectic and busy to actually see what other galleries were exhibiting.

Back in London, I sat down with Sophie Parker, Director of Photo London. I first met her when I asked her to speak to NXT GEN members and tell us about her career path. She started working at Photo London in 2018 as Gallery Development Manager, and has since worked her way up to Director. I sat down with her in an exciting pivotal moment for the fair, as they planned their move from their previous location at Somerset House to Olympia, an iconic venue in Kensington, West London.

---

*Sophie Parker is the Director of Photo London. She joined the team in 2018 as the Gallery Development Manager and later Associate Director. As one of the youngest female fair directors in Europe, Parker is forging a path for change in the commercial art world, as an advocate for inclusivity and accessibility, leading conversations on making, exhibiting, and collecting for a new generation in the medium. Parker also sits on the advisory board for the Ian Parry*

*Photojournalism Grant. Prior to Photo London, Parker worked at Cristea Roberts Gallery, RA magazine, and Lewisham Local History Society.*

---

**Alexandra Steinacker-Clark: Can you tell me briefly about your education and career path? What led you to the position you're in today as director of Photo London?**

**Sophie Parker:** I fell in love with art during my A levels, and thought that I wanted to study Fine Art. I had my heart set on Chelsea School of Art. It was the only school I applied to, and I didn't get in. It felt like a ruthless process. You just leave your portfolio in a room, come back, and just have a "no" on it. That rejection prompted me to really think about what it was about art that I enjoyed, and it was actually looking at other people's ideas. I decided to go study History of Art and Design at Manchester Metropolitan University, which was incredible. I then did a master's in Anthropology and Cultural Politics at Goldsmiths, which was wildly different from what I'd experienced at Manchester Met. There were a number of initiatives at Goldsmiths and one was at the Local History Society, where I worked to catalog their archive while curating exhibitions. After that, I worked for a small arts festival and, through my connection to Goldsmiths, I also got the opportunity to do a paid internship at the Royal Academy of Arts for the *RA* magazine. Following that, I got a job at Allan Christea Gallery, now called Christea Roberts, and was there for three years. I started off as an intern but worked my way into a full-time position in communications, exhibition organization, events, and art fairs. That experience gave me the insights of doing art fairs from a gallery perspective. Then I saw a job advertised at Photo London as Gallery Development Manager, worked my way up to Associate Director, and now Director.

*ASC: Can you describe some of the responsibilities that you have as director of Photo London?*

**SP:** The main one still is working with galleries. I recruit galleries from around the world by introducing them to Photo London and sharing what Photo London is. I choose galleries who have programs that I really want to work with and who I feel align to the fair. I am involved in every single department from the finances to fair management, production, and VIP partnerships — my role covers everything. I also do research which involves going all over the world to see what other fairs are doing.

*ASC: What does a day in your life look like for you in your job? It probably varies greatly depending on how far away from the fair you are in the year.*

**SP:** Exactly, each part of the year has a relatively different structure. In the summer, it's very much focused on recruitment of galleries from all over the world and speaking to them about what artists they should show at the fair. We think about what worked well last year and what we might need to improve on for this year. We start scheduling all of our global VIP events, and one thing that sets us apart from other fairs is that we want our galleries to feel supported year round, not just during the fair. I'll make sure that we're promoting them, taking our collectors to their galleries year round, and hosting events globally. I do the same with partnerships, working with our partnerships manager to make sure that our partners are happy. Or if our contracts are up with one, then we go look for another. Not only do we think about it in terms of financial partnerships but we also ensure they align with our audiences and values. Relationship building is hugely important in my job. Listening, and being open to feedback, is key because some of the best developments that we've had at the fair have been from listening to what galleries want. During the fair we have long days, with morning events from 9am when we'll be doing private tours of museums or other arts organizations with our collectors. I'll then be at the fair all day, checking on people and doing interviews with press, followed by events in the evening until around midnight.

*ASC: What other roles are there in your organization, and how does your position intersect with them? What are some entry or mid-level positions?*

**SP:** Our core team is partnerships manager, VIP manager, finance, and design, and then the founders have a PA. The partnerships manager looks after our partners and makes sure that they're getting everything that we agreed that they should get, from social-media posts to newsletter mentions, to activations on-site. Our VIP manager is responsible for growing our collector base and audience, and keeping them engaged. Our finance manager sets the budgets and targets, together with myself. The design team works on signage throughout the fair, our map, our branding, our adverts, the list goes on. We also work with external companies to come in and support the team from January onwards, due to the pick-up in workload. As we get closer to the fair, we work with a visitor-experience team, VIP tour guides, shippers, art technicians, floor managers, security, and caterers.

*ASC: Can you tell me something I wouldn't expect to hear about your job? What do you think many would be surprised to know?*

**SP:** I don't think many people realize the knock-on effect that art fairs have for the local economy. They can be seen as this "necessary evil" that causes galleries to get fair fatigue. They feel fairs aren't doing enough for them, and that they are resentful or reluctant to participate in fairs nowadays. An example is that during the run-up to Photo London a friend of mine was trying to get an artwork framed at a framer in Stoke

Newington. The framer apologized, not able to take the job, saying, "We just can't take on more work at the moment because we're so busy framing work for Photo London." It wasn't even the framer we partner with (because we do have one), but it was the natural influx of clientele to the small art businesses around London. I think that's something people don't realize!

*ASC: Have you ever made a career step that you've regretted or has there been something difficult that you've overcome, and what have you learned from it?*

**SP:** In terms of regrets, it's a pretty boring answer, but I really don't believe in having regrets. I've always thought, particularly when it comes to work, that things always happen for a reason. When I would go for job interviews and then not get the job, I was never too disappointed because I just thought, "Okay, that person who I interviewed with, they know the job and they know the role. And if they felt like I wasn't right for it, then I wasn't right for it and I probably wouldn't have been happy there." I've always felt like I stumbled into what I wanted to do. I've never had a big plan. It's about making the most of everything whilst you're there.

*ASC: If someone wanted to direct an art fair, what advice, or even warnings, would you give them?*

**SP:** If you want to work at an art fair, there are definitely some roles which would get you to a director level more easily than others. Working with the galleries when I joined was hugely beneficial because it was very much about learning from them and taking on their feedback. A bit of advice on being a director—no matter if of an art fair or more broadly— is to develop a thick skin but also be personable. Don't always feel like you have to pretend that you know everything. I think it's really important to feel comfortable saying, "Okay, I don't know that, tell me more" and being a sponge for knowledge.

*

Running an art fair means that you have two sets of clientele to cater to. Firstly, you have the galleries: recruiting new galleries to exhibit at the fair, maintaining relationships to previous exhibitors, and ensuring their experience with the fair is positive and uplifting. Then, the collectors and general audience: events programming, guided tours, PR, ticket sales, and keeping them engaged—not just during the fair, but year round. Both Christine and Sophie had non-linear career paths, not necessarily having planned on being directors of art fairs. That diverse experience is an asset in working with many different contributing factors—partnerships, galleries, collectors, and the general art-world audience—while liaising with shippers, designers, building managers, caterers, and more. It's a multifaceted role with deep engagement in a lot of different areas of the arts! As a final note, it's important to acknowledge that, yes, art fairs activate the local and international commercial art scenes, but some pivoting is needed in order for them to be more sustainable for emerging to mid-tier galleries. There is a large financial burden of shipping costs and fair-participation fees, not to mention staff travel and accommodation, plus any other extra costs involved. Currently, the market has a complicated relationship to art fairs, with some galleries choosing to organize international pop-up exhibitions instead of a booth, or deciding to be more selective about which fairs they participate in altogether. If this is something you take a particular interest in, there are plenty of articles, podcast episodes, and books on the topic, such as ArtTactic's episode with Art Basel Director Maike Cruse, or *The Art Fair Story* by journalist Melanie Gerlis, in the "Hot Topics in the Art World" series.

# KEY TAKEAWAYS IF YOU ARE THINKING OF EMBARKING ON YOUR OWN CAREER IN ART FAIRS

## Three Practical Tips

- Art fairs are pivotal for networking, client acquisition, and sales, providing unique opportunities for relationship-building with collectors, galleries, and institutions. Understanding the diverse roles involved can help you find where your strengths best fit within the fair ecosystem.
- The success of an art fair relies heavily on relationship management, effective communication, and maintaining a professional yet personable demeanor—practice these in whatever professional position you have, to grow these transferrable and valuable skills.
- Follow key figures on social media (like Christine and Sophie, but also Frieze and Photo London which have specifically fair-dedicated accounts) and attend major events to stay informed about trends and opportunities.

## Next Steps

- Visit an art fair in your area. See what the layout is like, pay attention to the details. Speak to galleries exhibiting, attend the talks program or a guided tour. Take in as much as you can!
- Some art fairs, like Frieze, aren't limited to the fair model. They have an exhibition space in London, for example, and a magazine that comes out online and in print. Look into what you can research that goes beyond the fairs you like, to learn more about what else they do.

- If you want to experience working at a fair, working for a gallery exhibiting at a fair is a great place to start. Some younger galleries could use assistance in manning the booth during local fairs, so be proactive and see if anyone would appreciate an extra hand. Volunteer your time to glean some experience from another perspective.

# CHAPTER 10
# WORKING IN AN AUCTION HOUSE

I first started working in an auction house in 2017, the same year I started my bachelor's degree. It was my first job in the art world, and I had gotten it as a result of a chance given to me after I had coffee with an employee there. I emailed a staff member who was from my hometown and, after meeting me, they recommended me for an interview for a casual position (meaning a zero-hours contract) in the Client Services department. I still had to impress at the interview, though, which I thankfully did due to my customer-service experience, which I'd gained while working in retail in high school. I know I keep sharing this sentiment throughout the book, but never underestimate how valuable your transferable skills can be, no matter what job you are applying for.

I worked in the Client Services and Bids department at Sotheby's in London for the next four years, as I finished both my bachelor's and my master's degrees. I handled high-pressure situations, traveled to different countries, and answered the phone more times than I can count. It was a role in the Operations department, whereas in the following interviews you will hear from staff in specialist departments. There are two auction houses that seem to rule the global market, and those are Sotheby's and Christie's. They have locations in London, New York, and elsewhere all around the world. There are also other large international auction houses, like Bonhams and Phillips, and regional auction houses like AGUTTES and Dorotheum. When we think about the other organizations covered in the book, some have larger teams but none of them are as large a corporation as these auction houses. To give you a rough idea, one of the biggest galleries in the world, Gagosian, employs around 300 people in total across their 19 spaces (as of 2024, at least). Christie's employs approximately 2,300 people. This is about as corporate as you will get in the arts. What are the pros of this? You actually have an HR department. Climbing the ladder is, in some cases, more straightforward because there are in-house strategies for promoting staff. There are processes in place that ensure efficiency whereas sometimes in a smaller organization, instead of a CRM system (CRM stands for customer relationship management), they just have an Excel spreadsheet. What are the cons? Some people describe it as being a cog in a machine. You walk down the hallway and don't know half the people you pass. In a gallery team of 15 people, that doesn't happen—you regularly cross paths with everyone. In addition, although on paper some of the progression strategies seem great, in reality it can be a really cutthroat business to be in. Auction houses are, in my opinion, the most commercial of all the art businesses. You don't work with artists, you work with the market. It's incredibly stimulating, but after being at Sotheby's for four years, I knew that I would rather work in an institution, thinking about public engagement and programming, or a gallery, still commercial but working with artists and supporting their career development alongside sales. That being said, as you will read in the following interviews, an auction-house job requires strong interpersonal skills and emotional intelligence, alongside broad and deep market knowledge. Working with consignors and buyers while assessing the art coming to auction, cataloging it, valuing it—it's all a big part of the huge production that is an auction.

Although my professional experience was in London, I wanted to go to the headquarters of Sotheby's in New York City. More specifically, I wanted to go to New York for the chance to speak to Lisa Dennison. Lisa worked at the Guggenheim Museum for nearly 30 years, and served as director for 2 of those years. She has been at Sotheby's since, joining nearly 20 years ago. Just two weeks away from the May 2025 auctions, I walked into the large First Avenue location. Lisa welcomed me with her confident, open, and friendly demeanor, which was helpful because

I'll admit I was quite nervous. We sat down on the sofas in her small office, with large windows facing both outside as well as into the vast open-plan office space. She put her stylishly stilettoed feet up on the table—an unexpected move, for sure—and we began our interview.

---

*Lisa Dennison, with a 29-year tenure at the Guggenheim Museum, including as Director from 2005, joined Sotheby's as Chairman, Americas in 2007. At Sotheby's, she specializes in international business development, leveraging her expertise in Modern and Contemporary Art. She has cultivated relationships with top collectors, artists, and experts worldwide. Dennison holds a BA in Art History and French from Wellesley College and an MA in Art History from Brown University, and is a highly influential figure in the art world.*

---

*Alexandra Steinacker-Clark: What has your career path looked like over the last 50 years, and what led you to the position that you're in today as Chairman at Sotheby's Auction House?*

**Lisa Dennison:** It started as a strictly museum career. I went to Wellesley College in Boston as a French major, which I really had a passion for. My mom called me one day and suggested I take an art history class as well, so I did. The minute I started, I realized that was my career path—I knew I wanted to be a curator. That summer, I applied to the Whitney, the Museum of Modern Art, the MET, the Guggenheim, every single one. The internship scheme that I felt especially drawn to was the Guggenheim because it was a rotating program where I could start in one department and rotate to others for two weeks at a time. The prize, of course, being the curatorial department. While I was there, the Director's secretary walked off the job, so I decided to jump at that opportunity. I went upstairs to Thomas M. Messer, in this fantastic old-world museum director's office, and the rest was history. It was a remarkable summer. He taught me so much. I was learning about the museum from the perch of the director's chair. He was asked to write an article for *Encyclopedia Britannica* on early Picasso, so I wrote it for him and he gave me the full $250 honorarium, which in those days was a fortune—we're talking 1973. It was the summer of the Jean Dubuffet retrospective, and every Friday Jean would come and we would sit on the terrace outside Thomas's office and have tea. It was like it was a dream come true, honestly.

The next summer, Thomas Messer invited me back to be the head of the interns, but at that point I had met someone and decided to get married that next summer—don't ask me why I thought that was a good idea. I went to tell him that I was so sorry, but I couldn't come to New York to do this, I had to stay in Boston. While I was in his office, he called Daniel Robbins, the Director of the Fogg Museum at the time and facilitated an internship there. So, I was living in Boston, working at the Fogg, and commuting to Wellesley. After my bachelor's, I did my master's degree at Brown and continued to work at the Fogg. After that, I was trying to figure out what to do next in the museum world. John Walsh, who had been the director of the Getty, had just started at the Museum of Fine Arts in Boston as the Curator of 19th- and early-20th -century art, and we got along incredibly well. There was an opening for an assistant curator role and the job was to create an exhibition of French impressionist paintings from the collection, which was my passion. So, I went home and told my then husband, the person I shouldn't have married, about the job opportunity and he said, "But our dream is to live in New York. And guess what? I got a job offer today and I'm taking it and we're moving to New York." As a result of that conundrum, I went to see Tom [Messer] at the Guggenheim again and asked for his advice. He told me there was a curatorial assistant position at the Guggenheim as well, which I also ended up applying for (and I almost didn't get it because the person interviewing me thought I was overconfident). The job was Exhibition Assistant, very low on the ladder, and they were going to pay me $8,000 a year, which was half of what the Museum of Fine Arts was going to pay me at a higher level with this golden opportunity in Boston. But, alas, I said yes, and I moved to New York in 1978, and stayed at the Guggenheim until I left for Sotheby's in 2007.

***ASC: Fast forwarding, how did you end up at Sotheby's, and can you describe some of the responsibilities that you have in your role today?***

**LD:** I came to Sotheby's on a leap of faith, not really having a fully formed job description. My title was Chairman of America, so I joined in the same position I'm at today. I was always intrigued with Sotheby's and thought that, if I ever left the museum world, this is where I wanted to land. I had conversations with Sotheby's many times throughout my career—sometimes they called me, and sometimes I called them, but the opportunities were always wrong. In 2007, I had been the Director of the Guggenheim for two years and I was probably the only curator that was religiously in the auction rooms for the major sales because I felt it gave me so much information. In May of that year, I watched *White Center* by Mark Rothko, consigned by David Rockefeller, sell for $72,800,000. The next night, I watched a work by Andy Warhol sell within the same range at Christie's Auction House. It was then that I realized that this was a turning point in the art world, these huge, outsized prices. The next time I had a call from Sotheby's, I said I would come for the right position, which was Chairman. But, again, the job was a bit amorphous—it wasn't clear what I was going to do, really. I was going to lend strength to the Contemporary department but I wasn't *in* the department. I obviously had an affiliation with Impressionist and Modern art given my training and background, but I wasn't in that department either. Nobody knew where to place me.

I had no experience pricing paintings. I'm still not good at that today. However, I'm a team player, very collaborative, and just wanted to do what everyone needed me to do. It took me a while to find my own way because there was no guidebook, no job description. I came here with expertise in client relationships, cultivation, development, and a kind of different expertise than that of an auction-house employee. My value was that I had a different level of knowledge that I brought in. I started to build a portfolio of clients because I had none, and you don't walk into an institution like this, and people go, "Let me give you my clients. Here they are." It's like, "Get away from me. Do not touch my clients." But it ended up being very organic. People had clients that they did not know or never met, but I knew them, or people would leave Sotheby's and I would get the clients. After some time, I built a very robust portfolio and most of my job is based on taking care of those people.

***ASC: What does a typical work day look like for you?***

**LD:** The beauty of Sotheby's is that there are two sides to everything. Half the job is proactive. You have clients that you want to have touch points with all the time. There is a very regimented auction calendar. You know that you have the marquee sales in May and November in New York and March and June in London. Then there's Paris sales and Hong Kong sales and everything else. You can plan around that calendar by sourcing and selling. The reactive side is what makes the job interesting, because you wake up one morning, you think, "Great day. I'm going to catch up on paperwork," and then you get to the office and *boom*. You get a call, and you react. Many times, it requires you to get on a plane sooner rather than later. I always say a day in the office, me just sitting at my desk, is a wasted day. A good day is when I'm out in the world, either meeting with clients face to face or traveling. I have to think, "Where are the clients?" They're in Palm Beach in the winter. They're in Aspen and Malibu in the summer. I go to Monaco in the summer because I have a lot of clients there. It's about following the money, finding that opportunity and going after it or responding to someone. Right now, though, because we have our sales coming up, I am going through every client in my portfolio, thinking about what in this sale I would recommend to them. I generate the ideas, my assistant generates the email, and we send it. Hopefully a lot of them say they'll come in, or maybe they'll say, "No thanks."

*

As we were speaking, Lisa got a phone call from one of her clients. It wasn't a call she was going to leave unanswered, so we stopped the interview as she made herself available to her client. I was allowed to listen in, completely off the record of course, but it was such a privilege to see her work. She had every auction lot in her head, gave recommendations based on her client's collection and interests, and understood what would be of interest to them, but also was transparent about what wouldn't. They said their goodbyes and she turned back to me.

***ASC: Back on the record?***

**LD:** Yes, back on the record. See? That's the reactive part of the job.

***ASC: It is so impressive because that's the sort of expertise that you want to be able to gain in your career to be able to do that so fluidly.***

**LD:** Yeah. That's exactly right.

***ASC: Why did you decide to move into the auction business after working in a museum for so long?***

**LD:** I was at a point in my career when I had been at the museum for a long time, and I was considering options. Before I was Director, I had worked my way up to Deputy Director and Chief Curator and then ultimately was in charge of a very talented international curatorial pool. It was very entrepreneurial and radical, the things that we did at the Guggenheim, and it gave me tools that a lot of curators didn't have. I used to say I was as comfortable making a spreadsheet as a checklist. I could do both. I also thought it was worth exploring the gallery world, which I was very tempted by because the pay would have been so much better than what I had earned my whole life in the not-for-profit world. I had always been interested in Sotheby's, so instead of a gallery, and instead of another museum outside of New York, it was the best opportunity out of all of those options.

*ASC: I've heard from a few industry titans that it's easier to move from institutional positions into commercial but very, very hard to do the reverse. Do you feel that that's accurate?*

**LD:** Back then, it was much easier to go from museum to commercial than commercial to museum, but I think that's changed over the years. I think there is much more of a back and forth than there used to be. And certainly, I think curators are looking at more commercial opportunities even within their own purview as curators because it's a hard world. You're fighting for space on an exhibition calendar, you're fighting for barely living-wage salaries, and it's a lot of work. You spend so much of the time that you think is going to be about creative thinking doing bureaucratic work and helping to raise money. These two worlds have become much more intertwined, I think.

*ASC: What is a surprising or difficult aspect of your job, would you say?*

**LD:** I think the hardest thing about this job is the competitive nature of the business. You have one single competitor that is just the bane of your existence, truly. While you want them to succeed—because what's good for the goose is good for the gander and if they have a strong sale season or do well with the consignment, that's good for the art market—it hurts when you lose. Even internally, when there's money at stake in a bonus structure or private sale income, it becomes a little bit more cutthroat. Another difficult scenario is when a client calls and you know that they should be buying something elsewhere. I think this may be a surprising thing, actually. I will tell a client when to stop bidding if I feel they're going too high, and I will advise them what not to buy. If there's something in another auction house that they should buy, I will tell them that. I put my clients first, above the company.

*ASC: If you were hiring someone to follow in your footsteps, what are some personality traits or strengths that you would look for in an ideal candidate?*

**LD:** Writing and communication skills. Even though it's so important to pick up the phone and talk, so much is done over email. When hiring, I always want to see a writing sample—not just an academic writing sample, but how you can frame something in an email to get one's attention. I would also look for someone who can manage a lot of juggling because that's what this job is. One day, it's deadly quiet. The next day, you can't even think about breathing or eating your lunch. Plus, knowing when to ask for help. Bad news doesn't get better with age, so I respect someone who's not afraid to say, "I made a mistake."

*ASC: If someone wanted to do what you do, what advice or maybe even warnings would you give them?*

**LD:** You have to be someone who's adaptable to change, because this is a world that changes on a dime. The auction houses exist in a real-time market, and it's impacted by geopolitical forces. It's global politics, it's wars, it's disease. All of those things have an impact. It's a marketplace that is cyclical and volatile. You have to be able to understand that and stomach it. It can go from great to terrible in two seconds, and you have to be able to put that smile back on your face and just wake up and do it again the next day. That's the advice I would give to someone. Make sure that you understand that this is a real marketplace. Every little thing revolves around the art, but the factors that impact that are enormously complex.

*

The role of Chairman at a world-renowned auction house . . . I guess there is nowhere higher to climb than that. In Lisa's role, you have to know your client and know them well. You have to know what's in their collection, remember what they've sold in the past, and predict what they could want now. Of course, you also need to memorize your catalog front to back. Lots, titles, sizes, prices, provenance, condition, art-historical relevance, and whatever else — and Lisa doesn't just focus on one department, like Contemporary, she works across categories, including Impressionist and Modern.

Lisa mentioned that one of the more difficult parts of the job is the competitive nature of the business. When she speaks about the one single competitor, I can only assume she is referring to Christie's Auction House, the other big player in the world of art auctions. Naturally, I needed to speak to someone on the other side, so I strolled over to their offices at Rockefeller Plaza to sit down with Shereen Al-Sawwaf.

I was interested to speak to Shereen because she has spent her entire career thus far at Christie's, starting as a graduate trainee in 2019 and growing in various roles throughout the last six years to now serve as Head of Online Sales in Post-War and Contemporary Art. She picked me up from the reception desk and we went into a room on one of the upper floors, with a latte in hand from their free coffee bar (which they also have in London, by the way!).

*Shereen Al-Sawwaf is the Head of Online Sales and Associate Specialist in the Post-War and Contemporary Art Department at Christie's in New York. She graduated from the University of Chicago with a bachelor's in International Studies and Pre-Medicine and began her career at the auction house as a graduate trainee. She gained experience as a sales coordinator, cataloger, and specialist, and is now the Head of Online Sales in Post-War and Contemporary Art.*

***ASC: Can you tell me about your education and professional path after uni? You majored in International Studies and Pre-Med. What led you to the position you're in today as Head of Online Sales in Post-War and Contemporary at Christie's?***

**Shereen Al-Sawwaf:** I have had a quite unconventional path to the art world, in the sense that I didn't really think that a career in the arts was possible until I got to college. I grew up in a family of health-care workers. My dad was a doctor. My mom was a nurse. I believed that I was going to go to medical school and become a doctor, but quite the opposite ended up happening. I went to the University of Chicago for my bachelor's, and I really leaned into the whole idea of a liberal-arts education. I was Pre-Med there. I did all the classes that I needed to and I struggled through Chemistry and Physics and so on. It was not fun. However, I also took advantage of the opportunities that Chicago afforded me both as a cultural city but also in terms of the school itself, the professors, and the access that I had to really incredible people. I started taking some Art History classes, and we had a class where we would go to a different Chicago institution every week, sit in front of one piece of art for three hours, and talk about it. That's where I really fell in love with art and art history, and being able to see the *Zeitgeist* through artists' eyes. I began to reimagine how contemporary history was happening around us. I became really interested in the intersection between art and business and how you could take something subjective like a piece of art, put a value on it, and sell it to someone. I learned that there was a training program at Christie's, I applied to it blindly, and here I am.

***ASC: What was that like, your first experience in the arts being a position as a graduate trainee at one of the biggest auction houses in the world?***

**SAS:** It was a two-year long program where I spent about six months in a specific department that I chose, and then I did three weeks in other departments to try them out. The goal at the end of the two years was to find our niche in the company and, hopefully, get hired in the department that we felt comfortable in. Graduate trainees do a variety of roles. They're an intern, a sale coordinator, a cataloger—whatever a team needs at the time. I was doing anything from literature checks to writing essays to helping manage a runner (a runner is sort of a long list of works in the inventory and what we have confirmed for the sale) to doing all the basic research for cataloging. I said yes to everything. You have to dive into whatever you can get your hands on.

***ASC: You've grown in your career in the auction house. Starting off as a graduate trainee, working as a cataloger and then as associate specialist, and now heading the online contemporary sales. What was that progression like, and how do your past experiences in those different positions define how you approach your work today?***

**SAS:** My progression was quite quick, as it comes. A lot of it has to do with being in the right place at the right time, but I was also willing to do the job above me even though that wasn't what I was getting paid for or what my job title was at the time. For example, although I was a graduate trainee, I was also helping out as a sales coordinator. Eventually, I got hired to be a sales coordinator. I did just under a year of sale coordination, which is a lot of project management, working with shipping, logistics, photography, marketing, really all aspects of the company. I strongly advocate that if you ever want to start off in an auction house or in the art world, being a sale coordinator is truly one of the best experiences you can have because you're the touch point for every single part of any sale. It's the best front-row seat that you could get to see how sales come together.

Anyway, while I was sale coordinator, we didn't have a cataloger. I ended up being the one prepping all the works to be cataloged, doing the basic research, putting it all into our systems. I would then shadow the catalogers to really soak up everything that they were doing, and eventually I got to a point where I was comfortable enough to fully catalog on my own. Even though I wasn't a cataloger on paper, I was a sale coordinator, I was still doing the cataloging job. When the cataloging job came up, I had the perfect resumé. Eventually, you gain the business-getting experience and you can take the leap to become a specialist. I was a junior specialist for a few years, until I was promoted to the Head of Online Sales. I had worked on online sales my entire career, and I was the one on the team that knew them the best. I've been Head of Online for about a year now and have also taken on the role of Associate Specialist, which means I'm doing a lot more pitching and business-getting, in addition to putting together the sales.

*ASC: What are some of the responsibilities that you have in your position now?*

**SAS:** First and foremost, I'm the Head of Online Sales. In our department, we have two major online sales a year called First Open, one in July, one in December. It entails overseeing a pipeline of about

400 to 600 objects a year, anywhere from $500 to $200,000. I'm the one in charge of making sure that we reach the target budget. I ensure we have enough lots, and a good variety. I'm the one pricing a lot of these things, going to see things in clients' homes, making sure that I can talk to people during the consignment process, working on negotiating terms, that sort of thing. I oversee a cataloger and a coordinator, who help me with research, logistics, and shipping. We're a tiny team, but we manage a lot of property, so it's pretty fast-paced. The other half of my job is being an Associate Specialist. Online sales are part of a wider core market team, which also includes day sales and midseason sales. Of course, I have my priorities set out for my own sale, but I also help out with the other sales, whether it's bringing in consignments, helping sell certain works, or walking my own clients through other sales in case they might be interested. We're a team at the end of the day. It's not just online sales, it's a core market.

**ASC: *Thinking about a typical work day, what would that look like for you from start to finish?***

**SAS:** No day is ever the same, which is the fun of working at an auction house. You really have to stay on your toes. On a typical day, if I'm in New York coming into the office, I spend my mornings doing a lot of my desk work. We're a global team, we have colleagues all over the world, so emails come in at all hours. London's been up for five hours, in Asia the day is ending, so there's always something to respond to in the morning. After that, I'll do pricing of collections that people are interested in selling and figure out which sale works best for certain objects. I also do any research or any reading I need to do in the morning. I like to spend my afternoons on my feet as much as I can. What that typically looks like is I will be in the warehouse with our cataloger who is the one doing all the hands-on work. We'll look at artworks together and run through the research. We'll finalize the condition report, which is also how I familiarize myself with the objects themselves. Sometimes there is a client visit trickled in here and there, too. There's art everywhere in New York City. It's really easy for us to peel away from the office for an hour or two, go walk around someone's house, take some photos, talk to them about consigning or buying. We're very lucky to be located within the midst of everything.

I also travel quite a bit for my job. On days where I have appraisals, I'm often cataloging entire collections on the go for days or weeks on end. When we're in our busy season on deadline preparing for a sale, I'm in New York, boots on the ground. It's a team effort to get every single sale up online. But when we're in our off seasons, we're never really in the office. We try to be wherever the art is, and that could be New York. It could also be the West Coast. It could be in the South. So that's what makes it really exciting.

*ASC: In our day and age, it's very typical to jump from place to place in order to climb the professional ladder, especially at big organizations like Christie's. What is some advice that you would give someone who is in an entry-level position, unsure of what the future holds?*

**SAS:** The biggest piece of advice I can give people, and something that I honestly try to do myself, is to remember your "why." Remember why you came here in the first place. For me, that was to be able to work with incredible objects and handle really important narratives and stories. It's not every day you get to hold an Andy Warhol in a warehouse. It's a really privileged position. A lot of my friends work in finance or consulting where there's more of a clear path of how you grow—and that's not necessarily something that happens in the art world. It can be tough, so remembering why you're here in the first place is important to ground you. Also, having the patience to keep faith that things will work out. It will all come back to you if you put the energy in.

In the first three or four years of my career, I felt that my personality as "someone that worked at Christie's" and "Shereen" were so intertwined that I didn't really have a sense of who Shereen was outside of Christie's. After something didn't work out the way I wanted it to—isn't that always the way!—thinking about who I was outside of work, who I would be if I didn't have art, actually helped me progress in my career. It prompted me to really think about myself and my goals. I was so focused on the next thing, the next thing, the next thing. And . . . It's not that I was in a bad place career-wise, but I felt stagnant after a while. I had to remind myself to have patience and remind myself why I'm doing this, but I was also able to remind myself that this isn't my whole life. You're a whole person beyond just your 9-to-5 job. That bit of space is what ended up helping me take the next step.

***ASC: What other roles are there in your organization and how does your position interact with them?***

**SAS:** I think people really get caught up in this whole idea of wanting to be a specialist, or wanting to be in a specialist department. But there is a machine behind this whole enterprise, whether it's in communications and marketing or PR to art handling to working in commercial art finance or the chairman's office and business development, the bids department, client services, post-sale . . . There are so many other departments that we have at Christie's that really make this whole machine run smoothly. When I was a graduate trainee, I worked in client strategy for a little bit, which was really fascinating. It involved researching the clients that we work with and all of the business development relating to how we match clients with certain artworks. There was a point in time where I was really interested in marketing and being able to learn how we create all these amazing campaigns to promote the art that we're spending so much time researching and selling. There's not just specialist departments. There are so many other auxiliary departments. Beyond auction houses, there's communication firms, there's artist studios, there's museums, there's galleries. You name it, there is an opportunity in the art world.

*ASC: Can you tell me something that I wouldn't expect to hear about your job? What's something that you think many would be surprised to know?*

**SAS:** Online sales are often the first avenue that new clients come to Christie's through. A crazy large percentage of new clients first transact with Christie's through an online sale. Due to this level of new clientele, both on the seller's end and on the buyer's end, there's a lot of hand holding that has to be done in my job. If I'm working with a first-time seller, I'm walking them through the auction consignment process. What it means to consign, how we price something, why we arrived at the estimate that we did, which sale we're putting it in, why we're putting it in that sale, the marketing that we're giving that specific work . . . There's a lot explaining how this process works to people that have never done this before. A lot of people seem to have the misconception that those who work with auction houses are just high-net-worth individuals that have people that do this process for them. A lot of the people that I work with don't realize that they have a hidden gem in their attic that they've been sitting on and they finally want to sell it. I find those moments where I'm able to have these wholesome moments with people, and celebrate amazing successes, the most rewarding. I've also had situations where someone will transact in an online sale for the first time and then, a few months later, we're talking about evening sale lots and we're transacting in an evening sale together. There are some not . . . not so successful stories. But, you know, everything's a learning experience. The magic of auction is you never really know what's is going to happen.

*ASC: And can you tell me a challenging part of your job? What do you find particularly difficult?*

**SAS:** Managing client expectations. Whether it's someone who had something that they thought was worth a lot more than it actually is in today's market, or someone who is not thrilled with our estimates. It's walking the fine line of being enthusiastic and wanting to champion Christie's and getting people to consign with us, but also being realistic and transparent about where the market is, what we think it'll do. It's our job as specialists and as the auction house to manage both sides on the seller and the buyer side. I take a lot of joy and pride in that, but also, it can get pretty hard at times.

***ASC: If someone wanted to do what you do, what advice or even warnings would you give them?***

**SAS:** I would tell them to dive head first. I give 110 percent of myself to whatever I do, whether it's work or outside of work, and it has led to a lot of growth. Say yes to everything. Ask to get coffee with the person that sits next to you, sits across from you, sits behind you. Network your way through the company. It's a very social job. Lean into your company and lean into the people around you by keeping your ear to the ground in terms of conversations that are happening. You can learn so much by listening to other specialists speak on the phone or hearing how people negotiate certain things. There's an art to a lot of that. I think the more you expose yourself or put yourself in the room where those conversations are happening, the more you learn. Be a sponge and soak it all up, while keeping in mind your "why." That being said, don't be afraid to take a step back for a little bit. Make sure you take time for yourself and find things that aren't art that let you kind of relax and stay steady.

*

Hearing from someone who has a more recent experience entering the sector and growing within it was incredibly enlightening. One of the biggest lessons I took with me from my conversation with Shereen was that it's so important to have your "why" with whatever you do—it will help direct you into what your next step should be, it will help ground you when things get hard, and it will shine through when you are speaking to potential employers. Both Shereen and Lisa are based in New York, and are employed at two of the biggest auction houses.

There is a lot of talk from established professionals in the art world, and within these chapters, about going to where the art is in order to be able to thrive in your career. For some paths, that may be true, but for others, it's about gaining experience and cultivating the cultural scene where you are, which can be just as rewarding. Auction houses are fast-paced, sometimes ruthless, and incredibly exciting. The commercial art world is, admittedly, where you can also maintain a higher salary in comparison to some non-profit careers. If you are interested in working with artists and creating exhibitions for audience engagement and impact, then this could be less of an attractive career path. However, if you enjoy the prospect of working with works of art from all over the world, speaking to consignors and collectors about the art-historical and economic value of the works, and you are interested in the art market, working in auction houses may be just the right fit for you.

## KEY TAKEAWAYS IF YOU ARE THINKING OF EMBARKING ON YOUR OWN CAREER IN AN AUCTION HOUSE

### Three Practical Tips

- Developing strong interpersonal skills can be a great asset. Working in auction houses involves continuous communication with high-net-worth clients, collectors, and consignors. Honing soft skills like emotional intelligence, tact, and persuasive communication is essential to build trust and facilitate sales. (You can do this by reading helpful books, watching instructional videos, along with gaining experience through internships, graduate schemes, and work placements.)

- Work on starting a career with internships or entry-level roles in smaller regional auction houses to gain foundational skills. This will allow you to develop excellent research, cataloging, and art handling skills early on, and will give you an edge if you are applying to the big two.
- Once you get your foot in the door, be proactive in offering to assist with auctions, client meetings, and research to stand out and demonstrate initiative.

## Next Steps

- Find your "why" — write down two or three things that define your reason for being in the sector. What are you passionate about? Where do you view yourself in a few years? What does that career look like, and why do you want it to be that way? Grounding yourself in these will fortify your resilience when you inevitably encounter a bump in the road in your professional progress.
- Start gaining market knowledge by reading the news and downloading market reports (there are a few in the reference section at the back of this book) to stay informed about trends and price fluctuations.
- Watch an auction. They are live-streamed online but they are open to the public (except for the big evening sales, which are ticketed). You can walk in and watch the action happen live! Write down the results, keep track of the type of art being auctioned, and learn what certain works sell for.

# CHAPTER 11

# WORKING IN ART LAW

When I was growing up, I had some exposure to law through my mother. She has an American law degree, and has taught me how to read contracts and advocate for myself should I need to negotiate terms. However, the more I learn, the more I realize how incredibly surface-level my knowledge is, especially when it comes to the specifics within art law. There are employment contracts that contain clauses granting IP (intellectual property) rights to your employer of anything you create both within or outside of working hours. There are loan agreements and consignment agreements and release forms for disseminating content online. Not to mention the ins and outs of trademarking and copyright. Of course, as an arts professional, you can always consult a lawyer to ensure you are navigating these topics correctly if you feel out of your depth. However, as we will hear in the following interviews, if you have a love for art and have found an interest in law, there are ways to combine the two professionally.

On a sunny Friday afternoon in London, I sat down with Mona Yapova, a lawyer specializing in art law at Mishcon de Reya LLP, a renowned law firm that has the oldest art law practice in London. She was having a busy day, running from one meeting to the next, but when we were conducting the interview, she dedicated her full attention to me and my questions. I have known Mona since spring 2024, when I approached her to speak on a panel at a conference I organized for the *All About Art* podcast (which was a precursor to NXT GEN). I was excited to see her and ask her more about her experience in art law, because her path to it emerged from practicing art—a rare occurrence of an artist turned art lawyer!

*Mona Yapova advises artists, artists' estates, collectors, galleries, art foundations, museums, government entities, and non-profit organizations on the creation of art, the art market, and heritage protection. As a lawyer, art historian, and former artist, Mona has a natural ability to navigate both the legal and creative angles of projects and disputes alongside clients. She is a published author and regularly teaches at leading institutions in the UK and abroad.*

**Alexandra Steinacker-Clark: Mona, can you take me through your education and career path thus far?**

**Mona Yapova:** I had a very international upbringing and carried a lot of it into my approach to my education and my professional path. I have two law degrees, an LLB in English Law from King's College in London and the French equivalent from the Sorbonne in Paris (which makes me a bit of a sucker for punishment). I also have an LLM and a postgraduate degree in Art History from the Courtauld Institute of Art. When it comes to my professional path, I stubbornly always try to reach for and to stay really close to what I love the most, which is why most of my professional experience is a little bit off the beaten paths of the legal industry. That is how I ended up working at the Peggy Guggenheim Collection in Venice and the State Hermitage Museum in Saint Petersburg, a philanthropic foundation in London, and at Phillips Auction House.

**ASC: What was your first experience in the arts — or maybe I should ask specifically in art law? — when you were just starting out?**

**MY:** Art was always first. My very first foot in the door was a foot in my own studio during an artist residency in Thailand in 2015. At that time,

I had a year to spend focusing on my practice. It was the first opportunity I had to completely immerse myself in art and learn from the creative scene in Bangkok, which was life-changing. It gave me a lifelong connection to Southeast Asia and also helped me understand the bridge between a creative practice and how the art world works. Up until that point, my only relationship with art had been focused on my own practice.

**ASC: *After that experience, what made you pivot into art law?***

**MY:** I always wanted to support creatives, innovators, people that are passionate about the arts as much as I am. Becoming an art lawyer was one way to do it that felt quite natural. I rarely tell this story, but what really made me pivot firmly happened when I was still studying law and starting to think about going back to the art world. One of the stereotypes that is true about the study of law is that it can be a little dry until you start practicing or engaging with a branch of it that you love—they can be two different worlds. While I was studying, instead of doing all my vac schemes* and legal internships, I was spending almost all my time off working in the arts. Halfway through my law degrees, through the most improbable circumstances, [renowned Chinese contemporary artist] Ai Weiwei gifted me a porcelain sunflower seed from his *Sunflower Seeds* work with the gentle instruction to do something decent with my law degrees. It stuck with me. He is somebody I respect hugely and law was something that I could use to support the arts—I couldn't *not* do it. I'm sure he doesn't sit around wondering what I am doing, but his poetic nudge made it sink in that there is no excuse not to do this.

**ASC: *Can you describe some of the responsibilities you have as a solicitor specializing in art law?***

------

*     Vacation schemes, or "vac schemes," are periods of work experience offered by a law firm to students looking to experience what it's like to work in a law firm.

**MY:** My work is to identify and solve issues in any creative, cultural, or art-historical context. It's very tailored advice in cases that can be disputes, transactions, or projects that aren't necessarily transactional but are a little bit more unique and creative. It's a broad range, but the heart of my job is to help clients in a way that enables their work and projects to thrive and protects their reputation.

**ASC: And what does a typical work day look like for you, with all those varying contexts?**

**MY:** There really isn't a "typical" day. If I step back, I can see a rhythm in my work, but the shape of individual days can be very different depending on what I'm working on. It always involves juggling a few cases in very diverse contexts. I work with artists, galleries, museums, art foundations, collectors . . . and their priorities and individual paces are naturally very different. My job is to guide and support them, so my rhythm depends on theirs a little bit as well.

**ASC: Tell me something that I wouldn't expect to hear about your job. What's something that many would be surprised to know?**

**MY:** There's an expectation that what lawyers do is quite cold and formulaic. It's somewhat tied to a completely fair expectation that lawyers should be efficient because time is a luxury in law as much as it is in the creative sector these days, but detached formulaic advice is just completely unnatural in my work. If I can't step back to see the big picture for a client and align the work that I do with it, I would not be making much of a difference to their projects, their practice, or their work. Stereotypes have a source and are difficult to break, but that steely mechanical way is not part of my approach. It's essential that I'm always immersed in the context of the advice that I give—whether it is creative, cultural, art historical, or just commercial context—and that's just as important as the legal analysis and the arguments that I craft around it.

***ASC: Can you tell me a difficult aspect of the job, something that you find particularly challenging about it?***

**MY:** The pace can be tough. In many ways, it's both one of the most challenging and rewarding parts of the job. Usually, if the pace at which you're working is fiery, it means that clients are coming to you for things they really care about. And it's an absolute non-negotiable to be able to work at the pace of a client's project and priorities. But when timelines and time zones overlap, it can become a bit of a triathlon.

***ASC: I've spoken to a few art lawyers and everyone keeps saying that when you're an art lawyer, one of the best things you can do is to understand the context of the art world, so having any sort of experience in it is incredibly beneficial both to your practice as well as to being able to serve your clients in the best way possible because you understand the nuances.***

**MY:** Exactly, you have to guide and empower clients in a way that allows them to achieve what they want to and protect what matters. If you do that just going off legal principles in isolation, they wouldn't be able to fully benefit from your advice. It's great to spend a bit of time working in the art world, whatever shape or form that takes.

***ASC: If someone wanted to do what you do, where do you think that they should start?***

**MY:** I would suggest getting exposure to the practice of art law itself, to find out if what it entails is really something that suits you. You have to enjoy the process of advising clients. You can do a vacation scheme or you could apply for an internship, which you can do without a law degree—the UK system in particular is very open to people qualifying into legal practice with a background in other disciplines. A large proportion of the lawyers in the UK didn't study law at undergraduate level, they may have studied music or politics and done a conversion course. In my view, that dual background can make them even better lawyers.

*ASC: How feasible is it to access this specific profession from either an art or a law background given how niche the field is?*

**MY:** If it's something you really want, anything is feasible. The opportunities are very rare because the field is very small. You tend to find art lawyers where you have bigger art markets, but usually just a handful. Whether you start with art or law doesn't necessarily matter. What matters—and this is a personal perspective—is to be the right type of unicorn with the right motivation. You have to enjoy working for clients as a lawyer and taking their issues and aspirations on as your own. You also have to make a dual commitment, both to really developing your skills as a lawyer and to the art sector. Both are key to thriving in a niche field and to ensuring you enjoy it.

*ASC: How restricted would someone be in terms of international job prospects depending on where they study and where they gain their first professional experiences?*

**MY:** Most of my work is international. Clients and their projects, disputes and transactions are spread across the world. Of course, lawyers can only advise on the law of the jurisdiction they're qualified to advise in, but you can qualify in an additional jurisdiction once you've already qualified in one. Something to keep in mind is that the common-law and civil-law systems are quite different. If you come from one, it's a little bit trickier to go into another, but not impossible.* Having studied both systems and having a multicultural background helps me hugely in cases with an international thread—I work with a lot of our French clients, for example. Being able to work with French lawyers by knowing the right questions to ask and understanding their approach is very useful in my work.

**ASC: If someone wanted to do what you do, what advice or even warnings would you give them?**

**MY:** You have to basically be bilingual, in a way. You have to speak the whole legal language, but you also have to speak the language of the art world. You have to be able to take clients' priorities on as your own in their context and make all that complex legal advice tailored to them. I wouldn't go into art law only as a means of being in, or staying in, the arts. You do have to enjoy the core of what legal practice is made of.

*

I left the interview with Mona feeling infected by her passion for both the legal field and the art sector. During our conversation, she mentioned that one will most likely find art lawyers where there are big art markets, which made me curious to speak to someone from the largest art market in the world—the USA. Strolling along the Upper East Side in Manhattan, microphones in tow, I walked up the stairs to a brownstone

---

* The core of civil-law systems are legal codes, such as an "Intellectual Property Code" or a "Criminal Code," i.e. they are heavily reliant on codified laws. Common-law systems are more rooted in uncodified case law that arises as a result of judicial decisions, recognizing prior court decisions as legally binding precedent — meaning the law evolves slightly more fluidly through cases that have gone to court. Both types of systems include both statutes and case law but have different foundations. An example of a common-law system is the UK, whereas you see civil-law systems across continental Europe.

just off of Madison Avenue to meet with Jonathan Illari. Jonathan has worked in the legal departments of several global auction houses, financial institutions, and e-commerce corporations. Not only that, but he himself is active in the cultural sector as a musician. The same as with Mona, it goes to show how valuable it is to have a passion for both the law and the arts.

---

*Jonathan Illari is a thought leader in the unique space of fine art as an alternative investment. Educated at Cornell University and Boston University School of Law, dual-qualified to practice in New York and London, and with extensive knowledge of corporate, commercial, data-privacy, and fine-art law, Jonathan has worked in the legal departments of several global auction houses, financial institutions, and leading e-commerce corporations. While personally a terrible visual artist, by his own account, he remains a lifelong musician.*

---

**Alexandra Steinacker-Clark: Hi Jonathan, it's great to be here with you today in New York. Can you take me through your career path thus far?**

**Jonathan Illari:** US lawyers start out in undergrad, which I did at Cornell University, and then go on to law school, which I did in Boston. Since graduation, I've predominantly practiced in New York, with stints in California and London. Along the journey, I became licensed in the UK which has been a huge help in the international art market. It is very rare to be able to do art law full time, so I started out in a medium-sized law firm that was doing litigation from a fine-art insurance perspective. I wanted to do something related to the arts since I was in law school, and

I'm a musician by trade, so I thought I would wind up doing intellectual property and copyright law, licensing, royalties, or things pertaining to music law. As I was taking different kinds of legal courses, I found art-law topics to be the most intriguing. "Art Law" is made up of a lot of different things. There is a commercial law element since you are buying and selling artworks. You're dealing with title and authenticity investigations and disputes. International law applies with the threshold question: "What jurisdiction are you selling them in?" and therefore what rules apply. For instance, tariffs have been a big issue since Brexit and the change in US administrations.

There are all these fascinating issues, so it's a hodgepodge of different things you become experienced in. After practicing for a few years, there was a temporary opening at Sotheby's, so I was privileged to work at one of the world's largest auction houses as a young lawyer. One piece of advice I would always give people is go where the jobs are. If you want to do art law, you're likely looking at New York, London, Hong Kong, Paris, and potentially LA or San Francisco. Later, when I stepped into the role of legal counsel for Bonhams, I moved out to San Francisco. Eventually, a position opened up at Phillips to lead their New York legal team, so I took it. I was General Counsel there for several years before moving to a platform that offers investments in works of art. At this point, I have developed a network of colleagues and clients to keep life interesting.

### ASC: What does a typical work day look like for you from start to finish?

**JI:** When it comes to art-law matters, it is highly transaction-based. It is looking at each individual deal to find out what's going on. When I am working on a deal, I focus on each contract. I think about what the team has already done: have we done title research? Have we seen the work of art? Where is the work now, and where is it going? Who is storing it? Who's shipping it? Who will those costs fall on? And making sure that all those details are covered. When working in an auction house, the evening sale would loom and it would be my responsibility to ask these questions. I would be watching the sale in a very different way than other people are watching it because I knew of the deals behind the deals. Who will receive an introductory commission? Where is the money going? Is there a guarantee on this work of art? I would have this mental sheet thinking, okay, what is the company actually making on the sale to ensure everything goes as planned?

**ASC: *How do you gauge success for yourself and in your role?***

**JI:** Personally, I would say that the deals get done, and they get done quickly. I pride myself on being responsive. For any lawyer, it's important to manage expectations, and if you're working in a gallery or an auction house, especially around sale time, things have to be done correctly and efficiently. There are a lot of things going on simultaneously, so deals getting through, never losing a deal, never getting sued, that's how I gauge success.

**ASC: *Have you ever made a step in your career that you regretted, and how did you go about navigating that situation?***

**JI:** Immediate regret, maybe. Long-term regret, no. I am generally quite curious, so I went to different places where I could get experience learning how to do different things within "the law." And at times, I may not love the individual job that I took on, but I learned something and I used that knowledge. Had I just been doing art law straight through and never tried anything else, I wouldn't have the diverse level of skills that I have now. When I say that I've had jobs I didn't really like that much, my thought process was keeping in mind that this is something that is going to help me down the line.

***ASC: What is something you would have wanted to know about this profession before getting into it?***

**JI:** Curiosity is fundamental. It's important to value different skills in different people. Working in-house, I have been fortunate to work with colleagues who possess a knowledge of art history that I do not have, so I will value that greatly. Or they'll have business experience I don't have. We're all learning from each other, and my role is another cog in the chain of making the machine go. I value the concept of "team," so I look at working in-house because you are part of that team. You kind of leave your ego at the door in that sense.

*

As illustrated by Mona and Jonathan, specializing in art law involves navigating complex issues ranging from copyright to contract negotiation, while also being able to creatively solve problems in a variety of contexts. It's an exciting career path as the role of an art lawyer goes beyond just knowing the law. It requires a deep understanding of the art world, because you're not just advising on legal terms, you're advocating for artists, galleries, and institutions while ensuring their rights and interests are protected.

## KEY TAKEAWAYS IF YOU ARE THINKING OF EMBARKING ON YOUR OWN CAREER IN ART LAW

### Three Practical Tips

- Blend law and art education: Consider pursuing qualifications in both law and art history to establish a comprehensive foundation for your career.

- Gain practical experience by seeking internships, vac schemes, or roles within art institutions, galleries, or law firms focusing on art-related cases to build an understanding of industry practices.
- Follow developments in both the art world and legal fields to anticipate changes that may impact your clients and practice.

## Next Steps

- Network with professionals through events that focus on legal aspects of the art market and consider additional coursework in negotiations, contracts, and intellectual property to bolster your expertise in art law.
- Sign up to professional associations that focus on art law such as the Art Lawyers Association (ALA), but also that focus on the arts, such as NXT GEN, to gain insights and access to resources.
- If you don't live in a metropolis "art hub," consider moving to one—even for a summer internship—to gain experience and see if it is the right fit for you.

# CHAPTER 12

# WORKING AS AN ART ADVISOR

Art advisors are key players in the commercial art world. There are art-advisory firms, with multiple advisors, there are independent advisors, and there are other companies that offer advisory services alongside the other main business services they conduct. Examples include Beaumont Nathan, Art Advisory Global, the UBS Art Advisory, and Art Bureau, to name a few — it's worth looking up some of the best-known art advisories, and learning the names of top advisors in the sector. There are some that are based in a specific city or country, but many are international, working across New York, London, Hong Kong, or other major art hubs. Internationality can be a huge asset to an art advisor, but so can a specialization in their regional art scene, so I wanted to speak to people who brought those perspectives to this book. Philip Hoffman is the founder of a world-renowned advisory firm, The Fine Art Group, and is a recognized authority in the art market not only in London but worldwide. Lele Barnett is a Seattle-based advisor looking at the local art scenes in the regions she advises, including for some mammoth tech companies building art collections in the area and around the United States. Working as an art advisor requires not only art-market expertise and skills in relationship management, but also an incredibly entrepreneurial mindset.

---

*Philip Hoffman leads The Fine Art Group, the world's largest art and luxury advisory firm. Under his leadership, the firm has built a global presence spanning the United States, Hong Kong,*

*United Kingdom, Europe, Middle East, and Australia. The firm collaborates with prominent experts and employs over 80 staff worldwide. Previously, Philip spent 13 years at Christie's, serving as CFO at 27, and then Deputy Chief Executive Europe and joining its global management board at age 33. He is a highly regarded industry expert frequently consulted by top media outlets such as the* Financial Times, Wall Street Journal, *CNBC, and the* BBC *for insights on the art market and investment trends.*

---

**Alexandra Steinacker-Clark: Can you tell me about your career path? I want to hear a brief history of your experience as CFO of Christie's at the age of just 27, and what led you to start The Fine Art Group?**

**Philip Hoffman:** I studied Economics, and after I left university I went to KPMG where I qualified as a chartered accountant. To be honest, I loved the team I was working with and the international quality of the companies I was auditing—Nestle in Vevey, Switzerland, Rolls Royce Vickers in Düsseldorf and Basel, or Maersk Shipping, for example—but truth be told, auditing was deathly dull for me. It was an absolutely superb training ground, though, and KPMG happened to also be the auditors of Christie's Auction House, who were under a lot of financial stress at the time. I had a reputation at KPMG of finding solutions to financial stress, as I had done that at a few companies prior. I was asked to come on board at Christie's as CFO when I was 27 years old. The interview process was extraordinary in that, because KPMG recommended me, there *was no* interview process. I was the first chartered accountant amongst the 1,200 people employed, so I came in to radically try to change the business. I stayed involved with Christie's for 13 years, but eventually I realized the options were limited. Did I want to aim to be CEO? Or did I want to be entrepreneurial and do my own thing? To be CEO of Christie's, I would have needed to be more of a politician and a diplomat than an entrepreneur, and that didn't suit my temperament. I left to set up my own company, which was originally called The Fine Art Fund. I was the first person to set up an art investment fund 25 years ago, and since then I have run nine art funds. The funds attracted private clients who began hiring us for advisory work, and the business evolved. Just before the pandemic, in a radical move on my part, we went from about 20 to around 80 employees and partners, growing the business fivefold in 5 years. In addition to that, together with Patti Wong, former Chairman of Sotheby's, we founded Patti Wong and Associates, and we also launched New Perspectives Art Partners, where I am working with people that I really admire who are at the top of the game in the world of art, including Patti. The others are Edward Dolman, who served as CEO of Phillips from 2014 to 2025, his excellent son Alex Dolman, an art-market specialist building major private collections across the Middle East, and Brett Gorvy, cofounder of Lévy Gorvy Dayan. In the last 25 years, I went from running a business with an art fund exclusively operating out of London, to a business that is multinational, advising and financing collections for over 350 families in 28 countries, and has direct shareholdings with other key players in the art market.

***ASC: I would love to know more about the work you do at The Fine Art Group. How does the company function within the wider arts ecosystem?***

**PH:** The company has five revenue areas. Number one is that we lend hundreds of millions of dollars against art, and are competitive with Sotheby's and Christie's in that regard. Number two is we are one of the leading valuation groups in the United States, conducting trust and estate appraisals. The third is our advisory, where we advise our clients on what to buy, what to sell, and give them holistic management consulting regarding their collection. The fourth is the art investment funds, and the fifth, we act as private sale brokers for major artworks from $500,000 to $50 million, ranging from a Stradivarius violin to a Van Gogh painting or a pink diamond.

*ASC: What are your responsibilities and duties as Founder and Chairman?*

**PH:** My focus has always been on growth and innovation. I create new structures, build partnerships, recruit talent, and develop products that respond to what our clients truly need. I also work closely with top collectors and raise capital for both our very significant lending business and our next art funds.

*ASC: What does a typical work day look like for you, from start to finish?*

**PH:** There is no typical work day for me! I travel constantly. In May alone, I was in 15 countries over five weeks. One week, I was in Vietnam speaking to 200 of Asia's wealthiest families about the art market; the next, I was in New York launching New Perspectives Art Partners. In Europe, I met with clients in London and Switzerland eager to invest in our lending platform. My days are unpredictable, and truth be told, that's exactly how I like them.

*ASC: How do you stay updated with current art-market trends? What is needed in terms of knowledge and expertise in order to do your job?*

**PH:** I attend most of the major art fairs worldwide—Basel, Hong Kong, Frieze—and some of the top New York or London auctions. I speak with dealers and auction houses at least once a week, if not more, and I read the art press daily; you have to keep your ear to the ground in this industry.

***ASC: How do you build and maintain relationships with clients?***

**PH:** Clients want three things: expertise, professionalism, and for you to be highly responsive. When they call, they want to be able to rely on you to know your subject, or bring in a team member who does, and for their question to be answered quickly with accurate information. One thing I've learned is to have humility in your knowledge, because in this business, no one can know everything. To value a Monet on Monday, a Twombly on Wednesday, a Canaletto on Thursday, and a diamond on Friday is not something I could do, even after 35 years in the industry. I roughly know what they might be worth, but what is more important is knowing who to ask as I have a team of experts around me.

It is important to be honest—to your clients and to yourself—about the services you can provide, and how you are going to bring in the services you can't provide, whether it be through the expertise of your partnerships or through your hired staff.

My three golden rules in business are:

1. Profitability, as every deal must make sense for both you and the client (otherwise, you can't survive).

2. Professionalism, i.e. always bringing in the right expertise.

3. Make it fun. Don't take it too seriously because art and luxury are passions, not necessities.

***ASC: Can you tell me something that I wouldn't expect to hear about your job? What's something that many might be surprised to find out?***

**PH:** That perhaps being eccentric is beneficial. I normally stand out because I often take the opposite direction, and I don't follow the herd, nor do I advise my clients to follow the herd. When people say something's impossible, I find a way to make it happen.

*ASC: Can you tell me a difficult aspect of the job, something that you find particularly challenging about it?*

**PH:** It's very difficult managing a big team. I'm good at ideas, seeing opportunities, and selling. But managing creative personalities can be extremely challenging. People in the art world don't always think conventionally, and learning to trust others and delegate has been a journey for me because I've had to do so much myself for the last 20 years. I've had to get used to a much bigger international team. That said, I'm proud of the culture we've built. Two of my former assistants, both quite new to the art world when they joined, were later hired by a chairmen of Christie's and a chairman of Sotheby's. The auction house staff obviously considered working with me at The Fine Art Group pretty desirable training, and I take that as a compliment.

*ASC: If someone wanted to do what you do, what advice or even warnings would you give them?*

**PH:** You need to have a vision and you need to have stamina to persevere. I speak to a lot of MBA graduates, and they all have great ideas, with great spreadsheets and numbers. But the hardest thing for an entrepreneur, especially in the art business, is to be able to see an idea through to profitability. I nearly gave up in the second year after starting The Fine Art Group, but I didn't. Our business has become one of the biggest in the art world, and it's iterated five times in the last twenty years. There will always be doubters and obstacles, but if you have conviction, resilience, and imagination (plus a bit of luck), you can build something extraordinary.

*

When speaking to Philip, I was reminded that, in some art businesses, the financial acumen needs to be just as high as the art-market acumen.

Although, no matter what, it's important to be honest with your clients and other business partners about your knowledge and skill set. As we have heard in previous interviews, the commercial art world can be a competitive industry. Admitting where you need other expert opinions can not only build trust with clients, showing you will bring in the right people instead of overreaching out of pride (or greed), but it can also lead to strategic and powerful partnerships. If you want to venture into the realm of art advising, don't pretend to be an expert in it all. Build a network of contacts (or, in Philip's case, a company with highly expert staff) who you can consult when needed, as clients value honesty over false confidence.

Philip built his business in London over 20 years ago, and has since expanded internationally. In the US, The Fine Art Group is headquartered in New York City, one of the global art capitals. Across the continent on the West Coast is Seattle, one of the global tech capitals. The city is known for housing the headquarters of tech giants like Microsoft and Amazon, alongside aviation giant Boeing and internationally renowned coffee chain Starbucks. Although not known for its art world, there are some innovative structures in place to support the creative scene there. For example, the Seattle Office of Arts & Culture receives funding from two primary streams: the Admission Tax and 1% for Art. When you attend certain cultural venues or events in Seattle (such as going to the movies or riding the ferris wheel), 5 percent of your ticket price goes towards the city's Arts and Culture Fund. Seattle was one of the first cities in the US to adopt a "percent-for-art" ordinance in 1973, meaning construction departments like Seattle Department of Transportation set aside 1 percent of their construction-project costs for art. This money goes into a Municipal Art Fund, which supports the commissioning, purchasing, installing, and maintaining public art all over Seattle. Finally, and this may not seem impressive to Londoners who are accustomed to free museums all the time, but everyone can visit the Seattle Art Museum and the Seattle Asian Art Museum on the first Thursday of every month for free. The scheme is supported by the Paul

G. Allen Family Foundation, founded by philanthropists Jody Allen and the late Paul G. Allen, cofounder of Microsoft. Even if some cities aren't known as "art hubs," there is always room to make space for the cultural sector to thrive with the right support.

Over on the West Coast, I hopped on a bus to downtown Seattle to speak to Lele Barnett, an art advisor who lives and works in the city. I met with Lele at her office over breakfast before heading to a meeting room for our interview. We enjoyed some scrambled eggs, fresh fruit, and hot coffee while we got to know each other a little bit, so that by the time we were sitting down for the interview, we felt like fast friends.

---

*Lele Barnett is an Art Advisor and Curator in Seattle with 25 years of experience, leading the ART (Artists, Researchers, Technologists) and Expansive Thinking program at a prominent technology company building immersive experiences. She has curated art collections for major global corporations based in the Seattle area. The former cofounder of McLeod Residence, she has also curated exhibitions for Tacoma Art Museum, Wing Luke Museum, and others. She is on the Frye Art Museum Board and a member of the APAA, ensuring impartial guidance. Specializing in emerging artists and New Media like XR and AI, Lele also works in private advising, consulting, curation, and project management.*

---

**Alexandra Steinacker-Clark: What led you to do the work that you do in the arts today?**

**Lele Barnett:** I grew up in California and moved to Seattle to study Art and Art History for my bachelor's. I was working through high school and college, selling luggage, and I was pretty good at it, which translated well as a skill set to start working at galleries. I then moved to New York for a while to work for a non-profit, doing art fundraising. When I moved back to Seattle, in around 2006–7, I opened my own gallery and bar, which was really fun, but it eventually got shut down by the fire department because we couldn't keep it up to code. When that happened, someone recommended me for a job as a curator with a major tech company in the area, where I worked for eight years. They have art in offices across North America and I came on to curate the collection across those spaces. I mean, spending a big corporation's money in support of the arts? What a dream! One of my first projects was curating the art in their Midwest offices, and they wanted to work with local artists. I knew nothing about local artists in the Midwest, so I needed to go on a trip to visit a bunch of studios and galleries. I met so many artists across the country, in all of the cities that the company has offices in. It was an amazing job.

However, every year, my budget got smaller and smaller. As a curator, you want to go bigger and bigger . . . So I began to have this dream of going off on my own and working with private clients. I started voicing this to people, which I see you post a lot about on your social media, too, Alexandra—I completely agree with that notion of being loud about what your goals are, because people do want to see you succeed. I had friends send clients my way, and I slowly built up my address book as I left my job as curator at the tech company. After around six months, I realized it wouldn't be enough for a full-time job, though. That's when I was approached by *another* major tech company for their Open Arts program. I started working for them as a contractor and was also independently advising, which worked out perfectly.

However, my whole team got laid off a couple of years ago. Arts are always the first on the chopping block, it seems. I was fortunate to be moved to the research team after meeting a director of research at the company. It was a stroke of fate, actually, because we didn't meet at work, we actually met at an event at the Seattle Art Museum (SAM).

When I informed that person that my team had been let go, they took action to keep me on board. I'm thankful for that SAM membership, because I'm always meeting people who want to support the arts in a big way. Being on the research team has allowed me to grow my own program, which is something I've always wanted to do, connecting artists and researchers and technologists. I still advise independently, and I curate exhibitions, too.

*ASC: Can you describe some of the responsibilities you have in your position when you are consulting and advising? And tying into that, I would love it if you could shed light on being a member of the Association of Professional Art Advisors, as it's the only accrediting body for the industry in the USA . . . what does that mean for you and your work?*

**LB:** For my private clients, I research artists and artworks and make recommendations. When they make selections, I oversee the acquisition, crating, shipping, insurance, installation, all of it. I became a member of the APAA when I was a corporate curator and have stayed as an independent advisor. They're very transparent as an association, and as soon as I started advising private clients, I reached out to a few of the other members and they guided me through how to set up my business, how to get paid, how it all works. Members within the APAA agree to a code of ethics so we're not double dipping, we're not being paid by more than one party. My clients see if I get a discount from a gallery—I have the gallery pass the invoice directly to the client, and then they pay me back whatever we've agreed on. It's all very transparent for all parties involved.

*ASC: As a consultant and advisor for corporate collections, what are your responsibilities? Do you have to consider the values of the corporation when thinking about what to acquire?*

**LB:** We had an overall mission and it was important for me to adhere to that, but also to work with the teams and stakeholders at the local offices. They would have ideas about what they wanted, and I would ensure that it worked with our mission. We thought a lot about investment value, but not because we had any intention of selling works from the collection. We wanted to show the stakeholders that the collection would go up in value every year. That was at the first tech company I worked at, though. At the second one, the one I still work for now, it's about being immersed in the art. There are a lot of murals, a lot of works directly adhered to the wall. We wouldn't be able to resell this art, so it's not considered a collection. It's about creating an environment. At the other company we said that we're investing in art, but at this company we say we're investing in artists.

*ASC: What does a typical work day look like for you from start to finish?*

**LB:** Three days a week, I come into the office. I work with tech researchers, and I've really spent a lot of time with them learning about what they're doing. We talk about how art and artists could enhance their work. The people I work with are like a think tank. They're thinking about the future, what it's going to look like, and how technology fits into that. It's really important to me that art is part of that conversation to inform the technology and our future, because art is what makes us human, and we really need it. The other days, I research artists, go to their studios, check out BFA and MFA graduate shows . . .

*ASC: What programs are here in Seattle?*

**LB:** I always love the MFA show at the Henry, which is the art gallery at the University of Washington. There's a digital arts program there, as well. When I am working with private clients, I'm constantly researching art and artists. Today, after this interview, I'm going to meet a new client at their house to talk about their vision for their collection and probably measure some walls.

***ASC: How do you build and maintain relationships with artists and clients?***

**LB:** I've worked with so many artists and I feel like we have fun working together. You build friendships. With clients, I've met people through going to fundraising events and being involved with the museums. I've been on the board of the Frye Art Museum for about a year and a half now. I go to nearly every event, and we've been doing a lot of collecting events where we travel together as a group to various organizations or art happenings.

There's a lot of newer wealth here in this area, because of tech. When I was starting out with advising private clients, I had a friend who is a stylist tell me she had a client who felt like they should be more cultured than they were. She told her client, "I'm going make you cultured as f*ck." That was the beginning of the "Cultured A F Club." We invited people to art and fashion events, and our little club grew and grew. A lot of people have now become clients, but they also refer me when they hear about somebody looking to collect art. That really helped me build a client base in the beginning.

***ASC: Can you tell me about the work you do more widely and how your work as an advisor intersects with it?***

**LB:** Working with artists, researchers, and technologists, the goal of the program at this tech company is to get to the next big thing. However, we understand that linear thinking is not what is going to get us there, artistic thinking is, so we aim to bring in different kinds of thinkers. My goal has always been to support art and artists and an additional, newer goal of mine is helping the future with artistic thinking, too.

*ASC: What is specific about your job in the Pacific Northwest? Seattle doesn't necessarily have the reputation of being a cultural capital like London or New York.*

**LB:** There are people here that are very new to collecting art, as I mentioned. There aren't these generations of collectors like there are in New York or London. So, they need that guidance a little bit more. Once they start living with art, they realize that they can't live without it, but a lot of people here have not grown up with art. I grew up with art on my walls and I know that I can't live without it, but this is new to so many of these people who are still discovering how rewarding it is.

*ASC: What are the biggest challenges you face in your profession?*

**LB:** Convincing people that art is important. Some people are just not going to understand. In almost everything I've ever done, I've spent so much time defending why I'm even here. And maybe that's just the arts. I feel like I've been successful when artists are being supported, and if my work has brought people to think in different ways. It's all part of it.

*

Being an art advisor can look so different depending on where you are based, if you are independent or work for a company, and what sort of art you advise on. As we clearly heard from both Lele and Philip, making contacts and having your ear to the ground are important activities for art advisors, especially when they are starting out and wanting to build their networks and their expertise. What I also gleaned from their interviews is that you need to develop relationships with artists, collectors, other advisors, and people in the wider art world in order to be able to thrive in your job. Relationships are key to being an advisor—whether it be to have the close connection to a gallery to acquire a work for your client that others wouldn't necessarily have access to (because, as we covered in the gallery chapter, the process of "placing" an artwork relies a lot on trust), or to be able to connect with local artists to build big corporate connections. Either way, your ability to build relationships will be one of your biggest assets.

## KEY TAKEAWAYS IF YOU ARE THINKING OF EMBARKING ON YOUR OWN CAREER IN ART ADVISING

### Three Practical Tips

- Ensure you have knowledge of art history and the art market, or you build a network who has that knowledge. As an advisor, you need to be well versed in why an artwork is relevant, both to you as well as to the wider market and art-historical discourse, because it may be important to your clients.
- Cultivate strong ethical standards and integrity. IIn a world where art advisors are going to prison and having glitzy books written about their fraud, trust and reputation are paramount. Adhere to a code of ethics, be transparent about commissions, and always prioritize client interests.
- Start building your network as soon as you can. Leverage digital tools like social media and put together a professional website. Go to events and, if possible, become a member at your favorite museum or other arts organization to meet like-minded people interested in supporting the arts.

### Next Steps

- Choose one membership club to join in your area that aligns with your goals. If you can afford it, join a patrons' program at your local museum. If that's not an option for you just yet, look into free associations—if you don't find any, take a page from Lele's book and start one!

- Reach out to artists in your city to visit their studios. Start having conversations about their work and becoming familiar with the structure of studio visits and how you like to conduct them so that both you and the artist feel the most comfortable.
- Think about how involved in the entrepreneurial financial market you want to get, and cater your next steps to that. Would you rather think about art as an investment for private clients? Or potentially work for a company, building their art collection and investing in artists that way?

# CHAPTER 13

# WORKING IN CONTENT CREATION IN THE ARTS

Instagram, TikTok, LinkedIn, YouTube, Substack, X (formerly known as Twitter), Threads — how to choose? Short videos, long essays, newsletters, episodes, stories, likes, views, comments — "engagement" and "following" becoming the defining metrics of success. The world of social media and content creation is a very recent addition to the cluster of potential careers in the arts, and it seems to be evolving at breakneck speed. I would consider myself a content creator, of sorts, but it isn't my main job. The *All About Art* podcast is definitely one of the pillars, though, and anything I post on Instagram, TikTok, or LinkedIn (where I, funnily enough, fall within the top 2 percent of creators due to my following, which grew unexpectedly) supports the greater mission of my work. According to a 2023 survey done by Morning Consult,* an American business-intelligence company specializing in online survey research technology, 57 percent of the Gen Z participants said they want to be influencers. It's understandable as to why! Successful content creators are high earners and their audience watches them go on brand trips and unbox lavish new product launches in beauty, clothing, and tech.

However, there has been a shift from what it means to be an "influencer" to a "content creator" or just "creator," and being online is fraught with problematic patterns. What was once a community-based, photo-sharing app has turned into a goliath marketing machine, and

---

* Morning Consult analysts, *Report: How Brands Can Succeed at Influencer Marketing*, Morning Consult, September 2023.

everyone is figuring out how to get the most attention to "hook" their audience. Issues of authenticity, privacy, pretty privilege, erotic capital[*] and the halo effect are some of the many reasons why approaching a career in social media is not as easy or glamorous as aspiring creators may think. In my experience, there is a constant push and pull between being yourself and maintaining a healthy distance, between knowing when to pull out the camera and when it is taking over your everyday life—and in the art world, you need to add another few layers of complexities.

In the arts, as you have read in a few of the previous chapters, reputation is key. If people know you as someone they want to work with, it will open doors for you. If you have an online presence and it is perceived as inauthentic, badly researched, or lacking a wider awareness of the arts in general, you may get attention—but institutions may not take you seriously. The arts industry values authenticity and impact outside of the social-media sphere, but there are massive benefits arising now as the art world catches up to other industries like beauty and fashion. In this chapter, you will read insights shared by Alayo Akinkugbe, who amassed a large following after launching her Instagram account *A Black History of Art* in 2020, as well as Marie-Odile Pantoja Falais, Paris-based social-media strategist and manager, and Robert Diament, gallerist and one half of the duo running *Talk Art*, an award-winning arts podcast.

Back in 2022, I sat down with Alayo to record an episode of *All About Art*, when she had just graduated from her bachelor's degree and not long before that had launched *A Black History of Art*, a platform amassing thousands of followers in quite a short amount of time. We have watched each other grow throughout the last few years, with Alayo working on amazing curatorial projects, launching her own podcast, and publishing a book in the summer of 2025 titled *Reframing Blackness*.

---

[*]  Constance Webb, *The Good the Bad and the Ugly Truth About 'Pretty Privilege'*, Gender at Work Blog by the University of Exeter, 30 March, 2023.

*Alayo Akinkugbe is an independent writer and curator, and the author of* Reframing Blackness: What's Black About History of Art? *She is a contributing editor at* AnOther *magazine, hosts the podcast* A Shared Gaze, *and runs the Instagram platform* A Black History of Art, *which celebrates the contributions of Black artists, sitters, curators, and thinkers from art history and the present day. She has contributed to books and exhibition catalogs and written for publications including* Dazed, Tate Etc., *and* The World of Interiors. *Her aim is to continually highlight the work of Black artists from across the globe and all periods of art history, in a bid to challenge the way art history is taught and presented in the West.*

**Alexandra Steinacker-Clark: Can you take me through your education and career path thus far?**

**Alayo Akinkugbe:** I studied History of Art at Cambridge for my BA, and then I went to the Courtauld to do an MA in Curating the Art Museum. Straight after that, I worked at the Royal Academy for a year as a curatorial researcher for the exhibition *Entangled Pasts*. I have been curating exhibitions since, notably contributing to *In the Black Fantastic* at the Hayward, and am the VIP Consultant, Africa for Frieze art fair. It was during my BA that I started *A Black History of Art*, in response to the fact that I hadn't studied any Black artists in my first year of university. I had a feeling that we weren't going to study many more in the second and third years, so I wanted to do my own research and post snippets online. I was inspired by *The Great Women Artists* run by Katy Hessel and also a page called *Paintings Daily*, which didn't provide any written information or context about the works of art but would post a painting a day. My aim was, in a way, to build an archive. In the meantime, I have started foraying into journalism, writing particularly for *AnOther* magazine. I've done a few pieces for *Dazed* and *Elephant* as well, but *AnOther* is where I have my regular column, 'Black Gazes'. I also have a podcast called *A Shared Gaze*, which is more of a passion project than anything else. I've been working on my book since 2021, and it came out in July 2025.

**ASC: *Would you say that Instagram was the way that you got your foot in the door for the opportunities that followed?***

**AA:** Instagram definitely created opportunities for me because a lot of them came from DMs from museums wanting to collaborate. The Instagram account is the root of everything, but other key parts of my career have developed since. For example, being known as a columnist for *AnOther* magazine has opened up so many opportunities with PR companies who reach out to me, not just for writing but also for my podcast. Initially, most of the opportunities came via Instagram, but since then, the other things have become springboards for further growth. Instagram has fed into these other things, which then have grown into their own entities that stand alone outside of social media. My master's also was extremely useful because it showed me how curating an exhibition actually works. Had I not had the Instagram account, the MA would have probably played the biggest part in my career growth.

**ASC: *Do you feel like you have a responsibility in running such a large platform?***

**AA:** For the most part in my career, it's been about discernment. I am always mindful of my responsibility to work with companies, institutions, or brands that actually align with what I'm doing. A key aspect of this has been trying to not be the token Black voice for whatever museum or gallery or institution. Moving forward, because I've now finished my book, I would like to seek out opportunities that make sense for where I want to take my brand next. Up until now, it has been a case of filtering and discerning to ensure I don't align myself with a company whose values don't actually align with mine.

***ASC: What does a typical work day look like for you?***

**AA:** When I'm in London for an extended period of time, I'll usually go to my sublet studio at Studio Voltaire to work. It makes a huge difference to have somewhere to go and be productive. Plus, it gives me access to a community of artists and arts professionals. When you're freelance, you are leading quite a solitary life. I usually try to wake up about 7.30 or 8am, and then I'll normally look through my emails or finish working on an article that probably needed to be done for the day before. I paper-edit the podcast, which is where I read the transcript and decide what to take out, instead of listening to the audio. In the afternoons, I could have a bunch of Zoom meetings including virtual studio visits, but if I can, I will attend a studio visit in person because that's preferable. There's an absolute lack of routine for the most part, though, because I'm working on so many different things, and no two days are the same. I feel like not having a set routine is a big challenge as a freelancer, but I'd rather have it this way than be going into a rigid structure five days a week. I work more than a 9 to 5, but some of these things feel like passion projects, so I don't mind doing them on a Sunday or late at night, and in exchange, I have more flexibility.

***ASC: As a curator, author, podcaster, presenter, and as someone who runs a large platform online, what type of content do you enjoy creating the most and why?***

**AA:** In terms of social media, my favorite posts to make are probably the reels that I do with museums because they have high-quality equipment and great editors. You put out something that you feel proud of. Sometimes you spend three or four hours for a one-minute video, so I don't make those videos myself because it is a whole production. I love continuing to build the *A Black History of Art* archive, posting about artists who people are unlikely to know or about sitters who people are unlikely to have seen. Outside of social media, I love interviewing people, artists especially. I find it very fulfilling to be able to have a conversation with someone and edit it into a format that's digestible for readers or listeners. That's also why I do the podcast as a passion project, because until I have a sponsor, the podcast doesn't give me any extra income. But it does create opportunities and I'm lucky if someone flies me somewhere to produce an episode.

***ASC: Are you ever going to move* A Black History of Art *off Instagram and have an archive elsewhere?***

**AA:** I did have a thought early on about the longevity of building something on Instagram. I thought, "What if Instagram dies, then my whole career is over." In addition, Instagram requires you to feed an algorithm all the time, and it might not necessarily be what you want to do—which is how I felt. That prompted me to think more deeply about what I want my career to be, separately from Instagram. I've been focusing on building that. But to answer your question, yes, I think it's important actually to move it off so that no matter what happens with Instagram as a platform, there is still access to the archive.

***ASC: Tell me something many would be surprised to know about your job.***

**AA:** I'm actually really bad at making content. I've made maybe two or three reels ever, and the rest of the reels have been made by museums or galleries with good video editors. I don't think I could, for example, work in a social-media strategy department in a big company, because even though I have the platform, I have not been focused on expanding its reach. I don't actually know that much about how to grow a social-media page—I think it was just the right place at the right time, and it has led to all these opportunities.

***ASC: Have you experienced negativity in the online space? If so, how did you overcome it?***

**AA:** Instagram creates these echo chambers, but when I collaborate with some institutions, it reaches their audience, who are not always the same demographic as mine. I have received comments criticizing the fact that I am "reading too much into the Black narratives." I feel like some audiences just have an aversion to seeing Blackness, and they follow museums like the National Gallery because it has a lot of white art in it, and they don't want to see a Black person talking about Black stuff. I remember the first few times it happened, I would respond and try to engage in a conversation, but it became clear that they didn't want to engage in a conversation—they just don't want a Black person on their Instagram feed. So, I just don't respond anymore and do my best to ignore the negative comments.

***ASC: What are your long-term goals for your career, and is content creation a part of that?***

**AA:** Long term, I really want to pivot into documentary filmmaking. I would like to start with subjects relating to everything that I've written about in my book, i.e. Blackness and where it sits in art history. It's about highlighting Black narratives, telling Black stories, seeing Blackness and Black people, and also, crucially, Africanness, represented in a way that I haven't yet seen in documentary and film. That's not to say that I want to stop everything else I'm doing, though.

**ASC:** *If someone wanted to do what you do, what advice or even warnings would you give them?*

**AA:** For me, a huge thing has been imposter syndrome, throughout everything that I've done. I would say if you're going to do multiple things, you have to be confident in your ability to do them because a lack of confidence will make you procrastinate. If you feel intimidated by the things that you're doing, they become infinitely harder. If you have the skills or the creativity to channel into multiple different things, you should. There's nothing stopping you from doing it. There's this saying "A jack of all trades but a master of none." I don't think it's true at all. The rest of the quote gets left off most of the time, but it is "oftentimes better than a master of one." You don't need to be a master of absolutely everything, or master of one specific thing. You can put what you can into all the things that you want to do, and build up the confidence to pursue it all.

*

In a world where half the videos I see on Instagram are about "how to gain 10k followers in 30 days, join my bootcamp," leading me to feel exhausted about always feeling the pressure to grow and grow and grow, Alayo's stance was refreshing. Her focus has never been on growing an audience online, and every opportunity she received through her social-media presence has been channeled into building a more sustainable, futureproof career in which she gained valuable experiences in other areas such as curating and writing. Her Instagram has served as a springboard, and it supplements her research and professional endeavors, but it is not the main source of activity or income for her.

I wanted to peek behind the curtain of social media in the art world a little bit more, so during a trip to Paris, social-media strategist Marie-Odile Pantoja Falais welcomed me to her home. We had connected during the COVID lockdowns, when we were all perpetually online, trying to develop professional connections and navigating our way through "unprecedented times." When you have known someone for a few years via their social media but have never actually sat in front of them or given them a hug, it feels like a phantom familiarity. It was gratifying to finally meet her as we sat down and put our phones on Do Not Disturb to spend an hour chatting about her career.

---

*Marie-Odile Pantoja Falais is a French–Brazilian content creator, social-media strategist, and consultant specializing in the art world. Marie-Odile studied Art History and started working the art market in auction houses and galleries. Throughout this time, she grew her Instagram account by sharing her exhibition visits and artistic discoveries, with which she was able to launch her freelance career. Marie-Odile lives and works in France and is a partner and social-media strategist at Aartemis, a company with solutions for Social Media Strategy, Cultural Engagement and Mediation, Influence and Communications for art and culture.*

---

**Alexandra Steinacker-Clark:** *It's really great to be here, after being in touch with each other online for literally years but never meeting in person.*

**Marie-Odile Pantoja Falais:** So true! I have Insta Friends, as I call them, who I've met and we bonded over sharing art on social media.

**ASC:** *It's something very distinct, isn't it? How did you get started in the social-media landscape, and more specifically in the arts?*

**MOPF:** I always knew that art was something that animated me, but had no idea of all the different jobs in the art industry other than being an artist, which wasn't my thing. After doing a bit of research, I found out that with art history, you could work in museums or galleries, and decided that was the direction I wanted to go in. I went to the Paris 1 Sorbonne University, which is more focused on the sociological and historic context of a movement, whereas L'École du Louvre is more focused on art history as a theoretical discipline and trains you more to be a museum director, I'd say. The main focus of my dissertation was on Brazilian contemporary art and art history, because I wanted to dive into my own culture. My mom is Brazilian, and I wanted to learn more about the history of the country, especially as we in Paris, or Europe in general, are very Western-centric regarding our art-history education. During my bachelor's, I did an internship at Christie's Auction House but was working alongside that in customer service at Swarovski in the Carousel du Louvre, which are the shops next to the Louvre Museum. It was actually very useful in learning how to deal with different kinds of clientele and was a transferable skill in my jobs later on.

***ASC: How did you get started in creating content in the arts?***

**MOPF:** In 2017, I got my first permanent contract for a job in the arts. It was for the position of gallery assistant, but during the job interview I told them that I also wanted to take care of their social media and ads because it can save costs compared to having articles in magazines, which are quite expensive in France. Social media was still very new back then, France is always so far behind regarding things like that. The French art world in 2017 was like, "We don't believe in social media." Of course, I didn't want to do anything *too* experimental on the gallery's Instagram, so alongside that I also started to share about art on my own account. It was where I could experiment and try things out with more freedom while also learning skills through developing the gallery's social media.

*ASC: How did your content creation, from that inception up to now, pave the way for your career?*

**MOPF:** I was, and still am, constantly learning new skills. Back then, Instagram was just pictures, so learning how to edit images and copywrite text were important skills. Now, learning how to video-edit is essential. I also learned so much about social-media ad campaigns and ads-manager functions using the Meta Business Suite, which is a skill in itself because that platform is horrible to navigate! In addition to all of those practical things, content creation was also a way to learn more deeply about the art I was sharing, because I would research while putting posts together. When I was still working at the gallery, after a few years and a promotion, I felt like I had progressed as far as I could in that job. My social media had grown and, as I mentioned, I had learned so much, so I decided to quit and start my business in consulting, video editing, and social-media creation.

*ASC: So there was the progression from gallery day job and social media back end, to being a known figure in the art social-media landscape, to leaving the day job to advise and support others in their growth on social media, all the while still growing your account?*

**MOPF:** Exactly. And now, it's mostly supporting behind the scenes. I don't have the time to focus on growing my account. I have a baby, and it's not my priority anymore. I have so many ideas for my clients, so when it comes to me, it's just not where my focus is right now.

*ASC: Do you think that clients look at your Instagram account with your level of following and think, "Oh, she's not big enough"? Do they expect someone to have hundreds of thousands of followers?*

**MOPF:** No, they are happy because it's the perfect medium: I'm not too visible, but I'm not invisible. It's a good balance.

*ASC: What does your job look like now, what are your responsibilities?*

**MOPF:** I am now a full-time social media manager and strategist. With clients, we agree on certain deliverables and a fee and then we get to work. In 2024, I became a Partner of Aartemis, a company that develops strategies for paid and organic social-media campaigns, cultural engagement, and communication for art and culture. Where my expertise is on Instagram, their expertise is on TikTok. When I had my maternity leave, they took care of my clients, and now we are working together and building the company. We think a lot about wider community engagement, and how we can bring art and culture to wider audiences, to people of all ages from children to adults.

*ASC: As an art historian, how do you balance educational content with entertainment for audiences? The balance of "edutainment," if you will.*

**MOPF:** It's all aligned with my mission throughout my entire time on social media, which is accessibility. A short backstory: before I met my partner, he wasn't the kind of man who went to museums. Why? Because he had a bad experience when he asked a question in a museum during a visit with his school and the staff condescendingly replied, "Oh, you don't know that?" As a result, he thought, "Okay, museums are not for me, my interests and knowledge don't fit here." Once I started taking him to museums again, and explaining things in the same way I was doing it on Instagram, he began to love it. I bring in my passion and combine it with my art-historical knowledge, presenting it in a fun and casual way. I want people to feel welcome in the art world, and that's how I approach each piece of content I create. It's important to define your reason why you do something because it will come across in everything that you do.

***ASC: On a practical note, what sort of hard skills are needed in order to work in content creation in the arts?***

**MOPF:** I started with free apps like InShot for editing. CapCut is another one that is incredibly useful. I also have knowledge in Adobe Premiere, but it's too complicated for what I needed it for. You don't need Adobe for creating social-media content, if I'm honest. You need to develop skills in script and caption writing, as well as just practicing. Practice filming, get to know the angles and lighting, and you will pick up on certain things you can do during video production that will make the post-production things like editing a lot easier. It takes time and practice! You also need skills on community management when it comes to connecting with people and being aware of who you want to reach with what you create.

***ASC: What is specific about being a content creator and social-media manager in the Paris art scene?***

**MOPF:** I don't know if this is a specifically French problem, probably not, but in 2017–18, a lot of museums and galleries bought followers. You can see it now because they don't have reach and we have clients coming to us saying, "When we post, we don't have a lot of views. We don't have a lot of likes." I can identify the cause quite quickly, because it's my job. I can tell that you bought followers. You cannot have 50,000 followers and 200 likes. It doesn't make any sense. So now, we have to have a hard discussion. You bought followers, but you need to tell me how many, because when I look at the numbers, it appears as though only 50 percent of your community is real. I don't know if the problem of authentic audiences is as prevalent everywhere, but I can see that this is a common theme here in Paris regarding my field. Why? Maybe because they were feeling like they missed the boat back then and tried to catch up in the wrong ways.

***ASC: If someone wanted to do what you do, what advice or even warnings would you give them?***

**MOPF:** You have to know your audience. Decide who you are talking to and adapt your content to that. You can't fake your knowledge about a topic to someone who has done research on it, it doesn't work that way in the art industry. If you are a content creator because you like art and you edit really well, but your knowledge of art, art history, and the arts sector as a whole is limited, it will eventually cause you to hit a wall. For example, I was listening to a podcast where they were saying that museum tickets are more expensive now because of the art market—and we both know the two are not directly correlated in the slightest. One is a private market and the other is state property, with two totally different funding infrastructures. It's just misinformation. So, a warning or piece of advice is that you have to acknowledge where your expertise lies and where you may need to do more research, in order to produce content and represent our sector responsibly.

*

The through-line I gleaned from speaking to Marie-Odile was that, no matter if it's to do with your audience or the research behind your content, being authentic is the key to maintaining a sustainable and valuable presence online. As a podcaster myself, hearing about such blatant misinformation in the podcast she mentioned was agitating.

There will always be moments where conversations veer into unknown territories, but it's important to question your own level of knowledge, especially if you have done absolutely no research about it prior. (Which is what sounds like happened with the podcast Marie-Odile was listening to . . . If they had done any research at all, it would have quickly debunked their hypothesis that high museum ticket costs are caused by the art market.) There are a few amazing art podcasts out there—of course, *All About Art*, the podcast I founded back in 2021.

Other podcasts I love are *A Week in Art* and *A Brush With*, both run by *The Art Newspaper* and hosted by Ben Luke. *The ArtTactic Podcast*, *Jo's Art History Podcast*, and *The Great Women Artists* are also some top favorites.

However, there is one particular podcast that I not only enjoy listening to, but that actually inspired me to write this book. *Talk Art*, a podcast hosted by the art-loving duo Russell Tovey and Robert Diament, has been running since 2018, so far having published over 350 episodes and achieving millions of downloads. They have written two books, the first published in 2021 and the second in 2023, both on the topic of discussing contemporary art and conversations with art-world figures inspired by or taken directly from their podcast. Robert, one of the two enthusiastic hosts, is also Partner at Carl Freedman Gallery, the leading contemporary art gallery in Margate, Kent. Early on a Tuesday morning, we hopped on a Zoom call and he took an hour out of his day to answer some of my burning questions about something that's quite close to my heart: podcasting.

---

*Robert Diament is Partner of the Carl Freedman Gallery, a contemporary art gallery located in Margate, Kent, and Counter Editions, a company that produces prints and multiples by leading contemporary artists such as Tracey Emin, Lubaina Himid, David Shrigley, and Frank Bowling. Before working in art, he was the lead singer of electro-pop band Temposhark and since 2018, together with actor Russell Tovey, has hosted the award-winning* Talk Art *podcast.*

---

**Alexandra Steinacker-Clark: Can you tell me about your career so far and how you got into the arts?**

**Robert Diament:** I started writing songs when I was 13. It was a way for me to get through trauma, because I wrote my first song the day after my brother passed away in 1994. It was weirdly connected to art because I had heard Madonna, the pop star, talking about Frida Kahlo and how Frida's work was very much about survival and overcoming trauma. At the hospital that day, I remember my parents telling me the news, and I immediately thought about Frida Kahlo—which was such a weird experience. That sort of creativity and connection to art and music is in the DNA of who I am and where it all began.

In the years following, I had a sort-of professional career in music. It was really hard to make a living from it but from 2002 (so quite a while after I started) I was able to make some money performing across the UK in different venues with my band Temposhark. I set up my own record label, too, and I got a lot of transferable skills that really benefited me later down the line. One of the things I learned when I was making music was how much support you can get from your peer group. Rather than thinking, "I can't do this because I don't know anyone that runs a big record label" or "I don't know anyone that is a super famous singer," you can actually do it by growing together with people. Especially if you think of the art world, it's totally transferable.

When I started making money from music, I would spend the little that I had made on art. I was buying Tracey Emin drawings for around a thousand pounds, which I would pay in installments. A friendship with Tracey began, and she became a mentor to me, in a way. The friendship with her is what gave me the idea to go and work for Carl Freedman as well. I had done a master's at Christie's Education for a year in central London when I was around 28 or 29 because I felt really inadequate, like I wasn't going to get a job in the art world because I'd never had any formal education. I did that course as a way of filling in the gaps, and to give myself self-confidence. I'm really glad I did it, and at that time in my life, too, because I went in there a bit older and very determined to apply myself. I also made amazing friends on that course who are now art advisors or gallerists in the sector. While I was doing that course, I was also out every single night networking, so by the time I graduated, I managed to get a few interviews with different galleries. One was called Max Wigram, which doesn't exist anymore, and another was for an internship at Gagosian, and then I had the interview with Carl Freedman. Carl didn't actually like me that much, I could sense it, but we kept meeting up and I ended up getting offered the job. It was a lesson in perseverance! I also got offered an internship at Anton Kern Gallery in New York, which I was tempted to take but decided against it. I also knew that if I were to work at Gagosian, for example, it could be great for the experience but I would have very limited range at such a huge gallery. I went to work with Carl because I knew I would be able to learn way more in the long run.

To be honest, a lot of the art world changed their relationship to me because before, they'd known me as a collector, as a musician, as a friend of other artists. When you go to work for a gallery, the rules change, suddenly you're competition. Back then, the art world was quite cutthroat in many ways. It can still feel like that at times, but I do feel like there is more of a sense of looking out for each other, and people are friendlier to each other even if they're competitive.

***ASC: How did your podcast,* Talk Art, *end up coming into existence?***

**RD:** That was really accidental and, again, I think there were lots of transferable skills, which is why it happened. Russell Tovey, my co-host, and I met at a dinner in Edinburgh celebrating Tracey's museum show there. After the dinner, we went to a hotel bar with our then-boyfriends who sat in silence while we spoke for around two and a half hours about Tracey's drawings and why they meant something to us. It was quite a neurodivergent, intense conversation and was literally the weirdest meeting of my life because, up until that point, nobody had understood why I loved art so much. We emailed each other that night, and we've emailed each other pretty much every day since. The idea for *Talk Art* occurred when I was invited to be interviewed on a podcast about Counter Editions, which is Carl Freedman Gallery's print house. The night before I was scheduled to do the interview, the producer of the podcast called me and asked, "So, who are you bringing?" And I was like, "What do you mean?" And they said, "You have to bring a customer of the business." The only person I could think of at that short notice was Russell. Luckily, he was free. During the interview, the host didn't get a word in edgeways. We just spoke for a whole hour. When they released it, my mum heard it, and she said, "I finally understand why you guys love art. You are so good together. I've never heard you two talking. You should do your own show." I told Russell and he said, "You're not going to believe this. My mum said the same thing." It wasn't like we sat down and thought, "Oh, we want to do a podcast." It was never driven by being successful or by money. Even though it's gone on to become a company that is making money, it was never the intention behind it. I believe that is also why it took off, it's 100 percent genuine. The podcast became an extension of what we were already doing, going to museums and artist's studios and talking about the art we love.

Before the pandemic happened, we only had about maybe 5,000 listeners, and through lockdown people binged all of the previous 2 or 3 seasons, and we suddenly saw this huge spike in listener figures. We got in *The New York Times*, and after that, our listenership skyrocketed. We responded to that by working even harder, putting out two episodes a week during the pandemic to that captive audience, and the listening figures were just getting higher and higher. When you've got people that have downloaded the whole podcast, it fluctuates a bit, but for the most part you have regular listeners. It's not dependent on the guest, so if you have an unknown artist, people still tune in, and it becomes this really amazing platform promoting different levels of people's careers, which is a really beautiful thing.

*ASC: What sort of hard skills, such as editing, and soft skills, such as the ability to get the most out of interviews and conversations, are needed for launching and building an award-winning podcast?*

**RD:** We ended up finding people to help us. Collaboration is a really important thing! Don't be put off if you think you can't do something. For the first four seasons of *Talk Art*, I would do all the edit notes, listening to every bit of audio and writing time stamps of where things should be cut. For example, if I said a swear word here, if somebody said something a bit strange that could be misinterpreted there, cut that out. It would take around two hours every week to listen and make notes, then I would send that to someone who knew how to edit quickly. It would cost around £80 an episode, so it made it possible at the time because we weren't making any income from the podcast. Once we started to make income from the podcast, we outsourced the editing, recording, and everything else technical, which makes it a lot easier when you've got a full-time job. We use Acast as a distribution website, which puts us out on Spotify and Apple and all of that, and it's great because their data knowledge is so accurate. You can see that you're being listened to in a hundred countries and that there are 40 percent men and 60 percent women, for example, which is useful for brands that want to advertise on your show. While it might seem a bit cringe or embarrassing to have advertising, it actually pays for the show. It means that it becomes sustainable and can actually continue while staying free for the listener.

When it comes to other skills, I have always had quite a lot of imposter syndrome. When we got the book deal, especially. I think we have the same publisher, don't we?

*ASC: Yes, we do!*

**RD:** Wonderful. Well, with the book, but also with the podcast, I had quite a bad bout of imposter syndrome. It reared its head in an early episode where we interviewed Pedro Pascal, who's now obviously a global superstar. Back then, he wasn't the level of star that he is now. Halfway through the episode, I broke down and started crying because I thought Pedro and Russell were annoyed with me. I said, "I don't want to do this, I'm rubbish at it, I don't think I'm doing it very well." Pedro just looked at me and said, "What are you talking about? I don't know that much about art, and you're making me really enjoy this episode. Stop crying and put the recording back on and keep doing what you're doing." And Russell was just like, "Rob is such a drama queen" because he knew me, and he knew I'd be fine. But it was Pedro and Russell saying to me, "We believe in you" even though I didn't feel comfortable that encouraged me to keep going. I had a lot of hang-ups because I felt like the art world was going to judge me, that it would be bad for my reputation. I kept thinking maybe I was stupid or that I didn't know enough. When we did the book, it was similar in the sense that it was very vulnerable. The day it came out was the most scared I've ever been in the whole of my career. That day, when everyone was posting pictures on social media sharing how much they loved it, and friends and artists were telling me how much they loved it, I suddenly realized how *Talk Art* and the book had really changed my life. Even in terms of just believing in myself and realizing that I was valid. I won't always be right and I may look a little silly sometimes, but what I learned is you just have to try. I love what I do, and it's such a privilege to be able to do that.

I have also learned to listen, to be aware that I do not, and will never, know it all. Making art or even making music or just being creative allows you to listen to yourself, it allows you to be heard, but it also allows you to listen to other people. The podcast itself is about listening to the guest. In the early few seasons, we used to talk too much (and sometimes maybe we still do). The key is to try not to impose too much of yourself, even when you get excited and want to share your passion. I'm better at it now than I was before. In the early days, Russell and I were constantly interrupting each other. It was quite a mess, actually, we were getting a lot of people criticizing us.

*ASC: With your large audience, have you experienced negativity in the online space? How did you handle it?*

**RD:** You just have to ignore it. For the amount of vicious people, there's a hundred times more positive people. Not everybody likes art, and you're never going to make everyone like art. But it's great to make a space where people that do love art can come together and celebrate that. I think when people strive too hard to "be mainstream" or to get a bigger audience, they actually sacrifice something in doing that because they're almost removing a part of themselves in trying to be a version of something that they think the world will like. In reality, you only reach bigger audiences when you are fully yourself. That was one of the scariest things during *Talk Art*—I felt like I couldn't really hide myself, because I'm there talking about what I think, and that is a vulnerable space. I had quite a few people in the first season come and tell me off. They were like, "Why are you interviewing actors about art? This is unacceptable." or "You're debasing the intellectual rigor of the art world." One of them even became a guest on the podcast later and apologized to me because they realized what the mission was. I'm just myself on the show. And if you don't like it, then it's fine. Don't listen to it. There are luckily lots of other art podcasts.

I would also say that sometimes having a smaller audience is actually a really powerful thing, so you don't necessarily need to go and have a giant audience. Whatever you do doesn't need to be mainstream entertainment. You've already got it. You are already enough. It's important to consistently remind yourself of that.

*

I was reminded of a few things in my conversation with Robert. Firstly, choosing where you go in the art world professionally can be given a lot of thought in terms of not just jumping into the biggest gallery with the most well-known name. When he started at Carl Freedman, which is where he has been for decades now, he joined because he wanted to be more hands-on and have a chance at developing himself in a smaller gallery in a smaller town. He lives in Margate, but does a lot of work internationally, and that is a great combination to have in a career in the cultural sector. I also took away a lot through what he shared about running a podcast. A sentiment echoed in Alayo's, Marie-Odile's, and Robert's interviews, when it comes to building communities online, is that when you keep going, show authenticity, and allow yourself to be vulnerable, you will find your people, and it will resonate with the right audiences.

## KEY TAKEAWAYS IF YOU ARE THINKING OF EMBARKING ON YOUR OWN CAREER IN CONTENT CREATION IN THE ARTS

### Three Practical Tips

- Develop a strategic use of platforms. Different social-media channels serve different purposes, so Instagram can be useful for visual art and archives, like Alayo with *A Black History of Art*, and podcasts are ideal for long-form conversations. Think about the format that fits best to you and what you want to create.
- Think about your content creation as an extension of your mission—it should not be the be-all-and-end-all of your work. It can expand into curatorial opportunities, book deals, museum collaborations, and more.
- Learn hard skills such as using editing tools like CapCut, InShot, Adobe Premiere, or Garageband. Practicing filming angles or audio takes can help you learn what you can do to enhance the quality without breaking the bank, and it will get you used to hearing the sound of your own voice (which can be daunting at first)!

## Next Steps

- Take a half an hour and ideate about what you want your niche to be and who your ideal audience is. Is it contemporary art? Historical? Are you talking about the art itself, or, like *All About Art*, the art world and its inner workings? Then write down 10–20 topics to cover in posts or episodes, to see how you can run with your concept.

- Build a network—whether it be online or in person, having people you can learn from and collaborate with will enrich your career. Start by connecting with people online by following accounts you like, and go to exhibition openings of galleries you enjoy the program of to meet gallery staff and artists.

- Do your research—both when it comes to the latest social-media trends, tools, and best practices, as well as on the topics you want to be posting about. Content should be well researched and accurate. Misinformation can harm your credibility and professional reputation, especially in the arts, where expertise is valued.

# CHAPTER 14

# CONCLUSION (AND SOME MORE CAREERS)

Throughout the process of writing this book, I have had the honor of interviewing professionals in various art-world jobs. We did deep dives into what it can look like to work in a museum, as well as curation, responsible culture, framing, art handling, commercial galleries, artist agencies, studio management, art writing, art fairs, auction houses, art law, art advising, and content creation. Although I did my best to create an extensive overview within the scope of this book, the jobs represented in these chapters, as well as the jobs mentioned by the interviewees that are connected to what they do, are just scratching the surface of what a career in the arts can be. So, within my conclusionary chapter wrapping this book up with a nice bow, I want to leave you with just a little bit more. In the coming paragraphs, you will read about some additional career paths in the arts, ranging from events to fundraising, from shipping to insurance, and an important note on making your own luck by creating your own opportunities.

In the art world, one thing that will remain is the need for events. Antonia Grosse, who is now the Head of Patrons at the Serpentine (where interviewee Sally Tallant worked for a good chunk of her career!) came to speak at a NXT GEN event in 2025. She told us about her time spent in the events department at Sotheby's auction house, and how much that has informed her career now. As a gallery manager, I also learned how to organize professional dinners, panels, and tours.

Learning how to organize large-scale and high-quality events will always be valuable, and it is another fun, social, and lively area of the arts to work in.

Antonia's position now, as Head of Patrons, is a type of fundraising role responsible for managing and developing relationships with the organization's supporters. Sponsorships, fundraising, and development are incredibly important areas to gain experience in. These are most likely relevant to public institutions (commercial galleries won't have these roles as they don't "fundraise," they sell directly to clients—and thus have a different business model). The skills needed for this role are strong relationship-building and event-planning abilities, a love of socializing and being around people, good time management, and of course, a passion for what the institution stands for, because how else will you raise funds for a cause if you aren't passionate about the mission?

These roles, i.e. event management, development, and relationship building, can be full-time jobs in themselves, but they are also needed as skill sets within other roles, such as museum director (with Salome Asega and Sally Tallant both including fundraising in their list of responsibilities) or curator (with Gražina Subelytė speaking about traveling to Naples and Mexico with museum patrons). Gaining expertise in these areas early on in your career can be transferable in a lot of different ways later down the line.

If you are pivoting from another industry, looking at positions in accounting, HR, finance, or IT at a cultural institution, museum, or auction house can be a great place to start. A friend of mine trained as an accountant in Austria and is now working for the Naturhisorisches Museum (the Natural History Museum) in Vienna. He tells me he has enjoyed opening nights of special exhibitions and attending panel talks, as well as being in the building of the museum itself, as the architecture, both inside and out, is a work of art. Although his job is still accounting, he gets to do it while also enjoying the exhibitions, attending events such as renaissance fairs as a part of his working day, and being intrinsically interested and passionate about the mission behind his work.

Thinking back to chapter 13 on content creation in the arts, another area connected to that is working in public relations. In this job, depending on the communications agency you work for, you can be working with leading organizations as well as key cultural leaders and top voices in the industry, connecting them to one another. Not only is this gratifying, to find audiences for organizations who do meaningful work, but it is also one of the most powerful ways to build your network. It will deepen your abilities to strategically build relationships and shape audiences in mutually beneficial ways.

Marie von Ribbentrop, the previous studio manager for artist Alicja Kwade who you heard from in chapter 7, has ventured into another hugely necessary area in the arts that I did not include in this book, namely fine-art shipping. At Convelio, where Marie now works, they offer services in fine-art shipping, art storage, inventory management, as well as a digital platform to manage quotes, shipments, tracking, and operations. Working in a company like that as a technician, as Keisha Prioleau-Martin suggested in chapter 5, could be a great way to build your expertise as an art handler. Marie works in sales, a role in which she uses her transferrable skills from the studio and applies them to both gallery and client relationships. Queens Fine Art Shipping and Crozier are two other companies widely used in the industry—so if you see a large truck sporting their logos, you can be confident that the contents within the truck are most likely art!

You can't really have fine-art shipping without fine-art insurance. ARTE Generali, Chubb, AXA XL, and Helvetia, to name just a few, are companies that specialize in that. These companies also support arts organizations through other means. AXA XL supports TEFAF (The European Fine Art Foundation), an international art fair in Maastricht and New York, while Allianz has a partnership with MoMA in

New York, sponsoring several of the museum's exhibitions. Not only insurance companies but also banks lend valuable support to the arts through similar partnerships. Deutsche Bank has an art collection and is the Global Lead Partner for Frieze art fair every year. UBS also has an art collection, which is one of the most significant corporate art collections in the world, and they support the production of art-market reports in collaboration with Art Basel, contributing greatly to valuable research on the current state of the sector.

Taking an example from Francesca Gavin's interview in chapter 8, there are a lot of professionals who aren't employed by one single company but instead wear many different hats. Nowadays, there are plenty of cultural practitioners who work full time as freelancers, but also several who combine freelance work alongside salaried work, which, in my opinion, can benefit you greatly as you grow within the industry. You can get so much out of the sector by learning how to create your own opportunities (even when the door is closed). Take this book, for example. When I put together the book proposal, I had no idea how the publishing industry worked. Via many late-night Google searches, I eventually came to the realization that the top publishing houses did not accept unsolicited submissions. This meant that I had to get a book agent before I could submit to the bigger publishing houses. I applied to various agencies and was waiting to hear back from them, but in the meantime I decided to do more outreach, sending my proposal to publishers that would accept them, as well as taking a chance to send a cheeky message to an editor of my preferred publishing house on LinkedIn, feeling like I might be overstepping but taking my shot anyway. I had a few lukewarm responses and follow-ups from other publishers, but nothing felt right. Six months after I sent that cheeky LinkedIn message, my phone pinged and, to my surprise, I had received a response—and it was the one that stuck. That one message, taking that one shot, was how I got my foot in the door with one of the biggest publishers in the world without an agent. I did still get an agent whose work aligns with my values and who I could see myself working with long term, but I didn't follow any of the set paths that I was told to follow. I didn't listen when I was told "Well, that's just how it's done." I didn't let a closed door get in my way. Of course, it also took the Octopus team accepting my proposal and standing behind my pitch, for which I will be for ever thankful—but the reality of the matter is that this book might not have come into existence if I hadn't taken a chance on sending a LinkedIn message . . . and tried to make my own luck.

A career path I wish I could have included an entire chapter on is working in academia. I would have loved to speak to university professors about how they approach balancing teaching with research, and what it feels like to carry the responsibility of shaping the future of the art world. It is crucial to encourage the next generation of arts professionals to keep building the sector, because now, more than ever, we need culture. In a world where we are receiving constant news cycles directly to our phones, where education and freedom of speech are under threat and where freedom of culture is at stake, careers in art are vital. I hope this book can support anyone who wants to join this incredible industry that fosters education and increases empathy, deepens connection and communication, encourages cultural exchange and tolerance, and everything else the art world brings with it.

There remains a negative rhetoric about having a career in the arts. Yes, there is a very dark underbelly of people exploiting creatives in the sector. There are incredibly commercial, superficial vanity projects posing as businesses instead of doing work as meaningful initiatives. And yes, it can be difficult to live in a big city like New York or London on an art-world salary—but that doesn't mean it can't be a fulfilling, successful, and bright career, working in an industry that does good for the world, for society. As was proven throughout the rich conversations within the book, there are so many paths you can take. Not everything is linear, and you don't have to focus on one specific idea of a career path in order to succeed. We can all continue to learn, grow, and play to our strengths while continuing to build a sector that is responsible for not only contributing billions to the economy, but fostering a more empathetic, educated, *happy* society—and we can do it together.

A note to you as I finish off this conclusion: I am sure there are still some of you readers whose questions have gone unanswered. A piece of advice from me would be to pick up the phone or send an email to someone who can give you the answers you need. Use this book as a template, ask them some of the questions I asked, and take it from there with your own curiosity.

# RESOURCE LIBRARY

## WEBSITES AND NEWSLETTERS (ALPHABETICAL)

- **Arthist** (arthist.net) – Provenance research resources (newsletter available).
- **Artplace** (artplace.substack.com) – Art history, contemporary culture, and perspectives from art world professionals.
- **ArtTechSpace** (arttechspace.com) – Resources for art technicians and art handlers.
- **Call for Curators** (callforcurators.com) – Opportunities and resources for curators.
- **Looted Art** (lootedart.com) – Provenance research and restitution-focused resources (newsletter available).
- **news.artnet.com** – Daily and weekly international art world news.
- **The Art Bystander** – In-depth essays, reviews, and cultural guides examining contemporary art and its markets.
- **The Baer Faxt** – Newsletter focused on art market news and analysis.

## NEWSPAPERS AND REPORTS (ALPHABETICAL)

- **Curatorial Toolkit** – Karen Love (Visual Arts Network Australia / visualarts.net.au).
- **SML x ArtTactic Talent Report** – Research report addressing transparency, equity, and career progression in the art sector.

- *The Art Newspaper* – International coverage of art, museums, and the market.
- The *Financial Times* (including *FT Weekend*) – Arts, culture, and market reporting.
- **UBS x Art Basel Art Market Report** – Annual analysis of the global art market.

## PODCASTS (ALPHABETICAL)

**All About Art** by Alexandra Steinacker-Clark
**Key episodes (ordered by date):**

- **Chapter 1: Building a Strong Foundation** – "Discussing Art Recruitment with Emma Restall"; "The Importance of Art History Degrees with Gregory Perry, CEO and Christina Bradstreet, Head of Programmes, Association for Art History".
- **Chapter 2: Working in Museums** – "Dr. Sabine Haag, Director of the KHM-Museumsverband"; "Working at MoMA with Ksenia Nouril, Assistant Director of the International Program".
- **Chapter 3: Working in Curating** – "Curating *Surrealism and Magic: Enchanted Modernity* at the Peggy Guggenheim Collection with Gražina Subelytė"; "Curating Frieze Sculpture with Fatoş Üstek"; "Dr. Dorothy Price on Teaching, Curating, and Researching Critical Race Theory and German Modernism"; "Curating at Tate Modern with Dr. Val Ravaglia".
- **Chapter 4: Working in Responsible Culture** – "Sustainability in Art with Caitlin Southwick, Founder of Ki Culture"; "Looted? Missing? Authentic? Why Art Provenance Research Matters with Angelina Giovani".

- **Chapter 5: Working in Framing and Art Handling** – "The Art of Framing with Gregory Baker"; "The Mind Control of Mount Making with Alex Abbott, Director of Dauphin".
- **Chapter 6: Working in Commercial Galleries** – "Ripping Up the Art Market Rulebook with Millie Jason Foster, Director of Gillian Jason Gallery".
- **Chapter 7: Working in Artist and Studio Management** – "MTArt: The Story with Marine Tanguy"; "Redefining Artist Management with Valeria Szabó Facchin, Founder of Studio Expanded".
- **Chapter 8: Working as an Art Writer** – "Writing About Art with Holly J. Black"; "The London Art Critic: Interview with Tabish Khan"; "Art in Fiction: Discussing *Tiepolo Blue*, a novel by James Cahill"; "Towards the Ethical Art Museum with Gareth Harris".
- **Chapter 10: Working in an Auction House** – "Discussing Contemporary Art Auctions with Kelsey Macpherson, Sotheby's".
- **Chapter 13: Working in Content Creation in the Arts** – "A Black History of Art with Alayo Akinkugbe"; "Professionally Bullshitting Art with Sophie Nowakowska"; "Content Creation in the Arts with Lucy Donovan"; "Why the Art World Needs Social Media with Cassandra Bowes" '.

## OTHER PODCASTS

- *A Shared Gaze* – By Alayo Akinkugbe.
- *A Week in Art* – By Ben Luke for *The Art Newspaper*.
- *ArtTactic Podcast* – By ArtTactic (market analysis and industry commentary).
- *Talk Art* – By Russell Tovey and Robert Diament.

- *The Art Angle* – By *Artnet News* (individual hosts vary; no single author credit).
- *The Art Business* – By Dr. David Bellingham for Sotheby's Institute of Art.
- *The Art World: What If. . .?!* – By Allan Schwarzman and Charlotte Burns
- *The Great Women Artists* – By Katy Hessel.

## BOOKS (ALPHABETICAL)

- *A Year in the Art World* by Matthew Israel. 2020, Thames & Hudson.
- *Get the Picture* by Bianca Bosker. 2024, Viking/Atlantic.
- **Hot Topics in the Art World** (A book series, edited by Jeffrey Boloten and Juliet Hacking, published by Lund Humphries and Sotheby's Institute of Art.)
- *Poor Artists* by The White Pube (Gabrielle de la Puente & Zarina Muhammad). 2025, Prestel/Particular Books.
- *Seven Days in the Art World* by Sarah Thornton. 2008, W. W. Norton & Company.
- *Ways of Seeing* by John Berger. 1972, Penguin Books.
- *Why Have There Been No Great Women Artists?* by Linda Nochlin. 1971 (essay); later collected editions incl. 50th anniversary edition in 2021, Thames & Hudson.

## COMMUNITIES AND MEMBERSHIP PLATFORMS (ALPHABETICAL)

- **Art Fund** – UK-based charity supporting museums and galleries (National Art Pass).

- **Association for Art History** – Academic and professional network for art history.
- **Association of Women in the Arts** – Professional support and advocacy network.
- **Creative Freedoms** – Support network for freelancers in the creative sector.
- **International Association of Art Critics (AICA)** – Global professional association for art critics.
- **NXT GEN: AWITA x All About Art** – Community for emerging arts professionals, co-directed by Alexandra Steinacker-Clark.
- **Saloon Network** – International feminist art network with multiple global chapters.

# ACKNOWLEDGMENTS

I would first like to thank each and every person who contributed to this book, including those not named in its pages:

Alayo Akinkugbe, Shereen Al-Sawwaf, Salome Asega, Greg Baker, Lele Barnett, Bianca Bosker, Maria Rita Cerilli, Victoria Damidot, Robert Diament, Lisa Dennison, Marie-Odile Pantoja Falais, Lauren Farrington, Francesca Gavin, Ophélie Guillerot, Mikei Hall, Gareth Harris, Céline Hersant, Philip Hoffman, Jonathan Illari, Millie Jason Foster, Elsy Lahner, Nicola Lees, Paula Marschalek, Christine Messineo, Sophie Parker, Keisha Prioleau-Martin, Marie von Ribbentrop, Thaddaeus Ropac, Jasper Sharp, Caitlin Southwick, Gražina Subelytė, Virginie Syn, Valeria Szabó Facchin, Sally Tallant, Séverine Waelchli, and Mona Yapova. A special thanks to the team at Sophie Macpherson Ltd for their contributions to the first chapter.

I would like to extend a thank you to the teams that helped make this book possible: Charlotte Brown, Jessica Stanley and the team at Christie's Auction House; Katie Vohr and the team at Sotheby's Auction House; Nina Sandhaus, Patricia Neusser, and Lisa Schmitt at Galerie Thaddaeus Ropac; Veronika Kailich with the Frieze team; Sarah Morris at the New Museum; Lorenz Ecker and the team at the Albertina; as well as arts professionals Liz Ainslie; Alice Acland; Ellen Bashford; Amy Cope; David Fisslthaler; Sigrid Kirk; and Martina Pohn.

This book would not have become what it is without the support of my editor, Ellie Corbett, who has been nothing short of brilliant in advocating for my vision on this project. I extend so much gratitude to her, as well as to Rachel Silverlight for taking a chance on me from a simple LinkedIn message, and the entire Hachette team for turning *Working in Art* into what it is now.

A special thanks to my agent Clara Foster, who has been a pillar in the entire process – thank you for being my sounding board, championing me and this book every step of the way.

I could not have written this book without the initial encouragement from Marc Kristal and the endless support and friendship provided by the brilliant Chiara Gallo in assisting me through the early stages.

Extreme gratitude to Bow Arts Charity for giving me a space on Shaftesbury Avenue to write, and to the team at Synergy Associates for always believing in the work that I produce (and giving me the tools to produce it).

To the listeners of the *All About Art* podcast, I would not have kept going if it weren't for you.

Thank you to my friends, who have supported me endlessly and encouraged me to keep going even when I felt unsure in my path – you know who you are. Thank you to Emilie for years of friendship and support, and to Fola for believing in my work sometimes more than I did.

And finally, to my family: thank you to my dad, who taught me the importance of reading, writing, and drawing from the moment I could properly hold a pencil. Thank you to Monika for providing a pillar of support. And most of all, thank you to my mother, who, with unwavering faith in me and my abilities, instilled within me that "You can achieve anything if you put your mind to it." Without her, I would not be the person I am today.

# INDEX


Aartemis 229, 232
Abbott, Alex 93
academia, working in 248
AI 157, 213
Ai Weiwei
    *Sunflower Seeds* 196
Ainslie, Liz 89
Akinkugbe, Alayo 242
    *A Black History of Art* platform
        222, 223, 226, 227, 242
    "Black Gazes" column 224
    *Reframing Blackness* 222, 223
    *A Shared Gaze* podcast 223, 224
Al-Sawwaf, Shereen 183–92
Alemani, Cecilia 60
*All About Art* podcast 4–5, 7, 55, 63, 93,
    106, 125, 161, 194, 221, 234, 243
Allen, Jody 213
Allen, Paul G. 213
Allianz 246–7
*AnOther* magazine 223, 224
art advisors 206–20
    The Fine Art Group 206–11
    Seattle 212–18
Art Advisory Global 206
Art Basel 247
art fairs 72, 134, 144, 160–73
    clientele 171
    entry pricing 160–1
    Frieze 160, 161, 162–3, 164, 165,
        172, 223, 247

    sculpture park 72, 132–3, 160, 161
    and galleries 115
    Impact Prize 165
    Photo London 166–71
    viennacontemporary 141, 143, 144
art framing 77, 78–81, 82
    John Davies Framing 78
art handling 42, 77–95, 114, 246
    Sotheby's Auction House 77, 78,
        81, 82
    Tate Britain 42, 77, 83–8
art law 194–205
    common-law and civil-law systems
        199–200
    internships 199
    professional associations 205
    vacation schemes 196, 198
Art Loss Register 70, 72, 76
*The Art Newspaper (TAN)* 152–8,
    235
art writers *see* writing about art
*The ArtTactic Podcast* 235
Arte Povera 102
Articheck 66–7
artist management 118–32, 137–9
Artists Space 162, 163
ArtPresentFuture 141
ArtTactic 10–11
Asega, Salome 24, 31–8, 42, 245
Association of Women in the Arts 17
Aster 118, 126, 128–30

auction houses 174–93
   *see also* Christie's Auction House;
      Sotheby's Auction House
Auerbach, Frank 108
AXA XL 246

Baker, Gregory 77–83, 94
banks
   fine-art insurance 247
Barnett, Lele 206, 213–18
Barney, Matthew 84, 86
Basel Art Fair 72
Beaumont Nathan 206
Beuys, Joseph 98
Bomberg, David 108
Bortolami, Stefania 163
Bosker, Bianca 11, 145–52
   *Cork Dork* 146, 148
   *Get the Picture* 11, 146, 148, 149
Boston museums 177
Bowling, Frank 235
Brazil 230
Breuer-Weil, David 77, 78, 81
*A Brush With* podcast 235

C/20 Association for International
      Curatorial Practice 119
Carl Freedman Gallery 236, 237,
      238, 241–2
Casiraghi, Francesca 128
catalogs 11
Cattelan, Maurizio 102
Cerilli, Maria Rita 24, 38–42
Chetwynd, Monster 84
Chicago 164, 184
Chora Media 40
Christie's Auction House 175, 207–8,
      211, 230
   Berlin 56

New York 183–92
   provenance research 69, 70–1, 74
Christie's Education 236–7
commercial galleries 96–117, 139, 245
   blue-chip 97
   cash-flow management 110–11
   different roles in 113–15
   exhibition cycle 115, 116
   Galerie Thaddaeus Ropac 97–106,
      115
   Gillian Jason Gallery 107–13
   internships in 14
   sales assistants 114–15
   team management 113–14, 115
conservation
   and picture framing 79, 81
content creation 221–43
   misinformation 234
   public relations work 246
   skills needed for 233
   *see also* Instagram content creation;
      podcasts
Convelio Fine Art Shippers 132, 133,
      136–7, 246
core values 43
Counter Editions 235, 238
Covid-19 pandemic 4, 119, 128, 160,
      228, 238
Crozier 246
Cruse, Maike 171
curating 45–62, 213–14, 223
   New Curators 61–2
Curtiss, Julie 150, 151

Dartington College of Arts 25
Dennison, Lisa 175–83, 192
Diament, Robert 235–42
Dolman, Alex 208
Dolman, Edward 208

Dostoevsky, F. 126
Dubuffet, Jean 2, 177

EAPs (employee assistance programs
    20–1
education 9–11
    art history degrees 2, 9–11
    art history in schools 2–3
    extracurricular education and
        training 16–18
    government-allocated funding
        for 6
    PhD degrees 11
Emin, Tracey 84, 235, 236, 237
EPOCH magazine 140–5
events programmes 17
    management of 244–5
    NXT GEN 17, 166, 194, 205, 244
extracurricular education and
        training 16–18

Facchin, Valeria 118, 125–32, 138
Farrington, Lauren 69–75
The Fine Art Group 206–7, 208–12
fine-art insurance 246–7
fine-art shipping 132, 133, 136–7,
    246
Fiorucci, Nicoletta 127–8, 129
Foster, Millie Jason 106–13
framing 42
freelance work 15, 247
    art handling 77, 90–4
    art writing 142
    artist management 122
Frieze art fair 160, 161, 162–3, 164,
    165, 172, 223, 247
    sculpture park 72, 132–3, 160, 161
Fritz, Leslie 163
fundraising 245

curators 48, 54
galleries 013
museums 29, 42–3, 44

Gavin, Francesca 140–5, 247
gender pay gap 22
Gerlis, Melanie 171
Gillian Jason Gallery (GJG) 107–13
Gorvy, Brett 208
Grausam, Alexandra 51
Grosse, Antonia 244–5
Guggenheim, Peggy 40, 55, 58
    *see also* Venice, Peggy Guggenheim
        Collection

Haag, Sr Sabine 13
Hailey, Andrea 163
Hall, Mikei 77, 84–9, 94
Harris, Gareth
    *The Art Newspaper (TAN)* 152–8
Hessel, Katy 223
Himid, Lubiana 235
Hirst, Damien 84
Hoffman, Philip 206–12, 218
Holt, Lilian 108
Holzer, Jenny 164
Hong Kong 206, 212
Huyghe, Pierre 142

Illari, Jonathan 200–4
imposter syndrome 18, 228, 239–40
Independent Curators International
    (ICI) 162
Instagram content creation 18, 221,
    224, 228
    *A Black History of Art* platform
        222, 223, 226, 227
    Marie-Odile Pantoja Falais 230–4
insurance, fine-art 246–7

internships 4, 7, 9, 11, 12, 13–15, 23,
    39, 96, 230
  in art law 199
  commercial galleries 111–12, 116,
    139
  curating 56, 60

Kahlo, Frida 236
Karan, Donna 162
Ki Culture 63, 64, 65, 76
Ki Futures 64, 65, 66–7
KPMG 207
Kwade, Alicja 118, 132–6, 137, 160, 246

Lahner, Elsy 50–5, 61, 96
law *see* art law
Leung, Betty 55
Levin, Golan 37
Lévy Gorvy Dayan 208
LinkedIn 18, 19, 221, 247–8
Liverpool Biennial 24, 26, 28
London
  Chelsea School of Art 87, 167
  Courtauld Institute of Art 56,
    126–7, 223
  Frieze Masters 46
  Galerie Max Hetzler 96
  Galerie Thaddaeus Ropac 97–106,
    115
  Gillian Jason Gallery (GJG)
    107–13
  Hayward Gallery 26, 223
  Max Wigram Gallery 236
  Mishcon de Reya LLP 194–200
  Nicoletta Fiorucci Foundation
    126, 128
  Photo London 166–71
  Royal Academy of Arts 167, 223
  Serpentine Gallery 24, 28, 244

Somerset House 127
Sotheby's Auction House 3–4,
    174, 175
  Studio Voltaire 225
  Victoria and Albert Museum 31, 153
Long, Richard 88
Longo, Robert 164
Los Angeles 161, 163, 164, 165
  MAK Center for Art &
    Architecture 120
Love, Karen
  *Curator Toolkit* 45
Luke, Ben 235

Macpherson, Sophie 10
  *see also* SML (Sophie
    Macpherson Ltd)
Madonna 236
Margate
  Carl Freedman Gallery 235, 236,
    237, 238, 241–2
Marschalek Art Management 13,
    118–25
Marschalek, Paula 13, 118–25, 132,
    138
Mehretu, Julie 164
mentorships 35–6, 44
Messer, Thomas M. 177
Messineo, Christine 161–6, 172
Milan
  Galerie Thaddaeus Ropac 101–2
money
  salaries 19–23, 248
Morning Consult 221
museums 24–44
  art handling 92
  curators 50–4
  mentorships 35–6, 44
  NEW INC 24, 31–8, 42

Peggy Guggenheim Collection 24,
   38–42, 46, 47, 55–61, 127
Queens Museum 24, 26–31, 42, 90
Seattle 212–13
team management 27, 28–9,
   29–30, 37, 43, 44
Vienna 12–13, 46, 50, 52–4,
   118–19, 120, 245

Nazi Germany
art looting 69–70, 72–4
networking 9, 14–15, 17, 246
NEW INC 24, 31–8, 42
New Perspectives Art Partners 208
New York
Anton Kern Gallery 237
art fair 161, 164, 165
art lawyers 200–4
Bortolami Gallery 161
Brooklyn Museum 27, 30, 164
Christie's 183–92
The Fine Art Group 212
Ford Foundation 32, 34
freelance art handling 89–93
Gagosian gallery 174–5, 237
Guggenheim Museum 46, 89, 90,
   164, 175, 176–7, 177–8, 181
Metropolitan Museum of Art 109
MoMA 27, 30, 89, 90, 164, 246–7
Museum of Art and Design 89, 90
NEW INC 24, 31–8, 42
New Museum 24, 31, 89
POWRPLNT 32
Queens Museum 24, 26–31,
   42, 90
Sotheby's 175–83
Nowakowska, Sophie 55
NXT GEN 17, 166, 194, 205, 244

Obrist, Hans Ulrich 54

Pantoja Falais, Marie-Odile 228–34,
   242
Paris
Aartemis 229, 232
Carousel du Louvre 230
content creation and the art scene
   233
Galerie Thaddaeus Ropac 100, 101
L'École du Louvre 230
Louvre Museum 230
Sorbonne University 230
Parker, Sophie 166–71, 172
Pascal, Pedro 240
Patti Wong and Associates 208
Photo London 166–71, 172
picture framing 77, 78–81, 82
Plan Your Vote 161, 163–4, 166
podcasts
   *The ArtTactic Podcast* 235
   *A Brush With* 235
   *The Great Women Artists* 223, 235
   on Peggy Guggenheim 40
   *A Shared Gaze* 223, 224
   skills for building and launching
      239
   *Talk Art* 235, 237–41
   *A Week in Art* 235
   see also *All About Art* podcast
Poledna, Mathias 49
Prague Biennial 163
Prioleau-Martin, Keisha 77, 90–4, 246
provenance research 63, 69–75
public relations work 246
publishing industry 247–8

Queens Fine Art Shipping 246
Queens Museum 24–31, 42, 90

Rapa Nui (Easter Island) 64
relationship building 245
Renaissance art writing 140
responsible culture 63–76
    provenance research 63, 69–75
    sustainability 63, 65–8
Ribbentrop, Marie von 118, 132–8, 246
Richardson, Jonathan 140
Robbins, Daniel 177
Rockefeller, David 178
Ropac, Thaddaeus 96, 97–106, 113
Rothko, Mark 178
Royal College of Art 25–6
Ruiz, Cristina 153

salaries 19–23, 248
Salzburg
    Galerie Thaddaeus Ropac 4, 14, 96,
        98, 100, 101
    Salzburger Kunstverein 50, 51
Seattle 212–18
    Arts and Culture Fund 212
    Cultured A F Club 217
    Frye Art Museum 217
    museums 212–13, 215
    tech companies 206, 212, 214–15,
        216, 217
Seligmann, Kurt 55, 56
Seoul
    Galerie Thaddaeus Ropac 100, 101
Sharp, Jasper 45–50, 61
shipping, fine-art 132, 133, 136–7, 246
Shrigley, David 235
Simmons, Laurie 164
Smith, Sidney R.J. 83
SML (Sophie Macpherson Ltd)
    on art history degrees 10
    Art Market Talent Report (2025)
        10–11, 21
    on internships 13–14
    on salary negotiations 19–21
    on short or online courses 18
    on social-media presence 18–19
    on transferring from
        another sector 16
    on volunteering 13
social media 18–19
    content creation 221–43
    and France 230
    influencers 221–2
    Meta Business Suite 231
    TikTok 18, 221, 232
Soho House 143, 144
Sontag, Susan
    On Photography 3
Sotheby's Auction House 174–83, 211
    art handling technicians 77, 78,
        81, 82
    art lawyers 202
    London 3–4, 174, 175
    New York 175–83
Sotheby's Institute of Art 17, 108,
        111, 152
Southwick, Caitlin 38, 63–8, 75
Studio Expanded 118, 125–32
studio management 81, 94, 118, 132–8
Subelytė, Gražina 55–61, 245
sustainability 63, 65–8, 123

Talk Art podcast 235, 237–41
Tallant, Sally 24–31, 37, 42, 244, 245
TAN (The Art Newspaper) 152–8, 235
Tate Britain
    art handling 42, 77, 83–8
    Turner Prize exhibitions 84, 88–9,
        129
    Women in Revolt! exhibition 107
Tate Modern 42

TEFAF (European Fine Art
    Foundation) 246
Temposhark 235, 236
Thailand 195–6
Tik Tok 18, 221, 232
Torres, Edwin 36
Tovey, Russell 235, 237–8, 240
transferable skills 43, 114
transferring from another sector 15–16
Turner Prize exhibitions 84, 88–9, 129
Tusch, Gerold 3
Tyler, Gary 165

UBS Art Advisory 206, 247
UCL (University College London) 3, 4
UK (United Kingdom)
    art law 199–200, 201
United States
    APAA (Association of Professional
        Art Advisors) 215
    art law 200–4
    curators 54
    Plan Your Vote 161, 163–4, 166
    see also New York; Seattle
Üstek, Fatos 161

Vasari, Giorgio
    Lives of the Artists 140
Venice
    Biennale 41, 46, 47, 49, 55, 60
    Peggy Guggenheim Collection 24,
        38–42, 46, 47, 55–61, 127
Vernhet, Leonard 142
Vienna
    Academy of Fine Arts 50
    Albertina Museum 50, 52–4

'Artist's Toolbox' platform 124
das weisse haus exhibition space 50,
    51–2
FOTOWIEN Festival 119
Kunstistorisches Museum 12–13,
    46, 118–19, 120
Naturhisorisches Museum 245
Parallel Art Fair 119
Phileas 45, 47–8, 49
viennacontemporary 141, 143, 144
volunteering 9, 11, 12–13, 23

Walsh, John 177
Warhol, Andy 178, 188
Washington, University of
    Henry art gallery 216–17
A Week in Art podcast 235
Wong, Patty 208
work experience, introductory 9,
    11–15
work-life balance 20–1, 122–3
writing about art 140–59
    art criticism 140
    Bianca Bosker 11, 145–52
    career benefits of 12–13
    and the digital world 155, 157
    Francesca Gavin 140–5
    Gareth Harris 152–8
    'International Art Speak' 11–12

Yapova, Mona 194–200, 201, 204
Yeo, Jonathan 143

Zurich
    Manifesta 11 biennial 141
Zwirner, David 162, 163

**Alexandra Steinacker-Clark** is an American-Austrian art historian, curator, writer, and podcaster living and working in London. She is the founder and host of the *All About Art* podcast, the co-director of NXT GEN: AWITA x All About Art, a program designed to support early-career arts professionals, and a TEDx speaker, having presented a talk asking 'Can Consuming Art Increase Empathy?' in 2023. Her specializations are in contemporary art and its markets, along with accessibility, engagement, and the demystification of the professional art sector.